POLITICAL STYLE

New Practices of Inquiry
*A Series Edited by Donald N. McCloskey
and John S. Nelson*

POLITICAL STYLE

THE ARTISTRY OF POWER

Robert Hariman

THE UNIVERSITY OF CHICAGO PRESS
Chicago & London

Robert Hariman is professor of rhetoric and communication studies and Endowment Professor of the Humanities at Drake University.

The University of Chicago Press, Chicago 60637
The University of Chicago Press, Ltd., London
© 1995 by The University of Chicago
All rights reserved. Published 1995
Printed in the United States of America

04 03 02 01 00 99 98 97 96 95   1 2 3 4 5

ISBN 0-226-31629-7 (cloth)
      0-226-31630-0 (paper)

This book includes material from the following previous publications by the author: "Composing Modernity in Machiavelli's *Prince*," *Journal of the History of Ideas* 50 (1989): 3–29, reprinted in *Renaissance Essays II,* edited by William J. Connell, vol. 10 of the Library of the History of Ideas (Rochester, NY: University of Rochester Press, 1993); "Political Style in Cicero's Letters to Atticus," *Rhetorica* 7 (1989): 145–58; "Decorum, Power and the Courtly Style," *Quarterly Journal of Speech* 78 (1992): 149–72.

Library of Congress Cataloging-in-Publication Data
Hariman, Robert.
      Political style: The artistry of power / Robert Hariman.
          p.   cm.—(New practices of inquiry)
      Includes bibliographical references and index.
          1. Rhetoric—Political aspects. 2. Style, Literary. I. Title.
      II. Series.
PN239.P64H37   1995
808.5—dc20   94-36285
                                                                                    CIP

for my parents

"For it is not sufficient to know what
one ought to say, but one must also know
how to say it."

— Aristotle

"Style is always something general. It
brings the contents of personal life and
activity into a form shared by many and
accessible to many."

— Georg Simmel

"Thus all manners are a kind of plea.
We judge according to the style of appeal
being made, the conditions under which
it is made, and the audience for which it is
intended; in short, in terms of how it
is *staged*."

— Hugh Dalziel Duncan

"Hey, man, what's your style? How do
you get your kicks for living?"

— Lou Reed

contents

acknowledgments

When I was an undergraduate, I assumed that scholarship only required ideas. As a graduate student I learned, somewhat to my dismay, that it also involved training and discipline. Only recently have I realized how much it depends on acts of generosity. The following essays have benefitted from a wide range of readers, all of whom were willing to give up time from their own good work to help with a project that often illustrated how "potential" means you haven't done it yet. Particularly helpful were those discussions of early drafts of several chapters by members of the interdisciplinary Faculty Rhetoric Seminar, sponsored by the Project on the Rhetoric of Inquiry at the University of Iowa, and by the participants in the Scholars Workshop on the Rhetoric of Political Argumentation, also conducted at Iowa under sponsorship of POROI and the National Endowment for the Humanities. In addition, I have incorporated many of the suggestions provided by the editors and anonymous reviewers for the *Journal of the History of Ideas, Quarterly Journal of Speech, Rhetorica,* and the University of Chicago Press.

Although I fear omitting any individual, special recognition should go to Fred Antczak, Frank Beer, Bob Boynton, Bob Cape, Maurice Charland, Ken Cmiel, Marianne Constable, Marlena Corcoran, Tom Duncanson, Kathleen Farrell, Dilip Gaonkar, Gene Garver, Tom Goodnight, Stan Ingber, Jim Jasinski, Robert Kaster, Anne Laffoon, Michael Leff, John Lucaites, Harold Marcus, Don Marshall, Tom Mayer, Don McCloskey, Robert McPhee, Allan Megill, John Peters, Jane Rankin, Joseph Schneider, Allen Scult, John Sloop, Ira Strauber,

Mary Stuckey, and Ron Troyer. I also thank Rachel Buckles for her superb secretarial work and both Kate Neckerman and the Drake University Center for the Humanities for their help with the index. Above all, I am indebted to Bill Lewis, for being the ideal colleague, and John Nelson, for his unrelenting encouragement.

1

Introduction

The dean guards her privacy, yet regularly eats her lunch while having her assistants work at the table around her, and her health problems, though not serious, are the talk of the office. She has little interest in the official procedures that are her responsibility, but she always knows the physical whereabouts of the provost and president. She is aloof, imperious, and can silence a room with a glance, yet she allows her staff to fuss over her clothing as if she were a child. She has a sterling record, yet remains a puzzle to her colleagues. The secretaries only laugh and say, "You just have to get used to her style."

The university's law firm doesn't seem to have a chain of command. The gaggle of younger partners are always chattering or arguing loudly with each other and the senior partners. The officers of the firm are infamous for making no statement without additional consultation, and they insist, when pressed, that they hold no power. When decisions are made, they seem to turn on the eloquence of the moment rather than any consistent principle or strategy. Despite its considerable success and obvious collegiality, partners will fret about their reputations. All agree, however, that the real power in the firm lies with the founder. This puzzles other practitioners, for the old guy hasn't handled a case in years. The partners shrug and say, "The legal details don't matter; when he talks, we remember what the law is all about."

The major donor of the university, who coincidentally chairs its board of trustees, is a no-nonsense kind of guy. He can cut to the meat of an issue, take control of a meeting, and get things moving. If he doesn't make any friends doing it, that doesn't seem to bother him. He can't abide listening to long reports or speeches of any kind—as his pained expression makes all too clear—and his company's office decor is noticeably austere. He handsomely rewards initiative, however, particularly when someone hasn't let a petty rule or custom hold up the job. His subordinates admire and fear him, but they are puzzled by his attitude. "He's on top of the heap," they say, "but he never relaxes. You'd think he was at war."

The regional accreditation agency examines the university on a regular basis and according to specific professional criteria. The official visit to the campus is preceded by extensive correspondence regarding the examiners' objectives. During the visit, they are uniformly courteous, work long hours, and frequently remark that they are not fault-finding, only updating the records. Afterwards, there are requests for additional information. The final report is extensive, with copies sent to the school and the state, but its authors are not identified by name. Faculty are puzzled about some of the report's observations. Upon inquiry, however, they are told that everything was done in strict accordance with the procedures and that the written report cannot be amended.

Stories like these are a common feature of our political experience. Their arrangement around an academic setting reflects only my own background, for the four modes of interaction portrayed here are a regular feature of day-to-day politics in the various boards, offices, schools, churches, families, agencies, and other institutional settings that make up a complex society. In each case, relations of control and autonomy are negotiated through the artful composition of speech, gesture, ornament, decor, and any other means for modulating perception and shaping response. In a word, our political experience is styled. This strange term, which can apply to everything from the fine arts to what happens at the hairdresser's, may seem additionally confusing when applied to politics. The fact remains that we don't have a suitable vocabulary for discussing an important class of widely distributed skills. These habitual communicative practices are only a part of the political environment, of course, for people also are acting according to laws, rights, passions, interests, principles, ideologies, and all the other subjects of political studies. But these other variables are mediated by the communicative practices of the

2

people making the decisions, and sometimes the decision turns on rhetorical finesse.

The following essays offer variations on a single idea: To the extent that politics is an art, matters of style must be crucial to its practice. This assumption can appear both commonplace and unsettling, and it is easily disregarded. Consideration of the artistry of civic life goes against the norms of realism dominant in the social sciences, while it seems to fall short of the powerful critiques of literary autonomy and political privilege ascendant in the humanities. Yet, even if realist or poststructuralist attitudes prevail, they leave too much unsaid. The modern human sciences have not yet produced a strong account of what every successful politician knows intuitively: political experience, skill, and result often involve conventions of persuasive composition that depend on aesthetic reactions. As long as this account is not available, theoretical understanding of the dynamics of political identity will remain detached from ordinary personal experience.

This project extends a traditional mode of analysis within rhetorical studies for the purpose of reconsidering the nature of political action. The Sophists, it seems, were fascinated with style; subsequently it became a standard division of rhetorical studies; periodically it has been the dominant standard; today the notions of style, sophistication, and sophistry are thoroughly intertwined and associated with the conventional disparagement of rhetoric.[1] Traditionally, the search for the ability to achieve power by speaking led to an inventory of the techniques of verbal composition, and the recognition that discourse has to be *appealing* if it is to be effective led to an account of the aesthetic economies available to speakers in particular situations. From this perspective, style ultimately is a significant dimension of every human experience.[2] More commonly, it is a particular expertise disposed, like any *technē*, to displace any other kind of intelligence. Thus, the critical task is to focus on elements of political composition that are indeed important to participation and outcome, without producing a merely formal understanding or reinforcing unreflectively a particular standard of judgment.

The following essays offer relatively expansive conceptions of both politics and style by identifying four specific styles of political conduct. Each essay develops the analytical construct of a *political style* to account for the role of sensibility, taste, manners, charisma,

definition

charm, or similarly compositional or performative qualities in a particular political culture. In brief, a political style is *a coherent repertoire of rhetorical conventions depending on aesthetic reactions for political effect.* The four main essays identify four particular styles of political conduct: They are the realist, courtly, republican, and bureaucratic styles. (In the previous vignettes, they were represented in turn by the donor, dean, firm, and agency.) The realist style radically separates power and textuality, constructing the political realm as a state of nature and the political actor as someone either rationally calculating vectors of interest and power or foolishly believing in such verbal illusions as laws or ethical ideals. Since this style operates as the common sense of modern political theory, its deconstruction removes a major obstacle to developing alternative conceptions of politics, particularly accounts—such as this one—that highlight artistry. The courtly style is centered on the body of the sovereign, displaces speech with gesture, and culminates in immobility. This style has little purchase institutionally in modern societies but seems to be particularly resurgent within mass media representations of political events. The republican style develops a model of oratorical virtuosity for public performance in a parliamentary culture. This model includes an appreciation of verbal technique, a norm of consensus, the embodiment of civic virtue, and a doctrine of civility that exemplifies the difficulties facing contemporary liberalism. The bureaucratic style organizes the communicative conventions that together constitute office culture, including jurisdictional definition, hierarchical structure, the ethos of the official, and the priority of writing. As this style operates, it places everyone in a symbolic drama of assimilation that is the dominant form of identity in the late-modern world.

These four styles are identified through close reading of four texts. Each of these texts has a particular rhetorical form and hermeneutical function suited to its purpose of representing a distinctive political intelligence. Each operates in part as a rhetoric: a catalog of the means of persuasion characteristic of a particular political culture that could be used by anyone attempting to secure advantage. As each text highlights how specific, quotidian conventions of address and display can impel, influence, and prevent action, it equips the reader to act skillfully within characteristic situations. Hermeneutically, as each highlights the elements of a particular political

4

style, it casts that style into a reflective space, thereby encouraging interpretation and criticism, even if only on its own terms. Thus, they are "mirror texts," reflecting public processes of textual composition at work in the world around them without themselves necessarily having the same effect as the designs they mirror. The individual essays will each develop different aspects of this manner of reading, as suited to the particular text, author, and history of interpretation. In every case, however, the text is somewhat of a pretext, and the point is to equip the reader to analyze general patterns of identification that operate across the diverse and often fragmented episodes of modern politics.

The realist style is articulated in Machiavelli's *Prince*, the quintessential statement of modern political thought. Previous scholars have emphasized Machiavelli's departure from his genre of the "mirror to the prince" to achieve the perspective of political realism, but they haven't developed the radical implications of this shift in political writing. I examine Machiavelli's primary rhetorical technique of defining his subject against an alternative textuality; this technique persuades the reader of the artlessness not only of Machiavelli's text, but of power itself. The courtly style is portrayed in Ryszard Kapuściński's *The Emperor: Downfall of an Autocrat*. This *tour de force* by a contemporary Polish journalist chronicles the last days of the Ethiopian court of Haile Selassie. Often read as an allegory of the decline of second-world totalitarianism, I read it as a compendium of courtly tropes that are now disseminated throughout modern society and especially active within the mass media. The republican style is reflected in Cicero's letters to Atticus, a vivid correspondence by the greatest stylist in the Roman republic. Scholars usually have read the letters as artless renditions of Cicero's political experience and used them only to illuminate his other works. I read them as Cicero's place for crafting a persona emblematic of public life. The bureaucratic style is chronicled in Franz Kafka's *The Castle*. Although typically read as a theologically oriented extension of *The Trial* which iterates its themes of alienation and injustice, I read it as a comic documentary of bureaucratic practice that is quite ambivalent about the organization of modern life.

The purpose of these interpretations is to guide understanding of political events currently found inexplicable, irrational, or uninteresting. Along the way, I hope to encourage the development of social

5

theory that recognizes how the richness and intelligibility of our social experience comes from its being ineradicably a mixture of persuasive techniques, aesthetic norms, and political relationships. If this also encourages the development of political theory that grants a larger role in political decision making to the full range of communicative practices, so much the better. Toward these ends, the concluding essay discusses the theoretical background for this project, identifies related research programs, and suggests briefly how the styles and texts I have featured provide still undeveloped resources for understanding political action.

My perspective can be described as a cautious postmodernism. The construction of modernity has included from the beginning a dismantling of rhetoric as a tradition of erudition (the old materials can be found scattered throughout the new structure), and the current revival of interest in rhetorical studies both results from and contributes to the breakup of the grand narratives of modern thought. The recuperation of style as a term for the analysis of politics is not possible within strictly modernist conceptions of either politics or aesthetics (as I shall elaborate below), and a more expansive conception of how all thought and action are stylized could be one element of a postmodern social theory. In this sense, one can think of postmodernism as modern thought moving beyond itself—deconstructing, refiguring, revaluing itself—by recourse to those intellectual traditions and symbolic materials that it had repressed.[3] This analytical vocabulary is further distinguished by the manner in which it cuts across the received categories of modern inquiry. It neither follows, nor opposes, nor disregards the analysis of institutions or occupations or other standard categories of liberal social science, or the analysis of class or race or gender, or the analysis of either high art or popular culture. If these problems are not solved, neither are they abandoned, but the emphasis primarily is on understanding what escapes the modern thinker.

Such side-stepping of modern categories of analysis can contribute to another sense of postmodernity: the sensation that our public culture is undergoing a period of accelerated, perhaps epochal, change somehow related to the continued transformation of capitalism and the development of global communication technologies. In order to suggest how the identification of specific styles can aid understanding of such changes, I have attempted to address in each essay still

6

pressing questions in social theory: questions of the nature of identity, community, and power. An account of political style should be more than a handbook of techniques for the enterprising politico. As a style succeeds, it articulates specific rules of usage for the composition of self and others in relations of equity and subordination. We then face certain choices. Of the four styles I discuss, the realist and bureaucratic styles constitute essentially modern worlds, while the republican and courtly styles evoke contexts that are largely premodern yet increasingly appealing during the breakup of modernity itself. Here I become cautious. Despite the value of the general critique of modernity, we need to recognize how that critique depends on the protections of first-world society, and we need to be aware that by weakening modernist discourses (for example, of universal rights or procedural justice) one can place some peoples at grave risk. (Imagine someone appealing to the universality of human rights while standing before the secret police, only to be told that human rights are but another set of power relations and that there is no contradiction between commitments to truth and practices of torture since all are polysemic performances. The Grand Inquisitor would smile approvingly.) This is not to endorse uncritically a world of autonomous individuals, social sciences, competitive markets, and bureaucratic states, but at the least it suggests that the choice of a political style ought to include an appraisal of the various risks involved on each side.

It might seem peculiar, however, to relate such high stakes to questions of style. Established academic conceptions of style hardly prepare one to take seriously the aesthetic dimension of political experience. Stuart Ewen has neatly summarized the problems facing such an inquiry:

This frustration hit me on the first day that I set out to "research" the topic. I walked out of my house, to the local subway station, with the purpose of taking the train up to the Butler Library at Columbia University. At the entrance to the station, I glanced and then stopped to look at the newsstand next to the station doors. Among the hundreds of slick and colorful magazine covers, the word "style" appeared again and again. On news magazines, sports magazines, music-oriented magazines, magazines about fashion, architecture and interior design, automobiles, and sex, "style" was repeated endlessly. It seemed to be a universal category, transcending topical boundaries, an accolade applied to people, places, attitudes, and things. Still not sure what style was, I proceeded to the library with the knowledge that I was on the trail of a hot topic, a universal preoccupation, a key to understanding the contours of contemporary culture.

What I encountered at the library was sobering. . . . Unlike the newsstand, the card catalog offered few clues. There was a predictable reference to "See Fashion, Clothing," . . . there were also some references to works of literary style . . . This was not what I was looking for either, I thought to myself, realizing that I was about to tackle a subject that was, at best, amorphous; a subject that had no clear shape to it, and lacked the kind of concreteness that has shaped the catalogs of knowledge that scholars and students depend upon for intellectual guidance.[4]

Ewen had encountered the chasm separating popular and academic interpretations of style. The accounts of style in literary studies are typical of the academic usage of the term: "Style" refers to correct or characteristic elements of composition for a medium, genre, historical period, or individual artist, often without regard for the content of the message.[5] Texts such as *The Elements of Style* have trained generations of writers and readers, who also have become familiar with such classifications as "the Romantic style" or "Hemingway's style."[6] Similarly, each of the fine arts articulates the elements of composition that define the medium and artistic repertoire, for example, of music, of painting, of color field painting, etc., or that serve as the signature placed upon the work by an artist.[7] The most important constant in these related conceptions of style is the autonomy of the pertinent cultural practice. To understand the style of a poem requires mastery of the techniques of poetic composition, including meter, rhythm, and the like, as those techniques are unique to poetry. To understand the style of a novel requires mastery of diction, plot, character, point of view, etc., as those techniques are used in the novel. And so it goes. Nor has this orientation changed with the recent revival of interest in rhetorical studies: For the most part, the canon of style remains identified with cataloging discursive forms in the artistic text alone rather than understanding the dynamics of our social experience or the relationship between rhetorical appeals and political decisions.[8] This strong sense of artistic autonomy reinforces the tendency in stylistic analysis to catalog elements of design independently of substantive meaning. Understanding is identified with an inventory of formal devices, and stylistic analysis generally seems condemned by Samuel Butler's remark that "all a rhetorician's rules but teach him how to name his tools."

In short, if you want to understand how power is composed, you can't get there from here. When one starts with "style," the road leads into the arts and from there into formalism, far removed from even the display of power. Although this familiar conception of style is challenged periodically by the argument that social norms or political relationships infiltrate artistic production and representation, such analyses remain focused on a very narrow range of cultural practices. Consequently, I also doubt whether one can best understand how politics is artistic simply by amplifying the idea that the arts are political. In order to identify the aesthetic routines and everyday inventiveness of political actors, we need a more expansive concept of style than is available within modern classifications of art and of politics. It is time to recognize that although the resources of modern thought might be necessary for understanding the contemporary world, they are not sufficient for doing so. In a postmodern context, "the aesthetic turns social, the social turns aesthetic."[9] In this context, although style still highlights aesthetic reactions it no longer enforces artistic autonomy. Style becomes an analytical category for understanding a social reality; in order to understand the social reality of politics, we can consider how a political action involves acting according to a particular political style.

One might question, however, whether the study of style should be explicit. Perhaps a tacit knowledge is sufficient or advisable. The suspicions here are both methodological and political. On the one side, the objection is that style is merely epiphenomenal, only an effect or symptom of underlying, more substantive determinants of political action. This perspective can grant that the analysis of style has some diagnostic value, but even then cautions against its displacement of better instruments. On the other side, the concern is that political artistry is dangerous. Variations of this concern range from the presumption that any stylistic accomplishment comes at the expense of the core values in modern democratic states to the claim that scholarly appreciation of style encourages an "aestheticized politics" conducive to fascism.[10]

I concede that in any given case political style might be unimportant or dangerous, but obviously it can't be both. Moreover, if it is dangerous, one wouldn't want to overlook it, so the wiser alternative is to assume that political artistry can be important while addressing any concerns about its appreciation. Although nothing prevents using this study (or any other) as a recipe or rationale for tyranny, one strength of the rhetorical perspective is that it already informs conventional liberal practices thought to be a defense against fascism. Ordinary political actors in our culture routinely persuade by mastering considerations of costume, tone, and timing without suffering moral deterioration. Furthermore, questions of freedom, equality, and justice often are raised and addressed through performances ranging from debates to demonstrations without loss of moral content. An attention to appearances doesn't disregard certain values so much as it looks for the problems and techniques shaping their successful performance, on the assumption that values only can be taken seriously once performed successfully.

The greater problem here is not rewarding fascism but of recognizing how modern societies have become unduly defenseless against aesthetic manipulation. This problem stems in part from the restructuring of learning in the early modern period (and subsequently), which defined politics and aesthetics as separate and autonomous realms of experience. As Victoria Kahn has observed of this transformation, "When mathematical certainty is taken as the standard of reason in politics as well as science, then the aesthetic realm of prudential deliberation, and with this the work of art itself, must be redefined in terms of mere subjective experience."[11] This transformation and confinement of artistic life is reflected in various experiments in modern social thought, whether in the nineteenth-century German attempt to imagine politics as an "aesthetic state,"[12] or in the twentieth-century American effort to rationalize politics according to norms of scientific objectivity.[13] In any case, the modern thinker has difficulty recognizing the aesthetic sensibilities and routine creativity informing ordinary political decisions. Not surprisingly, the typical response to overtly stylized political acts is to restrain, condemn, or otherwise suppress them. The aesthetic dimension of politics is largely unacknowledged within our own experience and, when seen in others, it appears as a dangerous confusion of categories. Ironically, we then give an advantage to those master stylists who should be feared.

Even if the specter of tyranny is set aside, one might be concerned that stylistic analysis will displace investigation of other, more substantive, components of political action such as relations of production, interest-group alliances, or institutional practices. There are several stock responses that can be made here by drawing on the long-standing debates regarding the various interpretive turns taken in the human sciences, but these responses only reproduce familiar standoffs and are unnecessary for another reason as well: No account of style, and certainly not this account, is likely to be so comprehensive, persuasive, and in accord with everyone's interests that it could preempt the many other, well-established enterprises of academic inquiry. Nor should it. There is more to politics than stylized conduct, just as there is more to politics than government. It is one thing to claim that particular rhetorical conventions are widely available, sometimes determinative of conduct (and of rational conduct beneficial to a community), and representative of important elements of human communication. It is quite another to claim that no other factors are active simultaneously or that only rhetorical factors determine all human action. Yet, too often claims of the first sort are taken as claims of the second.

To suggest how a typology of political styles might be a sensible addition to a comprehensive understanding of politics, consider the following analogy between politics and music. It is easy to think of the world of music according to basic, collective styles of composition: These styles include classical music—which contains, for example, baroque, romantic, and modern composition—and popular music—which contains, for example, country, rock, and jazz—and others as well. Each style is produced out of a common universe of sounds, and often from the same instruments, but is defined by different patterns and effects. Each constitutes a different culture but doesn't have a strict correspondence with the meaning ascribed to the music within that culture. Each style requires repeated reproduction of a limited number of motifs, yet allows continual improvisation, individual distinction, and highly personal identification.

Similarly, each political style draws on universal elements of the human condition and symbolic repertoire but organizes them into a limited, customary set of communicative designs. Each evokes a culture—a coherent set of symbols giving meaning to the manifest activities of common living—yet has no *a priori* relation with any issue, event, or outcome. Each is thoroughly conventional, yet the means for personal improvisation and intelligent, innovative responses to unique problems. In the same way that an account of the "reality" of music could not ignore its established styles of performance and appreciation, however much it featured economic or institutional analyses, so an analysis of politics should not overlook its organization through different styles.

This comparison goes farther. Today, all forms of music are promulgated across society around the clock without exclusive sense of locale, or context, or audience. So it is with politics. We still have structures of governance such as bureaucracies, legislatures, and boards (just as we still have concert halls), but we also live in a vortex of discourses. Bureaucratic speech can be heard in the bedroom, republican oratory in the sports section, realist themes in the synagogue, and courtly tropes in the evening news. To the extent that politics is the product of its discourses, it is capable today of being rapidly transformed at any time, in any place, for unstable duration. As we choose, often unthinkingly, between different speakers, we often are choosing particular styles that in turn shape our decisions. All politics might be local, but often the locale is discursive: a perhaps transitory set of rhetorical conventions directing speech and conduct. As Fredric Jameson has remarked, "We are after all fragmented beings living in a host of separate reality compartments simultaneously; in *each one of these* a certain kind of politics is possible." [14]

I also should point out in advance that the analysis of political style ought to go well beyond the cases presented here. I have no doubt that there are other styles—for example, a revolutionary style—and certainly other texts could have been chosen as well. The styles I have featured are no doubt identified incompletely and many questions of application remain. In any case, there is much to be learned from joining an expansive conception of style with a renewed interest in the dynamics of political experience. Standing at the border of modernity, it is time once again to appreciate the art of politics.

12

2

No Superficial Attractions and Ornaments: The Invention of Modernity in Machiavelli's Realist Style

[handwritten margin notes: "real world up. textual world with self control the strategist"]

According to Lord Acton, he was "the earliest conscious and articulate exponent of certain living forces in the present world." Max Lerner commented that although "it has become a truism to point out that Machiavelli is the father of power politics . . . it is still true." In Felix Raab's succinct statement, "As far as the modern world is concerned, Machiavelli invented politics."[1] Likewise, *The Prince* remains Machiavelli's most representative text, the sure embodiment of his innovative intelligence. The specific character of his innovation, however, remains a "radical enigma" that has been the subject of an astonishingly diverse and dense history of interpretation that belies the apparent simplicity of his text.[2] Nor has the book's reputation been diminished by the knowledge that it draws on classical models, ignores key dimensions of modern political experience, and offers little guidance for its application.[3] In this essay, I suggest that the appeal of Machiavelli's text comes from its masterful articulation of a characteristically modern political style that crafts an aesthetically unified world of sheer power and constant calculation. This *realist style* is the basis of Machiavelli's persuasive success, it has shaped his text's subsequent history of interpretation, and it operates as a powerful mode of comprehension and action in the modern world.

The importance attributed to *The Prince* might seem strange to someone picking up the book for the first time. It is a slim volume written in simple prose. The first eleven chapters deal with various types of autocratic government and are followed by three more on the conduct of war. In the next five chapters, the book takes a controversial turn by claiming that at times the successful political leader has to act unethically, but the tone is candid and reasonable. Four subsequent chapters discuss fortifications, propaganda, and the inner circles of government. In the final three chapters, the book expands its scope by discussing the interplay of fortune and prudence in all human affairs and by appealing for restoration of the independence of the Italian states. Throughout the book, the author illustrates the importance of understanding politics as a matter of skill and of developing those skills by learning from experience, while he emphasizes that political events are continuously changeable and that success or failure always can turn on circumstances beyond one's control. In short, the book seems more a compendium of common sense than something enigmatic or powerful. But, as Machiavelli has taught us, appearances can be deceiving.

My reading of the book cuts across the grain of both ordinary and erudite understanding of his work. The common view of *The Prince* is that it provides an objective account of the universal conditions of political life, which is an amoral, winner-take-all competition for power. Machiavelli had the intellectual courage to recognize that politics is one thing and ethics another, and he desired no more than to discover the secrets of political success. The text itself is transparent, a clear explanation of the nature of power without any designs on the reader. Scholarly understanding has qualified these themes, largely through careful attention to the political and literary contexts of Machiavelli's work, but it also has, in the main, reproduced them. For most scholars, *The Prince* provides the definitive statement of political realism, the doctrine that all successful political action requires relentless distinction between what is and what ought to be.[4] This claim has been augmented in some circles by the claim that Machiavelli was the progenitor of political science, on the model of our exact sciences.[5] In each case, there is a corresponding devaluation of both traditional and popular political literatures, which are assumed to be invariably compromised by artifice, partisanship, and idealism.

Yet one might ask how most readers know that his account of sixteenth-century Tuscany is accurate, or why twentieth-century scholarship has been so comfortable with the conventional wisdom

14

of its century's none too admirable political history. Such questions suggest a shift in perspective, which sees the many variants of Machiavellian interpretation, and of Machiavellianism, as traces of his text's most compelling designs for composing political experience. The achievement of *The Prince* may be philosophical or scientific, but it also is literary and rhetorical: Machiavelli devised a particularly elegant imitation of a form of political practice, and he did so in a manner that persuades the reader to accept his text as pre-eminent among others of its kind. The designs of his simple text demonstrate how the persuasive power of a discourse depends in part on the manner in which it is positioned in a competition for status.[6] The methodological implication is that sometimes one can discern a text's fundamental persuasive design—its most powerful definitions of its subject, speaker, and audience—by looking for those moments in the text when other discourses are subordinated. In order to discover Machiavelli's political style, I begin by examining those passages where he writes against other writers.

This approach to *The Prince* is congruent with established critical practices in Machiavelli scholarship, which return the text to the explicitly rhetorical culture of the Italian Renaissance to consider how Machiavelli's innovation comes from crafty reformulation of the conventions of the political advice-book.[7] The genre of the *speculum principis*, or mirror-of-the-prince, comprised those texts bearing such names as *De regimine principum*, *De institutione principis*, and *De officio regis*, all of which were directed to educate the prince toward the end of governing well. The distinguishing conventions of the genre proved remarkably stable, for the hundreds of texts all followed the same topics as they developed the same themes: for example, each would discuss the relation of king to counselors, caution against flattery, and observe that prudence comes from reading good books such as the one before the reader. As Lester Born observed, "We conclude at once that originality is not one of the prime essentials of a good treatise on the education of a prince."[8] This lack of originality probably issues from the corresponding high degree of intertextuality among the works. Born suggested as much when he again remarked, "There is little originality displayed; the main argument is nearly always supported by wholesale quotations."[9] The texts represented a tradition of political commentary that continued to thrive in the intellectual ferment of the Renaissance, and authors of varied backgrounds and affiliations relied on the authority of tradition to accomplish their object of persuading the prince to behave decently.

There has been little disagreement about defining the various texts as a genre: classification includes attention to the ubiquity and locales of the manuals, their allusions and direct references to prior texts, and the many instances of direct parallelism. Nor has it been difficult to place *The Prince* within this tradition, noting primarily the similarity of the dedication to Isocrates' letter *To Nicocles*, which was regarded at the time (and today) as the origin of the genre, the Latinate chapter headings (despite the text being in the vernacular), adherence to such conventions as the catalog of virtues, and Machiavelli's two oblique references to other political writers, which occur in the dedication and at the beginning of his review of the virtues.[10] The crucial interpretative tasks have been to answer the related questions of how Machiavelli appropriated the Renaissance culture of civic humanism and how he challenged the conventional wisdom of his genre.[11] Today there seems no doubt that Machiavelli was both imbued with ideas reaching back to antiquity and author of one of the decisive innovations in modern thought, and that his innovation includes not only his brilliant critique of the idea that the conventional virtues were effective means for political rule, but also his "appeal to recognize the crucial importance of force in politics" and "the significance of sheer power in political life."[12]

The question today is not whether a break occurred between *The Prince* and its genre, but whether the break has been presented in the most revealing terms. Although there is no doubt that Machiavelli challenged ethical sensibilities and related literary habits, these observations alone do not account for the full range of persuasive effects achieved by his simple text. Although Machiavelli remains a realist who can ruthlessly separate ethics from politics and political inquiry from wishful thinking, this perspective has been available at least since Plato and Thucydides, and the question remains how *The Prince* provides decisive reformulations of political power and practical wisdom that have become characteristic of modern political thought. I submit that Machiavelli's innovation is in a crucial sense a matter of style, at once somewhat tacit and easily reproducible in situations far removed from his own. The key rhetorical maneuvers of his text model the basic elements of a realist style, which places politics in a

16

reality outside of the grasp of political texts and promotes strategic thinking as the pure form of political intelligence. This style begins by marking all other discourses with the sign of the text: It devalues other political actors because they are too discursive, too caught up in their textual designs to engage in rational calculation. This maneuver activates the endemic assumption in modern thought that political power is an autonomous material force. It ends with the modern understanding that political texts are necessarily incomplete, awaiting realization in a material world.

The nature and significance of Machiavelli's political style are most evident in his celebrated announcement of his innovation. Chapter 15 begins the portion of *The Prince* that most directly addresses the *specula:* Although he will follow the conventional catalog of virtues and the standard disputations regarding their application (such as whether it is better to be feared or loved), he begins by directly opposing himself to the other (unnamed) writers of the genre. "And as I know that many have written of this, I fear that my writing about it may be deemed presumptuous, differing as I do, especially in this matter, from the opinions of others."[13] Now if this had been the extent of his description, we would still conclude that he was attempting to break with the genre but the break would be judged solely in respect to its originality.

This theme, however, becomes eclipsed by the following claim, which is original and more: "But my intention being to write something of use to those who understand, it appears to me more proper to go to the real truth of the matter than to its imagination; and many have imagined republics and principalities which have never been seen or known to exist in reality; for how we live is so far removed from how we ought to live, that he who abandons what is done for what ought to be done, will rather learn to bring about his own ruin than his preservation" (p. 56). Three ideas are stated here regarding the other commentaries: They are imaginative rather than realistic, normative rather than descriptive, and weaken rather than strengthen the prince. The key to this passage is not the truthfulness of the several claims themselves so much as it is their implicit association. In Machiavelli's world, political success (*lo stato*[14]) comes from seeing what is the case, and saying what ought to be leads to political failure. Any other equation is itself one of the fantasies leading to failure. Therefore, if one is speaking of what ought to be, the advice

17

cannot be realistic; if one is speaking of what is the case, the advice must be effective; etc.

If we are to be realistic about the design at work in the text, then we should see that Machiavelli is twice masked. First, the opposition between realism and idealism disguises the motive of writing for advantage. Whereas the more conventional writers competed for a reader's attention by their artistic evocations of artistically perfected government, Machiavelli suggests that his epistemological standard is the only legitimate means for measuring advice; the quest for advantage has been separated from writing and moved to the realm of the prince's actions. The prince reads to gain advantage over his opponents, but writers write (properly) only to record the real. Second, it should be obvious that the declaration that he will identify reality itself is no less presumptuous than the generic portrait of the ideal prince.[15] Perhaps this is why Machiavelli's artistry is so subtle at precisely this point. Aristotle's observation that "a writer must disguise his art and give the impression of speaking naturally and not artificially" had been refined within Renaissance culture to a preoccupation with suggesting mastery by ease.[16] As Machiavelli's contemporary Baldesar Castiglione advised: "So this quality which is the opposite of affectation, and which we are now calling nonchalance . . . brings with it another advantage; for . . . it not only reveals the skill of the person doing it but also very often causes it to be considered far greater than it really is."[17] By claiming to simply see the world as it is (while looking to one's own advantage as advisor) the Machiavellian narrator feigns the ease of his cognitive skills and emotional control. His simplicity and candor are means for amplifying both the importance of his subject and the extent of his expertise, and it follows that he can best establish his authority by shunning affectation.

Recall now Machiavelli's other allusion to the genre, found in his dedication. "I have not sought to adorn my work with long phrases or high-sounding words or any of those superficial attractions and ornaments with which many writers seek to embellish their material, as I desire no honour for my work but such as the novelty and gravity of its subject shall justly deserve" (pp. 3–4). Here the writer of *The Prince* is announcing himself. Whereas the other writers are described in terms of their textuality, he is aligned with the natural

18

world. Their texts are made of the stuff of words alone and are extrinsic to their subject; his text is indigenous to reality itself. Yet his own terms are false, for he is not entirely the individual set against others who are in turn known by their artifice and their conventionality. He is equally conventional: he follows the convention of implying virtue through nonchalance and lack of affectation. He is equally artificial: he crafts the illusion that his writing is only a transparent medium between reader and world. Machiavelli successfully affects a lack of affectation; he is a consummate stylist who persuades us that he is without artistry. The influence of *The Prince* on its readers begins with its author's artistic concealment of his artistry, a master trope opposing nature and ornament, a real world and the distractions of a text.

Machiavelli's skill at aligning himself with signs of a natural world is evident in his following metaphor. "Nor will it, I trust, be deemed presumptuous on the part of a man of humble and obscure condition to attempt to discuss and direct the government of princes; for in the same way that landscape painters station themselves in the valleys in order to draw mountains or high ground, and ascend an eminence in order to get a good view of the plains, so it is necessary to be a prince to know thoroughly the nature of the people, and one of the populace to know the nature of princes" (p. 4). Here Machiavelli is addressing a classical question of decorum: How does one speak to one of higher station? No wonder that he is concerned, for he already has repudiated the words conventionally used in addressing a prince; the implications of social leveling are obvious and not likely to be received kindly. Given the architectonic function of decorum in Renaissance thinking, his words also challenged basic assumptions undergirding the intellectual culture of his day.[18] Machiavelli recognizes that this act requires explanation. His answer adroitly maintains a social hierarchy while achieving nothing less than a paradigm shift. As only the subject matter (rather than the social position of the communicator) should determine one's diction, so conventional forms of address are subordinated to depicting the subject. Although prince and political subject have different standpoints, they gaze across the same terrain. They share the common object of knowing an external world, and speech becomes an instrument of representation. This metaphor substitutes observer for writer, vision for language, the subject for its mode of expression, observation for invention, knowledge for convention, and objectivity (with its corollary common sense) for decorum.

This shift from textuality to topography exemplifies the rhetorical stance of Machiavelli's text: it is the means by which the text asserts its authority and defines the standard by which all political texts are to be judged. We are brought to see the other writers as idealistic because they are subjects of their discourse; Machiavelli becomes realistic because he has shunned artifice. For an indication of the power of this trope, imagine political scientists today claiming that they are writers accomplished in the artistically pleasing invention of phrases to appropriately address a ruler, rather than methodologically rigorous observers capable of objective knowledge of their subject matter. Yet their confidence in grasping the real vectors of political explanation derives in part from the rhetorical maneuver of setting their discourse over political "philosophy" or political "commentary" or political "rhetoric." Likewise, political expertise too often consists of little more than unedifying repetition of the conventions of this political style, particularly when it is used for legitimation of established regimes. Before its full significance can be articulated, however, we need to consider the counterargument that Machiavelli was a devout disciple of the literary culture of the Renaissance.[19]

Most commentators find the essence of Machiavelli's relationship with his milieu in his letter of 10 December 1513 to Francesco Vettori and, once there, in the passage where he turns from the empty pastimes of daily life to his solitary evenings in his study.[20] This passage also is taken too quickly at face value, for what is read as a testament to the life of the mind also operates as the artifice of the Machiavellian writer. The letter is a chronicle of Machiavelli's daily life; its basic motif is to show him moving through one scene after another—a morning walk in the countryside to supervise woodcutting, later on to the tavern for an afternoon of gambling, and so forth. Each scene begins pleasantly enough but ends in dissatisfaction. The portrait that emerges is of an acutely self-conscious individual condemned to living among the multitude. There is more to it, however, for the multitude are consistently identified by their incessant wordiness. Thus, the cunning of the letter is that it turns on the subordination of other discourses to the medium of the writer's mind. For example, he describes the vulgarity of playing at the tavern games that "bring on a thousand disputes and countless insults with offensive words, and usually we are fighting over a penny, and nevertheless we are heard shouting as far as San Casciano." Machiavelli, playing the realist, admits to his enjoyment, even need, for such things; but Machiavelli the stylist has again made language extrinsic to reality and so capable only of the exaggerated expression of desire. Not surprisingly, the entire letter is a record of false or idle speaking: He kills time with the woodcutters, "who have always some bad-luck story ready," loses in business because of the bad promises of his customers, to whom he then responds in kind, and speaks idly with others to learn of the "different fancies of men." There are only two instances prior to the evening scene in which language seemingly has intrinsic value: He values Signor Vettori's letters as sure sign of his good will, and he reads poetry to learn of tender loves and "enjoy myself a while in that sort of dreaming." Writing becomes the more realistic as it is the sign of Machiavelli's relationship with his patron, and otherwise it remains explicitly the medium of desire. The realist hides the strategist, for language's capacity for fact is unquestioned within the relationship of patronage, denied otherwise, and the actual basis for the distinction is never admitted. Again, after the evening scene we return to a world where those capable of helping Machiavelli speak clearly, while others are represented by the potential plagiarist Ardinghelli.

We do not come innocently to the final scene, then, nor leave it unfollowed. And what is within? "On the coming of evening, I return to my house and enter my study; and at the door I take off the day's clothing, covered with mud and dust, and put on garments regal and courtly; and reclothed appropriately, I enter the ancient courts of ancient men, where I am received by them with affection, I feed on that food which only is mine and which I was born for, where I am not ashamed to speak with them and to ask them the reason for their actions; and they in their kindness answer me; and for four hours of time I do not feel boredom, I forget every trouble, I do not dread poverty, I am not frightened by death; entirely I give myself over to them."

We begin by leaving the world, a passage emphasized by a series of passages—from day into night, public realm into house and there into the study, a pause at the threshold of the inner sanctum to shed the day's clothing, known by the mud and dust symbolizing the world and its temporal finitude, which is echoed at the close of the paragraph by his fear of death. Then, to become fit to enter, he dons clothing "regal and courtly," the appropriate garb for one entering the ancient texts. Here Machiavelli enters the only community he can respect, and so he assumes all the conventions of speech repudiated in *The Prince*. He speaks grandiloquently while observing the principle of decorum and even celebrating its sensibility. He ornaments himself without shame in order that he may speak with the ancient *auctores*. Faced with the same problem he acknowledged at the beginning of *The Prince*, that of speaking appropriately with one of higher status, he here calls on the resources for resolving that problem that he rejects there for the better alternative of plain speech.

Yet the letter remains consistent with *The Prince*, for in both texts speech and action are opposing worlds. His time with the ancients is a time of reverie, melding theoretical curiosity with psychological recovery, and it is wholly separate from the world. When within the world of texts he behaves accordingly—speaking in a grand style for a grand place, happy to be clothed and ornamented with words, savoring good conversation far more than the naked truth. But it is a separate world. The world of texts is not the world of princes. There is only one connection between text and world for Machiavelli, and it is a strange one. "I feed on that food which only is mine and which I was born for." Language again becomes the medium of desire. The continuity between text and world is the same as between this letter and *The Prince*: the gigantic personality of Machiavelli. Here is the lion lurking behind the stratagems of the fox, the individual who devours the tradition that so easily absorbs the works of the other writers.

The letter can still be read as a mark of Machiavelli's education, yet it also reveals his innovative composition of the persona of the political advisor. While Machiavelli admits to his relationship with his precursors, he also renegotiates the relationship between their texts and everyone else. He not only reads the classical authors, he secrets himself with them. By consistently separating one world of great literature from another of petty tyrannies, the texts become hermetic, valuable to the world only via the interpreter. They are guides, but also misleading, so a basic trade-off is offered: they are removed from the world, in the sense of no longer providing a check upon princely power, and are replaced by the office of the princely advisor, who now reads for the prince. This is the rhetorical stance which we know too well today as the role of the expert. *He* might speak with the ancients, but the prince who would turn his eyes from the world could only fall.

We have come a long way from Isocrates' letter *To Nicocles*, the supposed model for the dedication.[21] Although the parallel is obvious, the resemblance also can be misleading. Consider this difference: Although both writers appeal for the king's attention by contrasting their work to gifts of material wealth, Machiavelli defines these conventional gifts as "ornaments" and goes on to contrast himself with other writers who also are marked by ornamentation. Each has the same rhetorical problem—the intellectual's competition for the ruler's attention—and each follows the obvious strategy of finding an advantageous basis for comparison with one's competitors, but there is an important difference between them. Isocrates could have set himself against other advisors—that is, against oral advice—just as Machiavelli could have been content to oppose those attempting to purchase the prince's favors. But each is writing a metaphysics as well. Isocrates opposes those bearing material gifts not because he alone of all the Greeks attempts to gain favor by advising, but because he is writing the spirit of his age by writing a textual politics. We can confirm this idea by looking to Isocrates' second letter for Nicocles. Here Isocrates produces one of his more brilliant passages when anticipating the very argument Machiavelli advances: that eloquence contains nothing useful to a king. Isocrates, an able realist in his own right, nonetheless lives in a textual world: "There is no institution devised by humanity which the power of speech has not helped us establish."[22] The key implication here is that what is made by language can only be known fully through language; although words have the power to distort, they alone have the capability for the reflexive consciousness required for understanding anything made of discourse.

Machiavelli follows a different strategy to a different end. He places himself over the other writers not because he alone of all the Florentines attempts to provide realistic advice, but because he is writing the spirit of his age by writing to liberate himself from a textual consciousness.[23] Whereas Isocrates understood power as an effective text, and implied that rulers can only rule effectively if they, like speakers, adapt themselves to the restraints imposed by their audiences, Machiavelli developed the modern metaphysics of power by writing in a manner that subverted the authority of textual consciousness, freeing those who would rule from the constraints of eloquence. He did so from inside, of course—in contemporary terms, he produced a deconstructive text—by artfully professing the artlessness of his text as the means of hiding his artistry. Machiavelli turned rhetoric against itself; his kin include Socrates before him and Descartes after, but not Isocrates.[24] Machiavelli would have us believe the *specula* distort their subject in the attempt to persuade, while he lets the subject appear as it is. His full implication is that the essence of his subject is something that is correctly communicated only through artlessness; he abjures explicit textuality because power is not itself textual. As rhetoric is extrinsic to reality, so power becomes objectified, something existing independently of language, texts, and textual authority.

This shift in consciousness required subverting the genre of the *speculum principis* because the genre was the symbolic container of the textual metaphysics. The basic implication of the formal elements of the genre was that power is the consequence of authority, thus, a social relation expected to conform to the culture's authorities, including not least of all its authors. Power was intelligible at all because it moved through the appropriate channels, was conducted largely by persuasion (and the norms of persuasion such as decorum), and was at bottom a form of speech. The writer of the *specula* inherited this metaphysic and reproduced it by writing conventionally. The basic orientation of the genre was persuasive—as Isocrates claimed that the first letter to Nicocles was "pleading the cause of his subjects"[25]—and the conventions stressed the authority of past writers, the value in restating commonly held ideals, and the necessity of clothing the king in the appropriate speech: "I, myself, welcome all forms of discourse which are capable of benefiting us even in a small degree; however, I regard those as the best and most worthy of a king, and most appropriate to me, which give directions on good morals and good government."[26] This idea operated in both the Isocratean school and in the Renaissance not as an opinion but as a program of study and political invention. Hence, "eloquence was the distinctive concern of the Humanists,"[27] and the premier example of how any political instrument was by its very nature—that is, its textual nature—continuous with ethics.[28]

The extent of Machiavelli's break from this set of ideas is visible in the structure of *The Prince*. Although highlighting Machiavelli's break with the genre does not entail that the text should be read *sui generis*—in fact, it is the imitations that set up the moments of innovation—there are several deviations in form that each reinforce his redefinition of political power away from an association with textual authority toward an association with material force.[29] First, the text gives unusual attention to military matters, and particularly to the place of instruction in military attitudes, strategies, and tactics in the education of the prince. Neal Wood has shown how this topic suffuses the text, and we can observe its special prominence in chapters 3, 7, 10, 12, 13, 14, 19, 20, and 24, as well as its odd intrusion in the final chapter's peroration.[30] Second, Machiavelli gives less than usual emphasis to the literary education of the prince. Whereas the other writers were laboring to create a Renaissance Man, Machiavelli "only glancingly mentions the question of the ruler's 'intellectual training.'"[31] The reason for this difference is simple: why study what will mislead you? Machiavelli fills the gap here by recommending hunting (chapter 14) because it provides both physical exercise and training in topography. In addition, Machiavelli substitutes instruction in propaganda for the standard discussion of eloquence. What were lessons in conventional pedagogy and composition become a treatise on the use of verbal deception, that is, a redefinition of the art of rhetoric consistent with his metaphysic. Chapters 18, 19, and 21 advise the prince to rely on personal deceit and false public display, while chapters 22 and 23 warn against those capable of persuading him. In the realist style, public discourse becomes the artifice that covers sovereign political movement, and the public functions only as a force to be controlled. Taken as a whole, then, where *The Prince* most obviously follows the format of its genre (in the dedication and chapter 15) it denounces the genre's entanglement with language, and it then deviates from the conventional topics of the genre by omitting attention to literary study while articulating ideas of force and verbal deception.

Machiavelli's break with his genre is evident in another manner as well. The gist of his innovation is that he repudiated the genre's most basic assumption—its belief that politics is circumscribed by words. Thus, an interesting sign of the break is his omission of the one element of the genre that most signified the metaphysic of textuality:

the frequent citation of prior writers. The citation of sources was a common characteristic of the genre, allowing the writer to incorporate political commentary into a reflective field of sacred and secular literatures. This habit seems trivial today, as Allan Gilbert observed: "The scholasticism and classicism of the majority of these authors, taken together, has hidden their import from the modern world, even from professed students of politics. Our forgetfulness of the relation of ethics and politics, . . . our assumption that citations from classical authors are merely pedantry, . . . such things have allowed us to suppose that the books of advice to rulers that casually come to our notice were always as lifeless as they now appear."[32]

This hint is a good one, for those citations gave life to the texts by giving them both persuasive power and meaning. The citation operated as a rhetorical technique—the appeal to authority—and as an epistemology—where knowledge was lifted above the confusions of *fortuna* by being based in texts—and as a sign of the nature of power being created and restrained by the *logos* known through both sacred and secular texts. But not in *The Prince:* Despite some allusion in the work,[33] and widespread appropriation in his other works,[34] *The Prince* refers to only two authors by name—Virgil in chapter 17 and Petrarch in chapter 26. Interestingly, these do the conventional work of shoring up his argument where it is most controversial. For the most part, however, *The Prince* is presented as a sheer text, directly communicating unencumbered experience. In short, I am suggesting that Machiavelli's omission of this convention operates as one of the changes by which he altered his form of expression to articulate a new political consciousness. Although this break with convention cannot demonstrate entirely his subordination of textuality, perhaps it can serve as an apt illustration of the difference in sensibilities that I am attempting to chart.

The importance of Machiavelli's omission of citations is suggested by comparison with two contemporary texts, Desiderius Erasmus's *Institutio principis Christiani,* and Augustino Nifo's plagiarism of *The Prince.*[35] The first comparison shows us a masterful presentation of the conventional form, while the second demonstrates the attempt by a lesser writer to "correct" Machiavelli's text by restoring the missing conventions. Erasmus's text was printed in 1516, ran through eighteen editions and several translations during his lifetime, and continued to be widely read and quoted through the seventeenth century, after which the record grows hazy.[36] Erasmus stands at every corner as Machiavelli's opposite: the scholar, writing in Latin, for a hereditary ruler, to nurture Christian government. The difference in literary consciousness can be marked easily, however, by observing Erasmus's "constant references to classical antiquity in true humanistic fashion."[37] The dedicatory epistle can suffice for this comparison, for it refers directly to Aristotle, Xenophon, Proverbs, Plato, Homer, Plutarch (who in turn is quoting Alexander the Great on Diogenes the Cynic), and Isocrates, as well as alluding to two biblical stories. As an interesting complement, when he does refer to the present circumstances of the prince he compares him (favorably) to Alexander, to his ancestors surrounding him on every side, and to his deceased father. The unbroken impression, then, is that the prince is inextricably immeshed in a society of prior authorities, some of whom are the authors of texts while others serve as texts themselves. The dead have become *exempla*, rhetorical figures having as much presence as the living and more authority, and any distinction between ancient author, prior ruler, and current prince is, well, something not quite determined. Power has been denominated as *personae* themselves defined simultaneously by their words and their affinities for each other. The political world is textual and texts social, so the personality of the prince can only be found in the common association of these prior authors and authorities. Erasmus is well aware of the abuse of power—witness his discussions of tyrants—but he sees them from within a textual universe where the difference between forms of power is determined by the influence of persuaders on the prince's soul. So it is that Erasmus can fret about the very order of the young prince's reading.[38]

A more extreme indication of the metaphysical tension created by Machiavelli's text is provided by one of his contemporaries. Augustino Nifo was an academic whose works include fourteen volumes of commentaries on the works of Aristotle and a defense of the doctrine of the immortality of the soul. He also produced a plagiarism of *The Prince* under the title *De regnandi peritia* in 1523.[39] This plagiarism demonstrates perfectly how a conventional reader of Machiavelli's time would understand his genre. Nifo is impressively credentialed as a conventional thinker, and his many changes are direct reactions to *The Prince*'s deviations from the genre's sensibility. For example, the work is written in Latin, the language of medieval cultural hegemony, and the title is changed to subordinate the concept of the new ruler to the concept of government understood as a process of administration. (Nifo naturally would assume that "Most of the works *de regimine principum* are based on settled hereditary rule."[40]) Most importantly, he supplied the missing citations, including Aristotle (repeatedly, with reference to his *Rhetoric* more than any other work), Cicero, Plato and Socrates, Herodotus, Hesiod, Varro, Plutarch, Ovid, Demosthenes, Strabo, and others. It is reasonable to read these changes as the chief signs of the difference between Nifo's mind and Machiavelli's—that is, between the genre as Machiavelli found it and as he changed it. Moreover, the greater the deviation from the original argument the more Nifo relies on his authorities: so the typology of the forms of government beginning the work is a relatively plain text, while the book's concluding argument for moral government follows a litany of authorities to the last paragraph's reference to Isocrates—the letter *To Nicocles*. Nifo has worked his way backwards through the turn Machiavelli constructed: Where *The Prince* began with Isocrates in order to repudiate him, so Nifo has begun with Machiavelli in order to return to Isocrates. If we apply the maxim that thinking is the manipulation of available symbolic material, then we can conclude that Machiavelli's elision of the textual authorities subverted one way of thinking, including its characteristic ideas, and that Nifo's attempt to maintain those ideas consisted primarily of recovering the elided material.

More modern commentators have not found Machiavelli's style so unsettling. As Felix Gilbert's fine essay has been highly influential, it is important to note how it relies on Machiavelli's master trope. Briefly, Gilbert argues that although all of the humanist writers were grappling with the new problems of their time, only Machiavelli succeeded in establishing realism as the basis of political thought, while the others had "no appreciation of the power-factor and the egoistic purposes which dominate the political life."[41] Gilbert's explanation exemplifies the pattern of thinking Machiavelli authored: First, the other writers continued to be misled by their literary sensibilities—"As soon as an author had literary ambitions, he felt it necessary to set an ideal standard and write of an imaginary political world"—and, second, reality itself had not intervened, in the form of an act of force known as the French invasion, to correct the writers.[42] Reinforcing this pattern is a strict association of tradition with illusion and innovation with realism. Both Gilbert and Quentin Skinner are correct in identifying Machiavelli's discovery of the significance of the "sheer power" residing in "force,"[43] but neither considers how Machiavelli created the very means for the compliment: the modern terms "power" and "force" are metaphysical terms, and that metaphysics exists because Machiavelli so artfully defined politics against its texts.[44]

As Friedrich Meinecke has outlined, Machiavelli's work gradually became translated into a discourse advancing and legitimating the rise of the modern European state.[45] This discourse of *Raison d'État* can be understood as both a doctrine and a manner of speaking, and its stylistic conventions can be the principal means for sustaining the doctrine and for legitimating specific policies and leaders.[46] Note, for example, how the strategy of contrasting reality with textuality is used to characterize the masters (and would-be masters) of statecraft. Metternich remarked of himself: "'I am a man of prose . . . and not of poetry. . . . I was born to make history not to write novels.'"[47] Henry Kissinger has used the same figure in his praise of Bismarck: "I think he is the first modern statesman in this sense: that he attempted to conduct foreign policy on the basis of an assessment of the balance of forces, unrestrained by the clichés of a previous period."[48] As Kissinger also has remarked, "The practice of diplomacy is not something that can be learned from texts."[49] His prince, Richard Nixon, saw things the same way: "Because of the realities of human nature, perfect peace is achieved in two places only: in the grave and at the typewriter. Perfect peace flourishes—in print. It is the stuff of poetry and high-minded newspaper editorials, molded out of pretty thoughts and pretty words. Real peace, on the other hand, will be the down-to-earth product of the real world, manufactured by realistic, calculating leaders whose sense of their nations' self-interest is diamond-hard and unflinching."[50] More recently, George Bush relied on this style when defending his "inherent power to commit our forces to battle," namely, near complete usurpation of the Congress's power to declare war: "Our founders never envisioned a congress that would churn out hundreds of thousands of pages worth of reports and hearings and documents and laws every year."[51] In every case, the speaker gives us a real world by contrasting it to a textual world and denigrates opposing perspectives by associating them with their means of expression.

These examples also reveal the second major design of the realist style. The realist's definition of the political scene requires a complementary definition of the political actor. Only a person of a certain type will survive in a world of hard realities and sovereign powers. When reality is defined against textuality, one is sublimating the sociality of politics. If a discourse is a true representation of its subject because it is devoid of ornament (that is, because it is not directed to please others), then it must stand independently of a social situation, free of social motives such as the quest for higher status.[52] Once one discovers the vectors of power in a field of material forces, there is no need to understand social practices, regulations, or entertainments except as they are to be manipulated. In like manner, the intelligence necessary to master an environment of forces can be separated from any sympathy with the needs, wants, rights, or privileges of others: Instead of the conventional conception of prudence, the calculation of means advantageous to oneself yet beneficial to the community, political genius becomes the distillation of strategic thinking in its unalloyed form.[53] In place of a prince educated to govern in a manner benefiting the governed, Machiavelli presents the modern strategist.

As John Geerken has summarized, "One of the themes of Machiavelli's work is to demonstrate the style common to the political and military arts."[54] I suspect that one reason The Prince has fascinated the West is that it is the best study of strategic thinking before Clausewitz, and our most elegant ever.[55] Although a strategic sensibility suffuses his text, Machiavelli's articulation of it as a mode of thinking can be outlined quickly by looking to his chapters on the virtues and his comments on arms. Key elements presented here include defining human affairs as contingent, employing the means-end calculus, accepting the necessity of deception, and adhering to an ethic of self-control. Although these elements are available in many of those other works on war, politics, business, rhetoric, and love that could comprise a literature of strategy, the achievement of The Prince is that they cohere as a mode of political intelligence superbly fitted to the author's depiction of political reality.

Machiavelli is most notorious for his repudiation of conventional ethics, but his readers have too often failed to notice the exact grounds for this move: the problem with those who would do good is

30

that they fail to recognize the condition of contingency. Machiavelli the strategist opposes not just particular virtues but the very idea of a norm in human affairs: "A man who wishes to make a profession of goodness in everything must necessarily come to grief among so many who are not good. Therefore it is necessary for a prince, who wishes to maintain himself, to learn how not to be good, and to use this knowledge and not use it, according to the necessity of the case" (p. 56). The flaw in the received model of princely conduct was not that it contained an ethical ideal *per se,* but rather that it was cate- ~*rhetoric*~ gorical—given as applying under all conditions. By contrast, Machiavelli stresses consideration of when "to use this knowledge and not use it"—and the moral quality of the means clearly is subordinate to the necessity of adjusting to changing conditions. "I also believe that he is happy whose mode of procedure accords with the needs of the times, and similarly he is unfortunate whose mode of procedure is opposed to the times" (p. 92). The received model's moral tendency in turn leads to a confusion of ends and of means and ends; so it is that Machiavelli reiterates the single end of holding one's position, which in turn allows all ethical precepts to be unmistakably classified as means.

The second element of Machiavelli's account of strategy appears in the central claim of his argument that it is better to be feared than loved: "A prince, therefore, must not mind incurring the charge of cruelty for the purpose of keeping his subjects united and faithful; for, with a very few examples, he will be more merciful than those who, from excess of tenderness, allow disorders to arise" (p. 60). This sentence offers nothing less than a reconstitution of the terms of political discourse. Before Machiavelli, "mercy," "liberality," etc. were terms of value applicable to all social relationships and accountable in respect to the social actors present. If punishment exceeded the crime, then one was cruel; if wealth was distributed, that was liberality, etc. In every case, the proportionality essential to the concept—its rationality, as it were—was determined by reference to the agents in the relationship: one was cruel to someone, liberal with regard to someone, etc. After Machiavelli, the virtues have been subordinated to the economy of virtue, and the ideal ruler has been replaced by the means-end calculus.

The choice, Machiavelli tells us, is not between virtue and vice, but between two strategies: pursuing many small acts to achieve an end gradually while minimizing risk of immediate failure (for example, "mercy"), or pursuing a few bold acts to achieve that end more quickly and decisively while incurring a somewhat higher risk of failure (for example, "cruelty"). Now we can recall that his justification of Agathocles followed the same calculus to parse better and worse forms of cruelty:

Well committed may be called those . . . which are perpetuated once for the need of securing one's self, and which afterwards are not persisted in . . . Cruelties ill committed are those which, although at first few, increase rather than diminish with time. Those who follow the former method may remedy in some measure their condition, both with God and man; as did Agathocles. As to the others, it is impossible for them to maintain themselves. (pp. 34—35)

This shift from virtues and vices to the *uses* of virtue and vice completes Machiavelli's subordination of ethical to strategic thinking.[56]

The second element in Machiavelli's theory of strategy requires a third, however. A competition between two rational actors would quickly become too predictable for either to gain great advantage (save by *fortuna*), as long as each could learn of the actions of the other. So it is not enough to replace virtue with the calculation of virtue; in a move not exactly in the spirit of scientific inquiry, Machiavelli asserts that a calculation can be most effective only if it also is accompanied by deception. "But it is necessary to be able to disguise this character well, and to be a great feigner and dissembler" (pp. 64–65). Although Machiavelli hardly invented deception, he alone makes it into a cardinal principle of the ruler's thinking by emphasizing the *necessity* of concealing one's motives. "Therefore, a prudent ruler ought not to keep faith when by so doing it would be against his interest" (p. 64). His argument here extends across the eighteenth chapter: Speech itself is naturally debased since men are bad and do not keep their promises, the means of deception are always readily available, and there are plenty of fools willing to be deceived. Moreover, the cunning prince is caught in a contradiction, for he must both act contrary to virtue and appear virtuous if he is to maintain his position. "It is not, therefore, necessary for a prince to have all the above-named qualities, but it is very necessary to seem to have them" (p. 65). Finally, in judging political actions nothing counts so much as results. Thus, in any particular case deceptions (like virtues) become factored into the strategic calculation as elements to be evaluated only as they are used effectively or ineffectively, while in general they are valorized as crucial to sustained strategic success. As a measure of the importance of this precept in Machiavelli's thinking, note how he compares it in the next chapter to military might: the prince defends himself against foreign powers with arms and against his subjects with his reputation.

This is not to say that the prince is ethically undefined, however. As the prince becomes skilled in the practices of deceit he must become more suspicious of others, assuming that his courts are full of flatterers, his cities full of conspirators, and his alliances grounded in deceit. Although no longer bound by any conventional virtue, the Machiavellian strategist nonetheless must regulate his own conduct lest he fall into the snares set by others. Thus, Machiavelli makes self-control another element of strategic thinking; he crafts not only a theory of strategy but also a strategic temperament. This may be Machiavelli's major contribution to the history of strategy, for nowhere else do we find the presentation of strategic thinking as more than a collection of means or a calculus. The enormous influence of *The Prince* comes from its composition of the *persona* of the strategic thinker, and the Machiavellian writer persuades by appeal to this distinctive political personality. Ironically, this presentation brings Machiavelli closest to the ethical norms of his genre, for his prince must not be impulsive, unduly acquisitive, or otherwise subject to desires. Nor can he exercise one faculty at the expense of all the others, or withdraw from the world, or be too common or worldly in his associations. He must affect a grand manner befitting his rank yet keep his feet on the ground, his eyes open, and his demeanor reserved. Although never advised to be a Christian knight, and always told to be virtuous only when it was useful to be so, there is a decidedly ethical cast to the Machiavellian prince that would have been quite "idealistic" when compared with the many overgrown children holding court throughout Italy.

Several examples should illustrate the particulars of this ethos of self-control. For all of the evil attributed to Machiavelli, it is noteworthy how little outright impulsive rapacity there is in the work. It is assumed that princes are imperialistic, or at least meddlers in each other's affairs, but the clear message is that this end cannot be had by

33

dashing off to war. The strong theme in the Caesar Borgia story is that he succeeded in freeing himself of his dependencies on the French and his father by acting on carefully considered plans; in fact, the Duke's plans are granted so much premeditation as to strain belief. And each of the incidents of savagery in the book are paramount examples of self-control. For example, Borgia kills the assembled Orsini and his official Remirro de Orco, Agathocles kills the assembled leaders of Syracuse, Liverotto kills the assembled leaders of Fermo, yet in every case the slaughter is the outcome of a strategically devised deceit, the success of which depended on the prince's restraining his decent impulses entirely and controlling his urge to murder until the appropriate time. In no case do we hear of a lord striking out in anger like a Lear, or reveling in his victory like a Thyestes. Appropriately, Machiavelli concludes this series of stories by demonstrating how cruelties, injuries, and benefits are all to be calculated and by reminding us that a wise prince never acts rashly to unforeseen events. Stated otherwise, the strategist subordinates conquest to control.

Of course, this is the ethos of the professional military. Machiavelli's use of the military model is unconventional only in his great emphasis on its value. "A prince should therefore have no other aim or thought, nor take up any other thing for his study, but war and its organisation and discipline, for that is the only art that is necessary to one who commands" (p. 53). This advice goes well beyond the reminder that states should be prepared for war; Machiavelli is activating a profound analogy between politics and war. As Neal Wood has observed, "Politics, then, for Machiavelli, is similar to warfare, and the style of the accomplished political leader should be something comparable to the art of war as practiced by the skilled general."[57] The common denominator between these two arts is a matter of style: a styling of oneself as the consummate strategist.[58] Interestingly, at this point (chapter 14) Machiavelli reverts to the custom of advising the prince to read: that is, to read histories of great military commanders in order to imitate their successes. Philopoemen, prince of the Achaeans, provides Machiavelli with the perfect exemplar of this style.[59] Observe him quizzing his associates while traveling through the country: "If the enemy were on that hill and we found ourselves here with our army, which of us would have the advantage?

How could we safely approach him maintaining our order? If we wished to retire, what ought we to do? If they retired, how should we follow them?" (p. 55). By training his mind in peacetime—rather than indulging such irresponsible propensities as enjoying the scenery while conversing about love—he would be able to react rationally in war. The soldier's discipline is a mental discipline and, specifically, the habit of calculating how the common means of the land can be used to the competitive end of military victory. Strategy begins with anticipation and ends properly when correct calculations are executed in a timely—that is, controlled—manner, so the strategic thinker acquires his independence at the expense of living freely.[60]

The story of Philopoemen also represents the topographical sensibility of Machiavelli's dedication. In place of political texts with their virtues, the prince lives in a denuded terrain to be used for advantage. The wise prince sees the ordinary political scene as a distribution of forces, and even radical disruption of that scene is understood in those terms. For example, *fortuna* is compared to a destructive river "that, when turbulent, inundates the plains, casts down trees and buildings, removes earth from this side and places it on the other; . . . And if you regard Italy, which has been the seat of these changes, and who has given the impulse to them, you will see her to be a country without dykes or banks of any kind" (pp. 91–92). This is not even the "book of nature," for the land is studied only to be used as a competitive field. Historical change has acquired the fury of nature, but that too can be contained by the prince who is trained to accurately map the terrain and discern its channeling of forces. This model subsequently has provided the terms for interpretation of his own work and much else besides. Once again, note how Felix Gilbert describes Machiavelli's world:

The Italian political situation in the *quattrocento* consisted of a number of known and calculable forces, and success was in the hands of him who knew how to calculate and give due weight to each. All the factors of the political situation were within the perspective of the intelligent observer. This ceased to be the case after the French invasion of 1494, which put an end to Italy's isolation and brought her once more within the orbit of the inexorable dynamics of world-historical events. History, in other words, once more appeared as the manifestation of an

35

MACHIAVELLI'S REALIST STYLE

incomprehensible and uncontrollable power. . . . Thus, all trace of the idealized human personality as such vanished from Machiavelli's portrait of the prince, and its place was taken by the superpersonal conception of reasons of state.[61]

Gilbert's "factual" description of political events is a highly stylized composition. This realist style produces an aesthetically unified conception of political scene and political actor: Whether ruled by will or *fortuna*, the political environment is an abstract world of forces (functionally equivalent, socially barren entities like military units or nation-states or transnational corporations), and one survives in this world through strategic calculation of others' capacity to act and through rational control of oneself.

Such portrayals of strategists in a world of forces have become more influential than Machiavelli could have imagined. For example, the famous essay by George Kennan on "The Sources of Soviet Conduct" schooled a generation in the realist style.[62] Kennan argued that the Soviets would understand only force, not diplomacy, and in doing so he crafted the image of the American strategist who can prevail against such an adversary. The Soviets, we are told, must be regarded as rivals, not partners, and are fundamentally different from us because of both national character and political indoctrination. (Kennan neatly overcomes the "idealism" presumed in his American audience by projecting onto the Soviets the coercive temperament that he is advocating. The general argument comes straight from *The Prince:* Of course, we would rather live more virtuously, but cannot due to the predatory character of others.) Because they have been indoctrinated, "the foreign representative cannot hope that his words will make any impression on them." Because Russian history has been one of "battles between nomadic forces over the stretches of a vast unfortified plain," they have "no compunction about retreating in the face of superior force," since their "political action is a fluid stream which moves constantly, wherever it is permitted to move, toward a given goal. Its main concern is to make sure that it has filled every nook and cranny available to it in the basin of world power." Consequently, the United States must adopt a "long-term, patient but firm and vigilant containment of Russian expansive tendencies," while recognizing that this diking of a naturally expansive force "has nothing to do with outward histrionics: with threats or blustering or superfluous gestures of outward 'toughness.'" (*Real* toughness is that which can be contrasted with a rhetoric of toughness.) Moreover, since the Russians know that "loss of temper and of self-control is never a source of strength in political affairs . . . it is a sine qua non of successful dealing with Russia that the foreign government in question should remain at all times cool and collected." (This effacement of personality was neatly symbolized by the essay's publication under the pseudonym "X.") In sum, "it will be clearly seen that the Soviet pressure against the free institutions of the Western world is something that can be contained by the adroit and vigilant application of counterforce at a series of constantly shifting geographical and political points, corresponding to the shifts and maneuvers of Soviet policy, but which cannot be charmed or talked out of existence."[63] Here Kennan has contained more than the Soviets. American understanding of international affairs has been channeled into the forms of realist rhetoric: Politics has been transformed into the strategic application of force, which is a material reality contrasted with verbal artistry and depicted topographically. Within this scene, political success is possible for only a single type of rational actor, one whose personality has been masked by self-control.

This aesthetics of plane surfaces and impersonal designs also is reflected in the language of *The Prince*. Perhaps it is not surprising that there has been insufficient attention to Machiavelli's prose style: Most readers do not read it in the Italian, minor variations in key passages are common in the multitude of translations, and no original manuscript survives.[64] In addition, we should credit the writer: Machiavelli's claim to be avoiding artistic virtuosity has been persuasive, deflecting attention from his writing and its effects. He is the master of a particular manner of selecting and arranging words, however, which reinforces the stylistic innovations and rhetorical power that have made *The Prince* a model of modern political intelligence.[65] In the classical lexicon, public address was graded from plain speech at one extreme to grandiloquence at the other, with each style having specific functions.[66] We know as much today: recipes are not likely to contain metaphors, and calls to salvation don't sound like recipes. What has changed is the presumption that politics is better conducted in plain terms than in a more amplified manner of speaking. Although this transformation in the norms of public address has occurred at different times in different places, certainly Machiavelli stands as one of its exponents. For the most part, he proved good to his word: The disavowal of ornamentation is indeed a principle of composition in *The Prince*.

If there are merely literary values, they are not evident in Machiavelli's artistry, for his text illustrates how literary simplicity is an element of the realist style. That is, this political style operates at two levels: most importantly, by activating master tropes for defining the speaker and subject of a political discourse, but also by speaking and writing with a simple diction and logical cadence that exemplify related aesthetic norms. Machiavelli's first chapter is a model of the characteristic features of this plain speech. He writes:

All the states, all the dominions under whose authority men have lived in the past and live now have been and are either republics or principalities. Principalities are hereditary, with their prince's family long established as rulers, or they are new. The new are completely new, as was Milan to Francesco Sforza, or they are like limbs joined to the hereditary state of the prince who acquires them, as is the kingdom of Naples in relation to the king of Spain. Dominions so acquired are accustomed to be under a prince, or used to freedom; a prince wins them either with the arms of others or with his own, either by fortune or by prowess.[67]

In a single stroke, Machiavelli has fused the subject matter of politics and the writer's intelligence into a uniform mode of comprehension that is marked by simplicity of manner and comprehensive scope. His diction and arrangement include only simple terms and straightforward syntax, yet his assertion has the grandest sweep: "All the states, all the dominions under whose authority men have lived in the past and live now have been and are either republics or principalities." The logical operator "all" declares that the proposition has universal reference, including every instance of the class of events under consideration; the two tenses for the verb emphasize that the class encompasses all present and past time; the predicate nominative's disjunction of "either . . . or" sorts all of the events into two mutually exclusive and jointly comprehensive categories. This correspondence of the diction and syntax of the plain style with the scope of the grand style offers a new alignment of political language with its subject, one that obviously is aesthetically perfect for enactment of Machiavelli's conception of the correct relation between political experience and the discourses of politics. Ostensibly, the description of reality has become the paramount concern, and the preferred mode of description allows one to see clearly a world without ambiguity. It seems that anything other than simple logical relations must come from flawed modes of address rather than from nature itself. Appropriately, the artistry of the sentence draws no attention to itself but, instead, exemplifies the assertiveness and well-chosen, decisive impact that Machiavelli celebrates in many of his portraits of successful rulers.

This simplicity is continued throughout the paragraph, while augmented with an elegantly drawn declension of logical relationships. All A are B or C; all C are D or E; all E are F or G; all G are H or I, and are J or K and L or M. The general sequence of the sentence establishes that the analysis is organized according to strictly logical relations, while the concluding clauses illustrate that this simple calculus can organize complex considerations. As precise discrimination of classes and elegant arrangement of their logical relations prevails, the text exemplifies the aesthetic sensibility of modern analysis, yet the author still succeeds at giving subtle emphasis to his major themes of fortune and ability without drawing attention to the interest or artistry involved in doing so. In addition, any specific sense of the writer's own personality—save for his logical powers—has disappeared.[68] Although just a moment before, in the last paragraph of the introductory note, Machiavelli was whining about "the great and unmerited sufferings inflicted on me by a cruel fate" (p. 4), now the language of the text seemingly carries only the outlines of the reality it describes.

Machiavelli can't stay with this simple manner of address, however, and even comes to violate his own injunctions against amplified appeals. Although it pervades his work, reinforces his most comprehensive persuasive designs, and becomes a new norm of decorum, the plain style doesn't contain the resources he needs to complete his book. In the last two chapters of The Prince, Machiavelli faces his most difficult tasks: first, of establishing the fundamental connection between his major theoretical terms of fortune and prudence and, second, of persuading the Medici prince (and others) to take up the cause of liberating Italy. When faced with these persuasive challenges, Machiavelli returns to the classical conventions that he denigrated at the beginning of the work. Fortune is not the subject of a logical analysis but instead becomes the subject of metaphor: first, it is a river destroying the ordered countryside and, then, a woman who will have to be taken by force. Machiavelli is still a master stylist—

for the first figure comes out of his topographical sensibility, the second substitutes force for the more conventional persuasions of romantic courtship, and both use a textual device to create a sense of nature—but he is no longer the severe, disinterested writer of the earlier pages. The next chapter goes even further down this road. Labeled an exhortation, it reads as a classical peroration, designed to inflame the passions and so impel action. Machiavelli pulls out all of the stops: He invokes God and the Church, appeals to honor and glory, and closes with a heroic stanza by Petrarch. Many commentators have noted the stylistic incongruence of this chapter with the rest of the treatise; from the point of view of his earlier passages about political writing, it is a disgrace.[69] Ironically, as Machiavelli turns to more explicitly rhetorical forms and a more amplified style, the writer begins to merge with the prince, stepping into the public space, attempting to be the forceful innovator, risking failure, and perhaps ending up betrayed by his language.

As he might have predicted, Machiavelli's call to arms did not succeed. His influence stems not from successful appeal to his immediate audience but from mastery of a style of political composition that fit with metaphysical and moral assumptions of the modern age. As the realist style persuades, it constitutes an abstracted world and sovereign self that have become key categories of modern consciousness. The modern epoch does not stand or fall with Machiavelli, of course, and in most cases it will be enough to consider whether realist rhetoric is accurate and what it motivates or excuses. Yet the full reach and significance of the realist style still might escape notice. Judgment of this style ultimately requires assessment in terms of the problematic of modernity, and perhaps such an assessment can contribute to the search for a rationale for the epoch.

I shall draw briefly on the sympathetic yet powerful analysis of modernity developed by Hans Blumenberg in *The Legitimacy of the Modern Age*.[70] Blumenberg has developed an impressive case against the claim that modern thought is the secularization of key concepts in medieval theology and on behalf of a careful reaffirmation of the modern age's capability for the production of a more humane world. His argument both articulates basic problems of the secularization thesis and supplies an alternative model of the historical process that features the susceptibility of innovations to "reoccupation" of the vacated positions in the prior epoch's cultural system.[71] This model provides the basis for a revisionary process of judgment: those ideas of our time that appear most sovereign, susceptible to critique, and illustrative of secularization—ideas such as "progress" and "the state"—are actually authentic and melioristic innovations that have become monstrous by reoccupation. By discriminating between the modest and imperial versions of modern ideas, we can discover the legitimacy of the modern age. Genuine modernity lies in the modest versions of such ideas as self-assertion and theoretical curiosity, and the role of the modern thinker is essentially the Kantian project of discerning the internal limits of any form of rationality in order to reverse the objectification of culture.

The application of Blumenberg's method might seem simple: We can indeed distinguish humble and imperial versions of Machiavelli's innovative stance—for example, between the humble idea of acquiring the skill to exercise political command in a world of contingency and the imperial idea of controlling all choice in all spheres of life by use of force and deceit—and the latter idea can be explained as an example of reoccupation, while the former idea can be used to criticize the latter. But the reoccupation model requires overlooking the origination of ideas in discourse. (Here is the cost of Blumenberg's having worked without benefit of a linguistic turn, which admittedly contributed to the distinctiveness of some of his assertions.[72]) The question here is not whether reoccupation can occur, but whether it can be avoided. The example of Machiavelli's composition of modernity suggests that there is nothing within such a process to favor the more "authentic" action or inhibit abusive overextension. The problem is that there is no discrimination at the level of discourse between the more or less limited concepts: Since both skill and dominion are created by removing textual restraints on power, each originates on the threshold of reoccupation. Furthermore, the shift from textuality to topography creates a gravitational pull toward imperial formulations. When power is understood in terms of speech, it is checked, relational, circumscribed by the exigencies of being heard by an audience or understood by a reader, and always awaiting a reply. When power is understood in terms of vision it is unchecked, expansive, requiring only the movement of the person seeing to acquire the means for complete control of the environment. Machiavelli is comprehensible as the exponent of the modern state not because he described the state but because he composed a discourse capable of carrying the expansive potential in state power. Thus, at the level of discourse, the basic division of ideas essential to Blumenberg's case breaks down.[73] There is nothing in the realist's composition of power to inhibit reoccupation; consequently, its dangerous distortion of modern ideas and impulses are likely to be discovered after the fact, perhaps too late. If we accept that Machiavelli figures prominently in the composition of modernity, then we perhaps should hope that the legitimacy of the modern age lies less in holding to weaker forms of now long-amplified tendencies to excess and more in recognizing possibilities for recovering, by reinterpretation, the terms of our own making.

Machiavelli's stylistic designs also complicate evaluation of the modern concept of self-assertion. It is no news to observe that he is encouraging princes to behave as individuals striving to dominate others in a hostile world. This is only half of the story, however, for a full consideration of this stance requires analysis of how the form of his text reinforces its content—that is, how the text itself is a form of self-assertion. *The Prince* depicts a natural world of predators in which the individual has to be self-assertive in order to survive, and it also is a text in which self-assertion is the essential speech act. The truly sovereign individual in the work is the author's persona, which is created explicitly as the assertion of an individual against the premodern community maintained through the rules of generic composition and the common sense of classical decorum. Furthermore, this individual then becomes the sole means for holding together what has been broken by his arrival: the personality of Machiavelli alone is the means for overcoming the contradiction between textuality and actuality. Once discourse (especially as it is known by its capacity for charming an audience) has been discarded as a means for completing a political scenario, and incapacitated as a source of political motives, the individual becomes the principle of cohesion by default, whether within a text or a polity. Thus, in its modern formulation, the state is defined not as a collectivity but as a supreme individual. Not surprisingly, "international law" then assumes all of the properties Machiavelli attributed to conventional political texts: it neither confers nor restrains the sovereignty states hold by force.

In other words, Machiavelli's technique of denigrating other political texts *as texts*, necessarily alienated in a material world, has become a rhetoric of self-assertion that now is reproduced endlessly.

So it is that diplomats can denigrate human rights as slogans, corporate executives can dismiss worker-safety laws as bureaucratic red tape, and journalists can debunk political speech as mere rhetoric. In every case, understanding the modern age requires reading Machiavelli not only as the proponent of self-assertion for the few fortunate enough to have *lo stato* within their reach, but also as the modern writer schooling all of us to attain self-assertion by overruling our texts.

This inventional design became established as a fixture of modernity in subsequent centuries, for example, in copyright laws, educational practices, and the new discipline of hermeneutics.[74] As David Quint summarizes this transformation in intellectual history, "The impulse to originality came to inform all realms of human thought and discourse, formerly closed, now irreversibly open-ended. . . . Originality had become the source of authority."[75] This impulse continues today in the stipulation that textual meaning is defined by authorial intention—that is, by the original act of self-assertion.[76] Consequently, it becomes difficult to identify political meaning with anything larger than or prior to the individual, such as "tradition," "common sense," "discourse," or "taste." (This is why the realist style undercuts the conservatism so often aligned with it, leaving a brittle sense of social order and a pessimistic view of history, neither of which is likely to be appealing to a modern audience.) Ultimately, empowerment itself is thought of as the individual's creative act—willful, perhaps wild, probably unpredictable and certainly inappropriate in some degree, however mildly so. Any idea of becoming powerful by drawing on traditional resources or assuming an authoritative role seems suspect or second-rate. (This is one point where the realist style resonates with romanticism.) In order to be taken seriously on these terms, a political text has to have an identity similar to individuality and an effect similar to a natural force. Furthermore, reliance on the individual as the principle of meaning and the state as the principle of political legitimacy results in trauma whenever the idea of the individual is weakened (for example, when Freud made the self a "parliament"[77]), or whenever a collectivity asserts itself independently of state representation (for example, when any "people" announces itself). One wonders if both the high anxiety and revolutionary euphoria occasioned by the "death of the author" or the rise of a "people" arises in part because these claims are aesthetically offensive to a consciousness shaped by the realist style.[78] Depending on whether one is relying on or suffering from political measures legitimated by realist discourse, the experience of stepping outside of its boundaries could be either the disorientation that comes from being unable to categorize reality or the sensation of the sublime that comes from exceeding a limit on one's perception.

These deep patterns of legitimation still leave considerable room for maneuver in more mundane communicative practices, however. Whatever advantages the style affords, the realist speaker doesn't escape the complexities of public address. Just as Machiavelli had to amplify his diction as he faced the challenge of motivating his audience, so do other realists have to step outside of their style as they enter the public sphere. Successful speakers in the realist style will have to learn both how to keep public debate on their own limited terms when that is possible and how to stretch beyond the style's own limitations when that is necessary. This artfulness recognizes that the realist style has a characteristic impact within the art of public address: both in the composition of specific speech texts and in its effects on the consciousness of speaker and audience.

The greatest advantage for the realist comes from constraining the wide array of public discourse—keeping deliberation within a vernacular of sovereign powers, calculations of interest, and the like. The demands of establishing consensus and motivating action often require additional, seemingly incompatible, verbal resources, however. Certainly, we can observe how realists have appealed ably to precedent, tradition, or history, cited philosophers, poets, and Scripture, and provided eloquent testimony to their belief in the highest ideals. Nor would it always be correct to assume that these appeals are given cynically, although that is a tone any realist would understand. Often there is another dimension to effective composition, for when the realist style dominates in a text or debate, it transforms aesthetically incongruous elements of the text according to its artistic conventions. For example, "history" becomes something at once material (rather than subject to interpretation) and abstract (rather than activating the sensibility of a particular historical period). In the realist style, history teaches universal laws of power, not the value of local knowledge or different forms of power itself, and it is invoked to inhibit argument rather than open the present to historical interpretation. Likewise, although the realist can invoke and even believe

44

in specific ideals, they exist at all as dispensable additions to the brute conditions of competitive life. The audience can rarely discern for sure, of course, and public debate need not turn on assessments of sincerity, but often the question has to be faced. I believe there is at least one cue to discerning whether any ideal is informing the speaker's argument—although now it, too, can be feigned. If the testimony to the ideal, no matter how provisional, provides coherent definitions of the basic nodes of rhetorical meaning—speaker, subject, and audience—then it probably informs the speaker's thinking; if it doesn't provide a full pattern of definition, then it is an instrumental appeal to the particular audience, no matter how eloquent its statement. Furthermore, if those linked positions are crafted in the realist style, giving us the strategist calculating forces to advise the prince, then all ideals are extraneous. When these definitions of speaker, subject, and audience are supported by the subordination of other perspectives to the realist's plain diction, a formidable persuasive strategy is in place. Although the realist style does not hold all cards in the game of public debate, a well-managed realism is trump.

Even realists believe in more than control, however, and the operation of a persuasive design in a speech need not be identical with the full consciousness of either speaker or audience, even as it is constituting thought and impelling action. If we consider how realism can be a style to be picked up and set aside in the interest of another set of commitments, we have to address the question of how this style is compatible with more substantive patterns of belief. One might look to the affinities between realist speech and other patterns of domination—patriarchy and imperialism come to mind—but there also is the problem of how any principled advocacy at some time has to adopt a "realistic" stance and whether that can be done without great risk to those principles. In the case of Machiavelli, such questions bring us to the debate over the relationship between his realism and his republicanism.

This debate has included consideration of both the composition of Machiavelli's major works, particularly the relationship between *The Prince* and his anatomy of republican government, *The Discourses on Livy*, and the subsequent history of his influence, particularly in England and North America.[79] Analysis of the texts has focused on their circumstances of composition and continuities in theme and argument, as well as larger concerns such as how he understood prudence or whether he expressed a political ideal.[80] The consensus today is that the *Prince* and the *Discourses* are aspects of a single perspective which includes the more sophisticated elements in Machiavelli's thought. One need not overturn this view to consider what it might neglect, however. Although it is obvious that important elements of both *The Prince* and *The Discourses* are to be understood as applying to all forms of governance, they also use markedly different appeals and they have had quite different effects historically. Their stylistic differences are evident from the beginning. For example, Machiavelli dedicates *The Discourses* to two friends who are defined by their civic virtues, which are contrasted with the raw power of the typical prince to whom such works, he tells us, are typically dedicated. In the introduction, he sets his work within the context of a worthy competition for praise, feigns humility before those who will say the same with greater eloquence, and calls for the inculcation of virtue and prudence through imitation of antiquity. Only in the next chapter does he revert to the calculative formula and universal reference of the first chapter of *The Prince*, but now it (and the analysis developed in the following chapters) is set within a more expansive discussion of the exemplary case of Roman history. Nor has the influence of the two texts been uniform: *The Prince*, not *The Discourses*, became the representative text of modern political consciousness, while the influence of *The Discourses* waned even within Anglo-American civic republicanism.[81] These discrepancies suggest that there might be a serious tension between Machiavelli's realist style and his republican commitments.

On the one hand, there is no question that Machiavelli was a dedicated civic republican and that he was enormously important to the development of that strain of political thought in Anglo-American political culture. On the other hand, he also was the author of modern political realism, which undercuts appeal to republican principles and certainly has been used to less noble ends. Although these attitudes can mix in particular persons or periods, there is a tension between them that was evident from the start and becomes acute as they are developed stylistically. In my terms, realism and republicanism operate as distinct political styles that can be joined in a single discourse but often are competing for influence and ultimately are incompatible. This tension begins with the opposition between the master tropes of each style: Where the realist assumes that power is extrinsic to political discourse, the republican finds it in successful public address. This opposition can be helpful, as it can correct the republican too disposed to assume that words will be followed by actions or remind the realist to not overlook the power stored in language. More often, however, the two styles offer different approaches to providing the "reality check" that any politician needs periodically. The realist will look for the gap between language and its referent, while the republican will follow a "linguistic 'realism'" that focuses on an intermediate range of thoughts and feelings intertwined in particular discourses.[82] Perhaps in Machiavelli's time there were stronger tacit affinities between these two conceptions of politics because of the rich understanding of language, politics, and history unique to Renaissance humanism. In the long run, however, the realist's repeated disparagement of political discourse and insistence on the plain style corrodes the persuasive norms that are the ground of republican culture.[83]

An additional consideration is suggested by the relationship between the origin and reception of *The Prince*. Although Machiavelli was devoted to the republican cause, *The Prince* inaugurated a radically nonideological vernacular for political theory and practice.[84] Whatever the author's intentions, his primer for the realist style has followed a trajectory of influence that has gone far beyond the confines of republican government. Perhaps an unintended effect of this work has been the substitution of realism for the civic republican tradition. The realist now is considered the exemplar of civic virtue, guardian of the republic, etc., even though all such terms are transformed through this substitution. More to the point of this essay, realism has reoccupied the position held by republicanism in the cultural system of Renaissance humanism. As the realist style prevailed in the formation of the European state system, the civic virtues became *virtú*, the heroic city became the sovereign ruler or autonomous state, the achievement of liberty in historical time became the monopoly on power amidst changing circumstances, and the reproduction of tradition in speech and action became the control of historical memory. Instead of operating as a corrective on other visions, realism now functions as the central conception and major mode of legitimation in modern politics.

This reoccupation might be an accident of history, but it could

47

occur because of the ability of the realist style to attack other modes of political experience while attaching itself to, and expanding with, the general structure of modern thought. First, the realist style, by devaluing discourse and reducing all values to the use of values, undercuts the discursive foundations of public deliberation and political philosophy. It provides in their place an ontology of power, model of political character, and aesthetic sense that together define political intelligence as the calculation of natural forces shaping the human condition. At that point, the realist stands alone as the only political actor properly oriented for the defense of the community. Once maintenance of the intrinsic qualities of that community becomes subordinated to their extrinsic defense, then "the style common to the political and military arts" transforms the community's indigenous political practices.[85] Any resulting deficiencies in political experience are met through amplification of newer terms (such as "nation-state") and transformation of the meaning of older terms (such as "prudence") to handle traditional tasks of political negotiation and legitimation. This reoccupation allows the older ideas (of civic republicanism) to persist, and even to play an important role at times in the constitution and conduct of government, but it inhibits development of those ideas on their own terms. More importantly, perhaps, this process of reoccupation contributes to the general deterioration of political theory and practice under the pressures of modernity. As Stephen Toulmin laments, "We have lost our feeling for all the respects in which social and political achievements depend on *influence*, more than on *force*."[86]

This essay has attempted to identify one characteristically modern assertion of force in order to discern how it operates as a pattern of influence. When confronted with the "realities" of politics, however, any interpretation might seem futile. Machiavelli looms ever larger in contemporary political thought because his political style generates both the metaphysics of modern political understanding and the paradoxical condition of political commentary becoming aggressively deconstructive. The classical rhetoricians had advised making one's discourse the more persuasive by making it appear natural; Machiavelli was a rhetorician with a vengeance, for he did the same with a world that was made of discourse. When political intelligence is presented as the calculation of forces in a real world, then political rhetoric becomes its shadow and political commentary the futile attempt to discern the light in the shadows. Thus, his strategies for aggrandizing his own text ultimately work against him. By setting his discourse over the other writers, Machiavelli set in motion an attack upon all political discourse that has to destroy his own position. *The Prince* is not enigmatic, strictly speaking, but the experience of reading it is paradoxical. Machiavelli's reader loses through the act of reading itself the resources for integrating this political treatise into the political world. This is the sense in which *The Prince* is a truncated text: it articulates a metaphysic requiring its own incompleteness. The world of political powers—of princes and principalities, of states and reasons of state, of "great powers" and "superpowers"—is set over the world of texts; politics is ubiquitous, suffusing all of our affairs, all of our texts, but power is autonomous, subject to no textual restraints, a sovereign mode of reality known only by its hard natural laws which never can be fully known within any medium clouded by desire.

Therefore, interpretation has to be endless, never capable of being surely validated, always somehow compensating for its own weakness before the force of events. Yet interpreters will feel a need to complete the truncated text, for it is never read without desire. Even in a world where power is a material force that manipulates discourses but never originates in them, any text still contains within it the reactionary turn to another world of pleasing words. This reaction can lead to the idea, certainly not a modern idea, that rhetorical practices are the sources of political community.[87] This idea is completed in a conception of politics where political, ethical, religious, aesthetic, philosophical, economic, and other discourses are unified through the achievement of eloquence.[88] This belief no doubt is idealistic, but it also suggests how much has been suppressed by the dominant style in modern political thought. Machiavelli's masterful presentation of that style at once sharpens perceptions of force and fragmentation and obstructs motives for political renewal.

social and physical
body of the king
immobility and silence

3

No One Is in Charge Here:

Ryszard Kapuściński's

Anatomy of the

Courtly Style

C ourt culture seems to be the antipode of modern life. However modernity is defined, it is not likely to be synonymous with terms like "monarchy" or "majesty." Those royal courts that persist in industrialized states have been reduced to a round of ceremonies clearly removed from the operations of government, and some are maintained for their contribution to tourism— surely the ultimate humiliation. In monarchies elsewhere, courtly functions are giving way to the bureaucratic administration and technocratic elite essential for modern development. Of course, some courts, however out of synch with modern habits, might still be powerful (if not in geopolitics, then in specific locales), and it is conceivable that courts could become powerful again (witness the many science fiction stories that fuse technological progress with political regression). Such arguments are far-fetched, however, and any discussion of courtliness today is haunted by the question of why monarchy should be studied at all.

Scholarly studies of court culture usually side-step this question of contemporary political significance while concentrating on either courts of Europe's past or marginal non-Western societies. Although they overlap significantly, several approaches can be identified. Historical analysis has examined aristocratic practices governing the major European periods and powers. Examples of this approach include Georges Duby's influential anatomy of chivalric society, Frank Whigham's superb account of Elizabethan courtesy literature, and, most recently, Patricia Fumerton's exquisite study of Elizabethan and

Jacobean practices of social ornamentation.[1] Although focused on examples from European history, the work of Norbert Elias provides a sociological analysis of court culture undertaken to identify general relationships between political behavior and social structure.[2] This project is situated in turn within a larger model of long-term developmental processes (for example, of the civilizing process, epochal transformations, and state formation) and also is used to highlight overlooked aspects of bourgeois sociality (such as its cult of manners).[3] A third approach has developed within cultural anthropology, particularly under the influence of Clifford Geertz. These studies have focused on royal ceremonies in order to identify the cultural determination and comprehensive distribution of power within traditional societies, as well as universal symbolic operations that permeate all cultural life.[4] They are distinguished also by their sophisticated reading of the written and gestural texts of political display.[5]

My approach branches off from these projects in two respects in order to discuss the recurrence of courtly manners in modern culture. First, I am attempting to feature conventions of courtly speech and conduct as they can operate independently of monarchical government or traditional social structure. Too often, the effect of both historical analysis of Western courts and anthropological study of traditional societies is to lock courtliness into a foreign institution and a distant time or place. Similarly, identification of abstract relations of culture and power can eclipse the analysis of how a *courtly style* can occur and prevail as an everyday practice within familiar locales of contemporary life. When examining a particular court, one should continue to focus on the relationships between courtly social forms and the cultural, economic, bureaucratic, and governmental practices of that particular society. But this analysis alone will not equip one to account for the persistence or reactivation of courtly tropes in the modern world. A discourse can persist after its "original" social structure collapses, and the rhetorical critic has to consider how that discourse can continue to influence people. In this case, the critical task involves isolating those conventions of persuasion that were dominant at court and then identifying how they can "float" through modern means of communication and become situated in particular social locales or reattached to other structures. Thus, my second emphasis is to consider, albeit briefly, how courtly tropes have been appropriated in the communicative practices of the modern mass

media and their constituent industries of entertainment and advertising. This persistence of courtliness without a court is an example
of postmodern culture in action: The premodern practice re-emerges
in modern life through propagation by the mass media, but in fragmented form that characterizes no specific social structure yet becomes a dimension of media production itself.

This approach also addresses basic reservations one might have
regarding my argument that political life is ineradicably a mixture of
persuasive techniques, aesthetic norms, and political relationships
working together in cohesive patterns of motivation activated
through speech. The most obvious example of highly stylized political experience comes from the pomp and circumstance of life at a
royal court. If the artifice of courtly life is incidental to understanding
and action there, then the concept of political style probably is not
significant anywhere. Furthermore, not all courts are alike: the totalizing theatricality of precolonial Bali differs considerably from the
pushy self-fashioning of Tudor England, and both differ from ancient
Egypt and modern Saudia Arabia.[6] Although all courts seem to have
some elements in common that represent powerful economies of human motivation, if the differences between specific political settings
far outweigh these similarities, then it would seem that no standard
type could be identified. This analytical breakdown in turn would
interfere with any attempt to identify how those designs might be in
effect more erratically outside of their original habitat.

In the hope of overcoming these suspicions, this essay features
The Emperor, a documentary account by Ryszard Kapuściński of the
last days of the Ethiopian royal court of Haile Selassie. Kapuściński's
work provides a superb pretext for analysis of the courtly style: It
highlights the conventions of an extreme version of a pronounced
case of courtly rule in a country defined as the margin between two
orders of civilization. At once African and darling of the West, Selassie appropriated the traditions and mythic history of a monarchy to
maintain a modern dictatorship, and while portrayed as a model of
royal prerogative and African independence, he served the interests
of European imperialism.[7] From beginning to end, his regime relied
on the full panoply and many dependencies of courtly performance,
which are portrayed brilliantly in Kapuściński's *tour de force* of investigative journalism. The perspective of the book comes from its
Enlightenment narrative of truth displacing power, reality overtaking

53

appearance, and reason replacing privilege. Some readers, particularly in the author's homeland of Poland (another border country), saw the book as an allegory of the decline of second-world totalitarianism. Others can read it as a theory for revolutionary change that emphasizes use of the world press and cooptation of the major symbols of the regime. I read it as a rhetoric—a catalog of the means of persuasion characteristic of a particular political culture. Kapuściński's interviews with courtiers and servants show us how the system works from within, how conduct is composed to create meaning, how conventions of address and display can impel, influence, and prevent action.

The book begins with a vignette:

It was a small dog, a Japanese breed. His name was Lulu. He was allowed to sleep in the Emperor's great bed. During various ceremonies, he would run away from the Emperor's lap and pee on dignitaries' shoes. The august gentlemen were not allowed to flinch or make the slightest gesture when they felt their feet getting wet. I had to walk among the dignitaries and wipe the urine from their shoes with a satin cloth. This was my job for ten years.[8]

The incongruity of high officials suffering a dog's urine might strike us as comic. But would we laugh were we there? As Kenneth Burke observed in his comments on Baldesar Castiglione's *The Book of the Courtier*, "In displaying his sense of the 'right' things to laugh at, the courtier thereby displayed the marks of his class."[9] In respect to Lulu, we probably would hold our tongues, for "His Majesty knew that a joke is a dangerous form of opposition" (pp. 6–7). At court, any interruption or critique of pomp can be subversive, for the rules of decorum are sovereign, and the courtier's success or failure depends on continually discerning the shifting applications of the social code governing all conduct.

The story of the pee lackey shows us a world of high decorousness. Although every political culture has a code of propriety, that code is intensified in the culture of the court, which follows a sophisticated, demanding etiquette that is linked explicitly to political survival. The court and its courtiers are distinguished first and foremost not by wealth or might or representation or law, but by their display of "highborn" behavior. Rather than merely ornamenting power, at court the rules of decorum serve as the primary means for accomplishing the essential task of any political system: regulating subordinate behavior without force.[10] Of course, the ceremony displays the emperor's hold on his courtiers, in this case his ability to humiliate them and their need to endure that humiliation, but much more is happening as well.

A male dog with a female's name quickly transports us into a realm of free-floating signifiers, yet he also activates a specific code of conduct. The dog inhabits a world of artifice while exhibiting a natural act that cannot be extinguished but is to be studiously ignored. In this world, meaning originates in decree, not through reference to a natural condition, and every courtier must restrain his nature (especially the inclinations to move on his own, appear angry, or laugh) if he is to reap the rewards of court. Lulu is nothing less than one means for the courtiers' instruction in the political style guiding their affairs. The court is defined as the realm of culture set over against the world of nature, and if there is any leakage between these contiguous orders, its effects are left to the care of the emperor. This disciplined ignorance in turn allows indifference to the government's failure to contend with the famines accompanying the droughts that reigned periodically outside of the court (p. 111). This lack of responsibility need not endanger the courtiers' legitimacy, however, for Lulu also represents the emperor himself. They are, among those present, the two smallest members of their respective species and otherwise unique as well. Dogs pee to mark their territory; the emperor does the same, marking the courtiers. The emperor, who is the Lion of Judah (or, animal of heaven), also symbolizes God who chastens the privileged to keep them properly humble while holding the superior positions they deserve. Through the ritual act of debasement the courtiers reaffirm their elevated status.

This legitimacy derives from their successful performance of the principle of hierarchy, which sets society over nature and orders all of society according to a succession of ranks often gauged by deportment. Hierarchies are not unique to courtly societies, of course, but courtly rhetorics are explicitly and profoundly hierarchical.[11] This symbolic structure is both a dominant appeal and a pervasive pattern of interpretation, and even for those near the bottom it is understood as a channel for the court's distribution of gifts and grace. "Even I took part in these worldly splendors, I who was only a member of the sixth decade of the eighth rank of the ninth level" (p. 89). These hierarchies are primarily distributions of rank, status, or favor, and they can have ambiguous or unstable correlation with the official titles and duties of the court or its complementary bureaucracy. In addition, the courtly hierarchy is defined by its material culmination in the personage of the monarch, itself a strange combination of social role and personal idiosyncrasy (as we shall see shortly). Above all, this hierarchy is not merely a stabilizing social structure, but the primary means for channeling initiative and exacting sacrifice. It is nothing less than a generative principle within the social group and the design that goads, drives, and dominates individual action. Witness how it works:

I was then serving His Most Sublime Majesty as an officer in the Ministry of Ceremonies, Department of Processions. In only five years of zealous and unblemished service, I bore so many tribulations that every hair on my head turned white! This happened because each time our monarch was to go abroad or leave Addis Ababa to honor some province with his presence, savage competition broke out in the Palace for places in the traveling Imperial party. There were two rounds in this struggle. During the first, all notables contended to be part of the Imperial party. In the second round, those who had triumphed in the preliminary stage strove for high and honorable places in the party. . . . Those who were lower were determined to rise. Number forty-three wanted to be twenty-sixth. Seventy-eight had an eye on thirty-two's place. Fifty-seven climbed to twenty-nine, sixty-seven went straight to thirty-four, forty-one pushed thirty out of the way, twenty-six was sure of being twenty-second, fifty-four gnawed at forty-six, sixty-three scratched his way to forty-nine, and always upward toward the top, without end. In the Palace there was agitation, obsession, running back and forth through the corridors. . . . on such an occasion a temporary hierarchy came into being alongside the hierarchy of access to the Emperor and the hierarchy of titles. Our Palace was a fabric of hierarchies and if you were slipping on one you could grab hold of another. (pp. 60–62)

This picture of "savage competition" continues the irony of the pee lackey, as their desire for social elevation reduces the courtiers to a raw state of nature. It also reveals how the persuasive appeal of hierarchy operates from the inside. Too often, hierarchy is imagined along the lines of a Gothic cathedral, as a grand, overarching structure ennobling all but well out of reach. Kenneth Burke gets caught up in this grandeur when he emphasizes how hierarchy "is a source of 'mystery' grounded in the very perfection of formal thinking" which persuades the individual and legitimates the society by providing the means for transcendence of social estrangement.[12] This "theologizing" (as Burke might say) of courtly motives, however, deemphasizes another equally important theme.[13] The courtly style involves not only a grand scheme of authority but also incessant plotting for higher rank and constant anxiety about the precariousness of one's position.

Thus, the courtly hierarchy doesn't just arrange practices of deference and patronage, or symbolic operations of distinction and identification, but animates them—gives them social energy and intrinsic appeal. Although hierarchy might entail a static worldview and has no implications regarding productivity—for life at court depends on place, not production—it places few restrictions on activity and motivates constant scheming and scurrying. So each stately entourage was assembled through "agitation, obsession, running back and forth through the corridors." Particularly as it is a mode of everyday experience, courtliness will include hierarchical motivations not only through spectacular displays of a vertical array of social roles (and its successive range of "mountings," to use one of Burke's puns[14]) but also through signs of finely honed anxiety, seemingly spurious activity, and creative appeals all directed toward improving one's place relative to the sovereign. Courtly hierarchy operates symbolically not only as a principle of order but also as a source of social invention and artistic creativity. It both goads the individual courtier to ingenuity as she vies for a higher station and equips the group to continually reorganize itself and incorporate larger societal changes. The social group organized by this style will become "a fabric of hierarchies," some permanent and others provisional, while the individuals are ever driven "always upward toward the top, without end." Obviously, this pattern is not always reassuring. While still providing a stabilizing function—"if you were slipping on one you could grab hold of another"—it operates through a process of ongoing disruption, for any position depends on the right combination of status and appointment, both of which are at risk. Everything is subject to a change in favor, which is the object of your competitor's persuasions and often the result of whim or happenstance. As Norbert Elias has noted about another court culture:

They pressed on each other, struggled for prestige, for their place in the hierarchy. The affairs, intrigues, conflicts over rank and favour knew no end. Everyone depended on everyone else, and all on the king. Each could harm each. He who rode high today was cast down tomorrow. There was no security.[15]

This is a world of jeopardy for all, including the emperor, who therefore has to rely on other designs to protect himself while perpetuating the court.

One such device is the doctrine of the "King's Two Bodies." As the lawyers of Elizabeth I declared:

The King has in him two Bodies, *viz.*, a Body natural, and a Body politic. His Body Natural (if it be considered in itself) is a Body mortal, subject to all Infirmities that come by Nature or Accident, to the Imbecility of Infancy or old Age, and to the like Defects that happen to the natural Bodies of other People. But his Body politic is a body that cannot be seen or handled, consisting of Policy and Government.[16]

This statement identifies not only a political philosophy with a specific history but also a more generally available pattern of definition capable of being invoked for influence. Note how Lulu reproduces the trope. Lulu's natural body is marked by the most explicit signs of mortality: an animal's form and bodily functions. His privilege of urinating on the courtier's boots without being kicked comes from his embodiment of the body politic: he stands for the emperor who embodies the state. His combination of animal signs and royal privilege displays the deep structure of the courtly style and serves as a constant reminder to the courtiers that they must not confuse the emperor's material deficiencies with his powers.

In other words, courtly politics differs from other political cultures by its emphasis on the body of the monarch, and in this symbolic system the king usually benefits from further division of his body into parts mortal and mystic. This is a symbolic system of great compass, for it provides both material and transcendental axes for royal power. As power is defined by the immediate presence of the monarch, it can be directly experienced and its extension calibrated, and through these experiential measures the entire ideological structure of the court is made manifest. Recall the courtier's scramble for places in the emperor's traveling entourage: Their power depended on actual physical proximity to the king, and those remaining behind in the palace had no more opportunities for advancement than one would find in an empty room. Lynn Hunt has made a similar obser-

58

vation of the Bourbons, who "had not only drastically circumscribed the political responsibilities of French subjects, as Tocqueville argued; they had also succeeded in making power virtually coterminous with the symbolic apparatus of monarchy, especially the monarch's person. Power was measured by proximity to the body of the king."[17] As Michel Foucault has summarized the issue: "In a society like that of the seventeenth century, the King's body wasn't a metaphor, but a political reality. Its physical presence was necessary for the functioning of the monarchy."[18] Yet the materiality of power carries its own limitations. Ultimately, it can lead to the execution of the king, and through that act, to destruction of the courtly style in the political rhetoric of the society. More commonly, the royal subjects will not encounter the royal body—they will be accustomed to its absence. Those wishing access then will have to hone the arts of positioning and waiting:

Life in the palace, however lively and feverish, was actually full of silence, waiting, and postponement. Each minister chose the corridors in which he thought he would have the greatest chance of meeting the distinguished monarch and making a bow. A minister who got the word that he had been denounced for disloyalty would show the greatest eagerness in this selection of itineraries. He would spend whole days trying to create an occasion for a obsequious meeting with His Highness in the Palace. (p. 50)

For those who prefer that their plans escape the king's notice, the situation is reversed; whether out of the king's reach, or watching his physical deterioration, the subject also becomes capable of measuring degrees of freedom from the sovereign.

The division of sovereignty into material and transcendental dimensions can counteract this empirical response to the concentration of power in the monarch. Because this division entails synecdochic opposition rather than contradiction, it creates a peculiar obsessiveness about the royal body. Although material and spiritual definitions of authority can compensate for each other, each also must represent the other as well; this fact focuses attention on the mortal body, as it is the visible element of the pair of terms. Thus, the Ethiopian court required a royal pillow bearer to slide a pillow under the emperor's legs as he sat upon one of the thrones.

This had to be done like lightning so as not to leave Our Distinguished Monarch's legs hanging in the air for even a moment. We all know that His Highness was of small stature. At the same time, the dignity of the Imperial Office required that he be elevated above his subjects, even in a strictly physical sense. . . . Therefore a contradiction arose between the necessity of a high throne and the figure of His Venerable Majesty, a contradiction most sensitive and troublesome precisely in the region of the legs. (p. 27)[19]

The emperor himself is subject to this discipline.

When he knew that someone was watching him, he forced a certain elasticity into his muscles, with great effort, so that he moved with dignity and his imperial silhouette remained ramrod-straight. Each step was a struggle between shuffling and dignity, between leaning and the vertical line. His Majesty never forgot about this infirmity of his old age, which he did not want to reveal lest it weaken the prestige and solemnity of the King of Kings. But we servants of the royal bedchamber, who saw his unguarded moments, knew how much it cost him. (p. 6)

From Selassie's perspective, this personal discipline was but a stitch in time:

The Emperor never showed the slightest sign of irritation, nervousness, anger, rage, or frustration. It seemed that he never knew such states, that his nerves were cold and dead like steel, or that he had no nerves at all. It was an inborn characteristic that His Highness knew how to develop and perfect, following the principle that in politics nervousness signifies a weakness that encourages opponents and emboldens subordinates to make secret jokes. (p. 6)

This disciplining of the sovereign spreads across the entire court culture, providing the conventions that discipline the social body of the court. In Foucault's terms, the embodiment of power beginning with the monarch generates the micropolitics of the social system.[20] These related conventions include the bodily performance of power, the displacement of speech by gesture, and, when the court is in trouble, the figure of royal immobility. Each of these figures is highlighted in *The Emperor*.

Court life often is used to illustrate how spectacles legitimate power in any political system.[21] The production of ceremonies, masques, rituals, plays, and the like obviously is an important part of court life,[22] but it does not cover all forms of courtly performance. The Ethiopian court was a constant round of ceremony, yet the experience of those involved turned on their individual embodiment of the power flowing through the symbolic apparatus of the court.

Yes, sir, the power of the Emperor's assignment was amazing. An ordinary head, which had moved in a nimble and unrestrained way, ready to turn, bow, and twist, became strangely limited as soon as it was anointed with the assignment. Now it could move in only two directions: down to the ground, in the presence of His Highness, and upward, in the presence of everyone else. Set on that vertical track, the head could no longer move freely. . . . Working as a protocol official in the Hall of Audiences, I noticed that, in general, assignment caused very basic physical changes in a man. This so fascinated me that I started to watch more closely. First, the whole figure of a man changes. What had been slender and trim-waisted now starts to become a square silhouette. It is a massive and solemn square: a symbol of the solemnity and weight of power . . . A slowing down of the movements accompanies the changes in the figure. . . . His step is solemn: he sets his feet firmly on the ground, bending his body slightly forward to show his determination to push through adversity, ordering precisely the movement of his hands so as to avoid nervous disorganized gesticulations. Furthermore, the facial features become solemn, almost stiffened, more worried and closed, but still capable of a momentary change to optimism or approval. . . . The gaze changes, too: its length and angle are altered. The gaze is trained on a completely unattainable point. . . . We realize that an attempt to convey our own thoughts would be senseless and petty. Therefore we fall silent. (pp. 34–35)

This description should not be entirely unfamiliar today—it could be a good account of the standard campaign picture used by our political candidates as they gaze confidently past us into future vistas of progress and re-election. The difference is that life at court consciously turns on the distribution of the charismatic energy of the sovereign. Consequently, questions of privilege and responsibility, and of prudence and principle, often will be understood and resolved with primary regard to the disposition of bodies. This orientation ultimately lead to its own form of absurdity. For example, one of the emperor's responses to the atrophy of his regime was to order the courtiers to engage in daily calisthenics. Such foolishness should not eclipse the successful use of embodiment for holding power within the court and garnering foreign aid, however, or consideration of how it contained the seeds of its destruction. Ultimately, this court was undone in part by the portrayal in the world press of the bodies of drought victims (pp. 108ff.). The prior celebrations by journalists of the emperor's splendid figure during his state visits and the denunciations of his indifference to suffering both stem from similar aesthetics of

61

representation, each placing a premium on the depiction of power through the bodies of sovereigns and subjects.[23]

The fixation on the embodiment of power works in tandem with another convention of the courtly style: the displacement of speech by gesture. Even in the chattering courts of Renaissance Italy, the supreme virtue of *sprezzatura* ("grace") was understood primarily as a gestural quality.[24] As the society of the *ancien régime* was collapsing, a courtier complained to Louis XVI about the demise of their world: "'Under Louis XIV one kept silent, under Louis XV one dared to whisper, under you one talks quite loudly.'"[25] At court, speech and gesture are competing principles of communication and political order, and the institution's survival requires the suppression of speech. As they held their urine-stained feet in the rigid stance of courtly display, the Ethiopian courtiers also suppressed their urge to speak out, exclaim, or complain. The dog received no comment, no verbal notice, his act went unnamed. All was wiped away with the pee lackey's satin cloth. The courtiers exemplified both the general rule that "bodily control is an expression of social control," and a specific form of social control that makes the decorous body the sign of order, and speech the sign of disorder.[26]

Although courts cultivate speech, it is regulated by placement in a hierarchy of different modes of communication. This hierarchy attributes the least status (but the most subversive potential) to written communiqués, upward through oral speech to gesture to the ultimate achievement of political order in silence.

His Venerable Majesty was no reader. For him, neither the written nor the printed word existed; everything had to be relayed by word of mouth. . . . It was the same with writing, for our monarch not only never used his ability to read, but he also never wrote anything and never signed anything in his own hand. Though he ruled for half a century, not even those closest to him knew what his signature looked like. (pp. 7–8)

In addition, "during working audiences His Majesty spoke very softly, barely moving his lips. . . . Furthermore, the Emperor's words were usually unclear and ambiguous" (p. 8).[27] What was clear, by contrast, was the power conferred by the emperor's gaze upon anyone singled out of the jostling, craning crowd of courtiers in the palace courtyard: "A passing notice, a fraction of a second, yet the sort of notice that later would make one tremble inside and overwhelm one with the triumphal thought, 'I have been noticed.' What strength it gave afterward!" (p. 14). And well it should, "as it was known that His Majesty, not using his powers of reading and writing, had a phenomenally developed visual memory" (p. 14). This preference for gesture over language was replicated by the courtiers' own embodiment of power upon receiving an assignment:

Nor is the Emperor's favorite eager to talk, since a change in speech is another postassignment symptom. Multiple monosyllables, grunts, clearings of the throat, meaningful pauses and changes of intonation, misty words, and a general air of having known everything better and for a longer time replace simple, full sentences. We therefore feel superfluous and leave. His head moves upward on its vertical track in a gesture of farewell. (p. 35)

This hierarchy culminated in silence. "Life in the Palace, however lively and feverish, was actually full of silence" (p. 50). It is important to recognize that this silence is more than the absence of sound; it is a form of consciousness. There are good and bad silences (p. 158), and silence is understood as a principle of order:

Whoever wanted to climb the steps of the Palace had first of all to master the negative knowledge: what was forbidden to him and his subalterns, what was not to be said or written, what should not be done . . . And since His Majesty had the habit of being silent, waiting, and postponing things, they, too, were silent, waited, and postponed things. (p. 49)

This strong association of strategy and silence permeated court life: "Everybody made his own choice, according to conditions and circumstances, whether to expose his tongue or to hide it, to uncover it or keep it under wraps" (p. 94). Thus, the rhythm of court life appears to come from a modulation not of sounds but of silences.[28] When speech is present, it is always measured against the value of its absence. "Each coterie started voicing its arguments, but voicing them secretly, in the underground manner, because His Highness didn't like factions and hated chattering, applying pressure, and any kind of peace-shattering insistence" (p. 126).

This suppression of speech not only creates a perceptual field for a rhetoric of gestures, it also has other implications. For example, by driving speech underground while observing silence as the principle of social order, the court associates speech with the vitality and amorality of nature. "Yet for the very reason that the factions appeared

63

and began slinging mud and drawing blood, biting and fighting, grinding their jaws and showing their claws, everything in the Palace came to life for a moment, the old verve returned, and it felt like home again" (p. 126). Thus, the court had its own symbolic drama of public gestures and private accusations, an imposing edifice of silent forms built over a snake pit of whispered intrigues.

Similarly, the courtly consciousness seems drawn to metonymic descriptions of human faculties, a definitional practice consistent with its gestural orientation. "It was said that one was more important if one had the Emperor's ear more often. . . . For that ear the lobbies fought their fiercest battles; the ear was the highest prize of the game, . . . and the fight for a piece of the Emperor's ear never stopped. . . . I will add that, in relation to his modest size and pleasing form, His Supreme Majesty had ears of a large configuration" (pp. 36–37). Those lacking the ear would compete for the eye, as they did every morning in the palace courtyard: "Face crushed face, but even the humiliated ones, the ones pushed away, the third-raters and the defeated ones, even those—from a certain distance imposed by the law of hierarchy, it's true—still moved toward the front, showing here and there from behind the first-rate, titled ones, if only as fragments: an ear, a piece of temple, a cheek or a jaw . . . just to be closer to the Emperor's eye!" (p. 15). When metonymy is the master trope, the result of the sovereign's physical embodiment of power is not an organic conception of the state (which would be a form of metaphor) but rather a pervasive partitioning of the elements of action. "In each person things were comfortably divided, seeing from thinking, thinking from speaking, and no man had a place for these three faculties to meet and produce an audible voice" (p. 146). If power infuses bodies, then the separation of body parts becomes a vivid representation of the division, locality, or loss of power. As the court deteriorated, "ears appeared everywhere, sticking up out of the ground, glued to the walls, flying through the air, hanging on doorknobs, hiding in offices, lurking in crowds, standing in doorways, jostling in the marketplace. . . . And everybody made his own choice . . . whether to expose his tongue or to hide it" (p. 94). Ironically, metonymic concentration of the monarch's powers can lead to visions of dismemberment. Kapuściński reaches this far when he quotes Procopius to capture the court's collapse:

On the other hand, the courtiers of Justinian who stayed at his side in the palace until the late hours had the impression that, instead of him, they saw a strange phantom. . . . all of a sudden Justinian's head would disappear, but the body would go on pacing. The courtier, thinking his eyesight had betrayed him, stood for a long while helpless and confused. Afterward, however, when the head returned to its place on the torso, he found himself amazed to see what had not been there a moment ago. (p. 107)

Have the courtier's eyes tricked him, or have his perceptions been shaped by his symbolism?

Metonyms such as these reinforce the reduction of diffuse political processes to moments of embodiment by king and courtiers, while at the same time they distribute power within that social system. Any political system must both concentrate and distribute power. Power not concentrated is not valuable, power not distributed is not useful. When power is concentrated in the body, then it must be distributed through the body. Whether attributing magical powers to the king's touch, or vying for and trembling under his gaze, or distributing the offices of the court through access and attendance to his body, the symbolic action distributes charismatically defined power. Thus, the actual configuration of powers at court becomes dependent, in part, on the health, configuration, movement, and partitioning of that body, and any serious decline in the sovereign's power is imagined as excessive partitioning, that is, as dismemberment.

These general dispositions toward the embodiment of power and displacement of speech by gesture became more evident as the Ethiopian court disintegrated. Perhaps the courtly style has its own subtle system of checks and balances, which, when working well, keep speech counterpoised against gesture and power evident in both the decorous body and an impersonal array of offices, titles, and court functions. As the court collapsed, its primary tendencies continued unchecked, becoming increasingly dysfunctional and culminating in immobility.

As Lulu walked among them, the courtiers could not "flinch or make the slightest gesture." At court, the rigorous schooling in self-control before superiors and the constant participation in public spectacle eventually produces the inability to act at all. As Norbert Elias observed of the court of Louis XV: "Etiquette and ceremony increasingly became . . . a ghostly *perpetuum mobile* that continued to operate regardless of any direct use-value, being impelled, as by an inexhaustible motor, by the competition for status and power of the people enmeshed in it."[29] Barbara Tuchman reports an anecdote from another court that also suggests declension from decorousness into, immobility: "There was another King of Spain at the beginning of the 17th century, Philip III, who is said to have died of a fever he contracted from sitting too long near a hot brazier, helplessly overheating himself because the functionary whose duty it was to remove the brazier, when summoned, could not be found."[30] What Tuchman calls folly is far more than that. It is a story of how rulers are themselves subject to their peculiar and dangerous conventions of domination. In this case, the ability to not act is an important element of court life, one aspect of its "negative knowledge." The emperor knew this lesson well. He outlasted a coup, for example, by not rushing back to the country, allowing the revolt to collapse on its own (p. 69). His undoing began (fittingly) with a fashion show, which

gave them a chance to form a crowd and begin a demonstration, setting off the whole dissent movement. That's where the big mistake was: no movement should have been permitted, since we could exist only in immobility. The more immobile immobility is, the longer and surer its duration. And His Majesty's action was strange because he himself knew this truth very well, which was evident, for example, from the fact that his favorite stone was marble. Marble, with its silent, immobile, painstakingly polished surface, expressed His Majesty's dream that everything around him be immobile and silent, and just as smooth, evenly cut, forever settled, to adorn majesty. (p. 146)

Like silence, with which it is closely aligned, immobility is more than the absence of motion. It represents a principle of self-control, an ethic for courtly life. Like other ethics, it is not a persistent quality of ordinary activity so much as it is a principle resorted to during difficult times. Immobility is the position from which the court can recollect itself, draw upon a secure source of power—spectacular display of its symbols of legitimacy—and gauge the time and place to assert itself into chaotic circumstances. As the court deteriorated, however, this immobility spread, dominating daily life as it had not before. "We could feel the temperature falling, life becoming more and more precisely framed by ritual but more and more cut-and-dried, banal, negative" (p. 83). Palace life became increasingly torpid; the emperor gave the same response to all proposals for counterinsurgency or reform: he listened and said nothing. His only actions were to stage additional ceremonies. By the end, "Immobile, he would meditate for hours in his office" or sit at his desk in silence (p. 156).

So the last days of Haile Selassie's court were spent observing increasingly empty protocols as others, quite unhindered, were dismantling his government. The emperor's only recorded moment of protest to his usurpation was when he was ushered into a Volkswagen. "'You can't be serious!' the Emperor bridled. 'I'm supposed to go like this?'" (p. 162). Dethronement can be accepted, but a monarch should never have to suffer a breach of decorum. Subsequently, he spent his imprisonment as if at court: each day "arranged within the framework of an inviolable program," all of his activities conducted "according to protocol" (p. 163).

This would hardly seem to be a model for imitation. Once again, a monarchy collapses, its achievement no more than persisting too long in the modern world, only to have its greed, insensitivity, and rigidity exposed. Kapuściński's story can reassure the modern reader while it nonetheless preserves the essential form of the regime it consigns to the dustbin of history. The book's last words epitomize the author's genius for melding his premodern subject and modern frame of perception:

"The Ethiopian Herald
Addis Ababa, August 28, 1975 (ENA). Yesterday Haile Selassie I, the former Emperor of Ethiopia, died. The cause of death was circulatory failure." (p. 164)

Here the king's body lies in repose within a modern text: It is circumscribed by the decor of the public sphere and the discourse of medical science and controlled by the current political regime (which, as the unstated presence signified by the term "former," is constituted in the realist style—an unnamed material power underlying any entitlement or publication). The "circulatory failure" provides the last irony, the final contrast of courtly artifice with the vitality of modern life. And yet, this brief text also is organized by the courtly dialectic of social and natural identifications, its hierarchy of rank, fixation on the king's body, and figure of royal immobility. The text has indeed been "an exhibition of the old art of governing" (p. 23), yet its story of a particular court's collapse has become imbued with courtliness as a mode of symbolic action, capable of being reactivated at another time or place.

The Emperor is not the only example of this condensation of the courtly style in the records of its demise, and other accounts reinforce my identification of its major conventions. Note, for example, how the style is displayed in a description by P'u Yi, supposedly the last emperor of China, of the royal entourage:

Whenever I went for a stroll in the garden a procession had to be organized. In front went a eunuch from the Administrative Bureau whose function was roughly that of a motor horn . . . Next came two chief eunuchs advancing crabwise on either side of the path; ten paces behind them came the centre of the procession—the Empress Dowager or myself. If I was being carried in a chair there would be two junior eunuchs walking beside me to attend to my wants at any moment; if I was walking they would be supporting me. Next came a eunuch with a large silk canopy followed by a large group of eunuchs of whom some were empty-handed and others were holding all sorts of things: a seat in case I wanted to rest, changes of clothing, umbrellas and parasols. After these eunuchs of the imperial presence came eunuchs of the imperial tea bureau with boxes of various kinds of cakes and delicacies, and, of course, jugs of hot water and a tea service; they were followed by eunuchs of the imperial dispensary bearing cases of medicine and first-aid equipment suspended from carrying poles. . . . At the end of the procession came the eunuchs who carried commodes and chamber-pots. If I was walking a sedan-chair, open or covered according to the season, would bring up the rear. This motley procession of several dozen people would proceed in perfect silence and order.[31]

Selassie would know just what to do in this scene, for it features basic elements of his political style, including the display of hierarchy through the entourage, royal embodiment and the distribution of offices through the partitioning of the body, and the identification of order with silence. P'u Yi goes on to tell how he, a small child at the time, delighted in disrupting the procession, but this only animates the story, giving the court the characteristic pleasures and powers that come from continual alternation between pressing nature into the forms of political order and breaking up those forms as they become stultifying.

These designs also inform another correspondent's account of another royal collapse: Thomas Carlyle's chronicle of the French revolution includes several sympathetic portraits of the last days of monarchical rule, which follow the contours of the style he is recording. The work begins in the sickroom of Louis XV, whose mortal illness symbolizes the state of "not the French King only, but the French Kingship."[32] When it turns to the events unfolding elsewhere, it celebrates "a silence which is better than any speech," which also is contrasted with the stillness that is symptomatic of institutional collapse, and associates the emerging powers of modern life with unchecked speech and writing.[33] These motifs and their nostalgic mood are returned to near the work's end, when he records the trial of Marie Antoinette:

The once brightest of Queens, now tarnished, defaced, forsaken, stands here at Fouquier Tinville's Judgment-bar; answering for her life. The Indictment was delivered her last night. To such changes of human fortune what words are adequate? Silence alone is adequate.

There are few printed things one meets with, of such tragic almost ghastly significance as those bald Pages of the *Bulletin du Tribunal Révolutionnaire,* . . .

Marie-Antoinette, in this her utter abandonment, and hour of extreme need, is not wanting to herself, the imperial woman. Her look, they say, as that hideous Indictment was reading, continued calm; 'she was sometimes observed moving her fingers, as when one plays on the Piano.' You discern, not without interest, across that dim Revolutionary Bulletin itself, how she bears herself queenlike. Her answers are prompt, clear, often of Laconic brevity; . . . At four o'clock on Wednesday morning, after two days and two nights of interrogating, jury-charging, and other darkening of counsel, the result comes out: sentence of Death. "Have you anything to say?" The Accused shook her head, without speech. . . . This Hall of Tinville's is dark, ill-lighted except where she stands. Silently she withdraws from it, to die.[34]

We might wonder how Carlyle's secondhand account could be so vivid. He didn't have to be there, since he already had all he needed to compose the event as a model of royal authority. Stripped of the hierarchy of rank, the queen recurs to another: She is elevated by her command of gesture and code of silence over her accusers, known by their bulletins and oral arguments. This silence is both the symbol of royal order—and one of its mystifications, as it is further aligned here with Eternity—and the principle of conduct relied on in the crisis. As Carlyle fills out the portrait by noting the general bearing and minute, metonymic details of her gestural performance, she becomes draped in powerful appeals to courtly deference. Although "defaced," she remains a model of self-control; while being accused, her body betrays only an aesthetic memory. Against the "darkening of counsel," she alone is a figure of integrity, glowing in theatrical spotlight as the scene ends. By now, the scene strains belief, yet it persists in the reader's imagination. Carlyle's sympathy for the institution of monarchy has been expressed through masterful appropriation of the courtly style to compose his political history.

The style need not be limited to these exemplars, however. By turning to other records of court life, one discerns not only the continued presence of the tropes I have identified but others as well. The key to seeing the style's full range of persuasiveness is to look through the eyes of the women of the court. In *The Pillow Book of Sei Shōnagon*, for example, we see not only the importance of rank, but its splendor, not only intricate codifications of decorous dress and deportment, but also the "cult of laughter" that both discharges the tensions of artful living and reinforces the artistic code.[35] Likewise, in *The Confessions of Lady Nijō*, we see not only the court's various hierarchies of rank, favor, and duty but also their coercive power over high and low alike, and the tension between the graceful dance of courtesy and the court's trafficking in bodies is registered through another metonymy: the tears that flow frequently and stain her ornate garments.[36] These accounts, at once firsthand and marginal and alternating between public display and backstage manipulations, expand the style aesthetically as they also reveal its costs. Here the style is a more self-conscious artistry of daily life and (somewhat) less a field of political competition; it is represented less by silence and more by the court poetry and music that fill up the idle hours and relieve the practice of waiting, and it culminates not in action but in prize moments of aesthetic contemplation.

At this moment the style resonates with a modernist aesthetic and so becomes masked: It seems to be a beautiful but inert form having no relation to the forces of modern politics. By contrast, Selassie's shabbiness becomes a virtue if it encourages a more critical frame of mind. However foolish or corrupt it might have been, the Ethiopian court ruled for several generations. It probably deserves an award for parasitism, but the field is crowded and not the subject of this essay. Instead, let us note how an effective basis for political action was supplied by a code of conduct that valorized hierarchy, the distribution of power through the king's body, the subordination of speech to silence, and other such courtly tropes. Although sometimes these conventions of display were no more than a mask for the real operations of power, at other times the power of the court was strictly synonymous with the symbolic operations characterizing its public performances and ritual interactions. Furthermore, this courtly style could constitute political experience because it also contained related conceptions of power and selfhood. In other words, at some point a political style can be understood as the artistic expression of a political theory (and some political theories might be considered rationalizations of specific styles of interaction). The theory lurking in the courtly style is intriguing because its basic conceptions of political phenomena are incompatible with modernist conceptions of power.

Selassie was not known for philosophical discourse, and his understanding of power was summarized not in constitutional doctrine but in the practice of visiting the provinces. Faced with the decision between an unannounced arrival that might discover mismanagement and a scheduled stop with a proper reception, the choice was clear:

Government can't work under threat, can it? Isn't government a convention, based on established rules? . . . Just imagine it, friend. His Most Extraordinary Majesty steps off the airplane, and around him—nothing. Silent emptiness, deserted fields, and everywhere you look, not a living soul. No one to speak to, no one to console, no welcoming arch, not even a car. What can you do? How can you act? Set up the throne and roll out the carpet? That would only make it more ridiculous. The throne adds dignity only by contrast to the surrounding humility. This humility of the subject creates the dignity of the throne and gives it meaning. Without the humility around it, the throne is only a decoration, an uncomfortable armchair with worn-out velvet and twisted springs. A throne in an empty desert—that would be disgraceful. Sit down on it? Wait for something to happen? . . . So what remains for His Majesty to do? Look around the neighborhood, get back into the plane, and fly north after all, where everything waits in excitement and impatient readiness: the protocol, the ceremonies, the province like a mirror. (pp. 40–41)

There is no question who is king, but there is no king without the successful performance of kingship, and successful performance requires that both king and subjects play their parts. Some royal power might precede its display, but most of it is created through the command of ceremony and audience participation, and all of it can be lost if the stage becomes dilapidated or the audience smirks. This awareness easily leads to characteristic abuses, including lavish expenditures to guarantee that the stage will always be splendid, along with neglect of other responsibilities. Yet even royal majesty can't disguise the fact that power is something conferred by others. The throne in the desert is absurd because there is no political power in a state of nature. Politics begins with the creation of meaning, which is always shared, reciprocal, a process of display and response. There is nothing to be appropriated that cannot also be withdrawn, and nothing so useless as a prop without a play.

In brief, the courtly style activates social and aesthetic awarenesses that are sublimated in much of modern political theory. One way or another, the courtly actor understands that power often is decentralized in its location, irregular in its operation, and potentially both available and unstable at any time. The power achieved by an individual is a by-product of successful performance, and the power located in an institution is distributed through its network of audiences, whose membership always is fluctuating. Even in the Ethiopian court, which seemed completely focused on the person of the emperor, the day-to-day political activity for most of the courtiers consisted of acting out their parts before each other. The extreme case of a court in decline suggests how a structured need for audience approval gives institutional life its tension. As Frank Whigham observed of another courtly culture,

> If all utterance in this context comes to have primarily epideictic force; if the manifestation of style transcends issues of substance; if subjects of conversation increasingly become querelles; if conversation is not listened to but watched; then the power relation between speaker and hearer becomes skewed normatively toward the audience. Speech and other significations reveal not power but powerlessness, a pleading with the audience for a hearing, for recognition, for ratification.[37]

Moreover, this relationship is inherently capricious since the roles of performer and audience are frequently exchanged and the standards for appropriate performance always negotiated through performance. "In fact, no one is in charge here."[38]

Thus, the courtly style provides an extreme case of an effect that occurs every time political relations are regulated by aesthetic atti-

72

tudes about rhetorical practices (as they are some of the time in any political culture). As Frank Lentricchia notes in his reading of Kenneth Burke's fusion of politics and aesthetics in rhetoric: "At some level aesthetic effect is out of control," and "there is no universal, perfectly 'centered' reader because there is no universal, perfectly 'centered' ideology: hence no universal text and no universal power effect."[39] Lentricchia has grasped the radical implication latent within any recognition of political style: To the extent that power is a product of performance, it is spontaneous, actualized, and unstable. As one Ethiopian courtier mused, "It's so very difficult to establish where the borderline runs between true power that subdues everything, power that creates the world or destroys it—where the borderline is between living power, great, even terrifying, and the appearance of power, the empty pantomime of ruling, being one's own dummy, only playing the role, not seeing the world, not hearing it, merely looking into oneself" (p. 145). In this conception, power is available potentially to anyone because it is entirely crafted, and sufficient to command the entire human being, but dependent on the thousand contingencies of audience response. This is why critical awareness of decorum is disturbing to those accustomed to the routinization of charisma. In place of rational governance, organizational structure, and political accountability, the analysis of political style suggests that often political decisions turn on transitory aesthetic perceptions, that a political system is continually reinvented through performances both scheduled and spontaneous, and that political power is very difficult to grasp.[40] In other words, power can be a relation created through performance, or a residual property of previous or repeated performances, but it is not likely to be the same thing as the application of force or the rational operation of administrative practices.

This conception of political power need not be the only idea of power available at court—obviously, identifications of power with force, rule of law, and bureaucratic organization all could be at work as well. In any case, the idea of performative power usually is an immanent idea. Its importance, however, is underscored by its reciprocity with the conception of selfhood that is another element and effect of courtly rhetoric. Richard Lanham's discussion of *sprezzatura* provides the point of departure into this aspect of the courtly style: "A poetic lurks in all of this, as in all political theory. . . . The self emerges from *The Courtier*, then, as aesthetic rather than moral entity, as a matter, finally, of taste."[41] To restate the matter, the conception of selfhood that is constructed within courtly discourse is radically different from the modern conception of the self: It lacks both psychological autonomy and moral foundation.[42] The person can only achieve the prerequisites of personal worth—identity and effectivity—through a persona conferred by the court. This attribution of identity comes as a response to performance, and when subjective considerations of taste, refinement, and grace are matched by audience assessments of their display, they become objective elements of political behavior. The more autocratic the system, the more this persona is dependent on the approval of the sovereign and the more minutely it has to be coordinated with "his vanity, his self-love, his passion for the stage and the mirror, for gestures and the pedestal" (p. 154). No wonder they would crowd forward hoping to catch the emperor's attention: "Now the face and the name are joined, and a person comes into being, a ready candidate for nomination. Because the face alone—that's anonymous. The name alone—an abstraction. You have to materialize yourself, take on shape and form, gain distinctness" (p. 15). In such a system, the courtier can never to one's own self be true and can get along quite well without a conscience. "Everyone gave in to such manipulation because the only reason for their existence was the Emperor's approbation, and if he withdrew it they would disappear from the Palace within the day, without a trace. No, they weren't anything on their own. They were visible to others only as long as the glamorous light of the Imperial crown shone upon them" (p. 29). Yet even when authority is less centralized the courtly self is an irredeemably social self, always oriented toward others as they in turn are oriented toward it. The courtier sees his own image only when looking into a hall of mirrors.

The courtier's sense of self is aesthetic because it is an achievement of theatricality confirmed by the act of pleasing others and rewarded in part by taking pleasure in one's own performances.[43] To be is to be in performance, and those elements of selfhood that moderns would prize—autonomy, integrity, stability, interiority, etc.—are, if present, available only as by-products. The more immediate and important elements of courtly selfhood are such qualities as performative mastery of a scene, expressive distinctiveness within a common repertoire, estimation of one's resources and effects according to others' attributions of status, and modulation of one's bodily desires and effects. In addition, the ethical probity and consistency that moderns value so highly is, although not necessarily absent, never valued as such. Instead, ethical considerations are translated into and conducted through a vocabulary of aesthetic terms. Conduct that would appear to a modern to be unprincipled could, but need not, become something for a courtier to avoid, but largely because it would be in bad taste. Conversely, there are some things a courtier would not do because that would be a breach of good taste, whereas moderns blithely transgress, assuming that no harm is done since no principle of moral conduct is violated.

This translation of moral terms into aesthetic terms carries with it additional nuances as well. Although the current text does not provide sufficient resources to chart the range of moral life in a courtly culture, it does suggest two elements of that spectrum. First, courtly ethics are highly personalized, and personal presence is established through decorous performance. One's obligations are to specific personages (the distinction from persons is important as well) and are to be honored to the extent that they can be signified in courtly display. Hence, the enormous importance of being at court, and there in the right place at the right time, and, above all, of being recognized by the emperor. This is not to say that responsibilities only extend to individuals, for the courtier can represent other constituencies, but there is nothing equivalent to the contemporary liberal sense of ethical obligations toward aggregates. Second, in courtly rhetoric, motives are assumed to always be mixed. There is no fault in having dual, or even contradictory, motives, and no virtue in having a singleness of purpose. (Quite the contrary: singleness of purpose is dangerous, and so always defined as a form of bad taste and potential subversion.) The ubiquity of mixed motives, in turn, accounts for the functioning of some of the courtly tropes some of the time: Metonymic description is a useful means for parsing motives, when, for example, my heart says one thing, my head another, and I have the good sense to vote with my feet. Likewise, the consideration of one's placement in a variety of hierarchies allows some latitude in choosing among different obligations.

Despite being grounded only in virtuosity, this self is quite quotidian. It is made up of well-known conventions that operate habitually in courtly discourse: As Whigham has demonstrated, the courtier's identity is registered as a set of points within a mesh of hierarchies and established dynamically (and self-consciously) through tropes of promotion and rivalry.[44] As Elias has shown, the courtier's self-preservation depends on arts of observation and inter-action, whereby one interprets minute and complex signs in anoth-er's behavior to discern information and motives while disciplining one's emotions to provide similarly subtle texts for others.[45] As Geertz has illustrated, the general equation of power with pageantry exerts a continual subordination of private, interior regard to the pre-vailing fictions of public display.[46] I have augmented these studies by identifying how courtly discourse activates a demanding code of de-corum, a generative principle of hierarchy, identification and division of power through the body of the sovereign, bodily performance of empowerment, subordination of speech to silence, a symbolic drama of public gesture and private accusation, metonymic description of political conduct, and an ethic of self-control culminating in immo-bility. As these and other tropes are deployed, related conceptions of power and individual identity are jointly activated and become means for the constitution of a political order, however provisional or temporary it might be. In any case, the courtly self carries all the anxieties of depending on the mastery of appearances. If locating one's identity in expressiveness continually opens up new opportu-nities for renewal and advancement, it also requires constant, ulti-mately futile, regulation of every aspect of one's desires and gestures.

One response to this situation is to search for all of those tech-niques by which decorous presentation activates power and estab-lishes selfhood. The example of the courtly style reveals at least one additional design in the conversion of decorum to power. A code of conduct emerges by overruling another code—more specifically, by overruling another, putatively lesser version of itself. This dialectic can be most visible as a competition between codes: for example, celebrities and street people snub each other outside a New York nightclub, all the while offending middle-class spectators.[47] The story of the pee lackey reveals the inner workings of decorum not only by showing a code of conduct rigidly adhered to, but also by showing how observing one form of propriety requires enduring the violation of another. At the Ethiopian court, it was proper both to be free of urine (otherwise, why the lackey?) and to be urinated on in public (otherwise, why the dog?); the decorousness of the court was achieved in part by inducing and managing this contradiction.

But surely we would not live this way. We are not courtiers and few of us have been the guests of an extant court culture. Yet I submit that the conventions of this culture persist today, albeit as "a range of persuasiveness usually found but in fragments" and "covertly."[48] Examining the political culture of the Ethiopian court can help us understand those fragments of courtliness that remain lodged in our political affairs. In contemporary American society, this style can emerge as both an occasional means for empowerment, whether at the society luncheon or family reunion, and as the dominant style in a particular locale or group, whether a corporate office or the traveling entourage of an entertainer. In any case, most people are unwittingly familiar with its persuasive techniques, as they have been embedded in everything from children's literature to pulp novels to *National Enquirer* or *Time* coverage of the British royalty. Anyone could be influenced by someone appropriating these tropes in a particular persuasive exchange. Most of the time, however, the attempt would be likely to fail as it would be going against the grain of more familiar and institutionally instantiated persuasive habits.

The question remains of how to discover courtliness without the court. The most obvious first step would be to follow attributions of monarchy: for example, Lewis Lapham is quick to describe Washington politics as a world of imperial masques, feudal relations, aristocratic prerogatives, and courtiers' insinuations.[49] Lapham's aim often is deadly, but however apt these descriptions may be in some cases, in others they are only metaphors for unwarranted privilege, unchecked selfishness, unscrupulous acts, and other vices that hardly are limited to any particular style of politics. In addition, condemnations of courtly power are a minor convention of civic republican discourse. One suspects that if the republican critic couldn't point to the court he would have to invent one and that sometimes the language is not well suited to doing more than condemn. Another point of departure would be to look for specific courtly tropes, reasoning that where one was apparent the others must be nearby. Unfortunately, from this step it is easy to stumble into the fallacy of the excluded middle: for example, although both the courtiers and schoolchildren use metonymy, it doesn't follow that the children are courtiers. Although the visibility of a trope, like a story of kingship, always should be considered a possible sign of courtliness, it alone is not enough evidence. Consequently, interpretation of the courtly style has to include several assumptions about where it is likely to operate in modern society and then demonstrate that it operates as a fairly comprehensive mode of persuasiveness within the particular locale.

Let me offer a provisional account of its dissemination in the contemporary period: First, the courtly style persists beyond the court, floats through modern society's universe of discourse, and attaches itself to other social structures. Second, it becomes a readily available and effective means for organizing experience, conferring meaning, and persuading oneself and others within those social settings that are focused on a specific individual's decisions or performances and are relatively isolated from democratic accountability. Third, at least to the extent that it operates as a pattern of identification within the mass media, the style coalesces around the metonymic representations of beautiful or powerful bodies.

The style persists because it is a coherent repertoire having a proven motivational economy, because it involves archetypal political relations that are widely propagated, and because it continues to work for those who have mastered it. It floats because it is no longer limited to or controlled by a political elite and because it is marginal to the major discourses and institutional legitimation strategies of modern society. It attaches to a specific locale because it constitutes communicative relationships having intuitive form, stability, and assurances suited to the social relations structuring that environment and because it provides a tacit means of persuasion for those holding or attempting to gain advantage there. This activation of the style is most likely to occur where social experience already is organized around some form of personal sovereignty: Courtly tropes facilitate communication around and about focal individuals, they both define and enhance personal authority, and they distribute power within a social order oriented toward an individual's display of political authority or aesthetic distinction. The style can dominate when this display features some body. Particularly when the social setting is oriented toward visual representation, performers and audience acquire the heightened attentiveness to and subtle discriminations of bodily display that are the lingua franca of courtly politics. As the style is coordinated with the social practices and communicative technologies of a particular setting, whether MTV or the dean's office, it acquires the full range of referential and performative functions that characterize an operational discourse. Once an audience becomes habituated to intensive attention to bodily form, adornment, and gesture, and particularly to the metonymic description that communicates diffuse attitudes, emotions, or experiences by segmenting bodily images, they become unconsciously receptive to the full array of courtly appeals.

The critic can assume that a political style is potentially available whenever one of its tropes is used repeatedly and without interference or nullification by other styles, ideological codes, etc., and that as more of its tropes are activated it becomes capable of shaping decision and action in the particular setting. In every case, the proof that a style is active in a particular setting requires more than simple observation or deductive inference: Saying "realistic" needn't make someone a realist, nor does "virtue" necessarily mark a civic republican or "rule" a bureaucrat. In the case of the courtly style, one has to be a bit more imaginative than usual, because it is more likely to be officially unacknowledged in a modern, democratic society. Hence, the critic has to identify likely places where it could occur and then consider how the full array of appeals could be at work. The cues can be either social or rhetorical: that is, one can either look for social practices that are relatively unregulated by institutional codes but feature individual actors or look for persuasive practices that make repeated use of one or more of the courtly tropes. In order to fill out the style, one then looks for other elements or effects of the style and considers how they correspond to the political relationships and aesthetic habits of the communicators.

Although I don't want to dismiss the instances of courtly persuasion in mundane interactions in everyday life, the style seems to be most active in specific discursive locales that are the result of or under the direct influence of mass-mediated communication. Three sites of courtliness seem prominent: celebrity culture, particularly in the entertainment industry but also including figures from government and business (for reasons that should not be mysterious); advertising, particularly as it involves images of the female body; and the American presidency. The courtly style seems especially available in each of these locales, and given their relationship to the mass media, they are likely to shape other instances of its use.

It is a commonplace to say that the Hollywood elite are America's royalty. This is as much a statement of reassurance as a description, however, for it also suggests that there is little threat to the democratic political order since this elite is so thoroughly circumscribed by entertainment. The act of containment in this definition is epitomized in the use of the synecdoche, "Hollywood," a small locale far away from the center of government. When political considerations are raised, they usually have involved stories of the importance of "big money" in politics or the typical denunciations of Ronald Reagan's showmanship. These approaches miss an important point, however: As media success confers celebrity, it also organizes those involved according to its conventions of production. Among its other effects, media coverage creates its own aristocracy of representation, which I believe is conferred through fragmentary projections of the courtly style and confirmed when that style becomes reproduced in the organization of the celebrity's daily life. Ultimately, the relationship between this subculture and the national government is less one of money or access and more a question of how much the courtly conventions will become a pattern for imitation.

As courtly conventions of speech and conduct are activated within the culture of media production, they become a basis for persuading others within and without. The basic structures of extreme status consciousness, hierarchical definition of access, deference, and action, and empowerment through personal display should not need documentation. In fact, a steady stream of biographies, novels, movies, television dramas, talk shows, gossip columns, and other media reports concerning celebrities reproduce these conventions daily as they document their operation in a myriad of details regarding personal life, media production, corporate operations, and the like. The extent of the courtly style's organization of celebrity becomes more evident as one discovers how its subsidiary tropes also are at work. To take one example, consider how media stars are defined through gestural metonymy. Success in the media requires that one distinguish oneself through performance before an audience of spectators. These performances, from R-rated films through rock concerts to nightly newscasts, are largely gestural. To become a celebrity, one has to master and distinguish oneself within a rhetoric of gestures—virtually every star has a defining gesture or gestural effect. (This also explains how some can become stars despite little artistic ability—they only need have the rare knack for achieving gestural distinction.) As the individual becomes individuated through a gesture—cocking an eyebrow, pointing a finger, licking the upper lip—the body part becomes a form of focal knowledge. Power is concentrated in the body, and the body becomes the means for segmenting power. As the body of the celebrity assumes the position (for the moment) of the sovereign, so it becomes a model of the distribution of power radiating out from the royal personage.

This process is situated most mundanely in the media practice of preparing the body of the actor for performance. Just as royal offices were defined by the dressing of the king, the media celebrity is defined in part by the tasks of preparing his or her body for performance. If great power does not lie today with those in wardrobe, hairstyling, and makeup, they nonetheless represent a pattern of courtly definition and are important elements in the process of generating and distributing charisma. Power does come from being dressed and made up by others, and that process uses the segmentation of a favored body as a form of social organization. "Demi Moore, for example, has six assistants: one for her clothes, one for her hair, one for makeup, a bodyguard, a nanny and a general-purpose personal assistant, who has her own personal assistant, who is thinking of hiring one of her own. But Demi is the queen of Do It Yourself compared with her husband, Bruce Willis, who required twenty-two assistants on the set of *Billy Bathgate,* including four or five bodyguards, a driver, a personal chef, a personal trainer, a masseuse and a hair and makeup stylist."[50] This organization of the celebrity's lifeworld according to the segmentation of the body is matched by the mass-mediated fetish of the celebrity's body part. As an actor is idolized for his shoulders or an actress for her legs, the distribution of charisma through dismemberment is accomplished. Only the few can have access to the whole person, but everyone can have a part of the part.

Needless to say, this distribution of power through the dividing of the sovereign's body coincides with the subordination of speech to gesture. Ideally, the royal life is confirmed in communication through gestures subtle or forceful, themselves evidence of exquisitely managed silences.

81

Julio Iglesias was seen walking onto the lawn in front of his cabana followed by a blonde in a bikini and a squatty butler. Selecting the ideal spot for sunning himself, Julio snapped his fingers and two towels were placed on the ground for him and his companion. After fifteen minutes, the sun's position had changed, and Julio stood up. His assistant bounced to attention and produced fresh towels, which he then placed on the ground a few degrees to the west of the first two.[51]

It's not that nothing need be said; power is performed by not having to speak to one who can only speak when spoken to.

The other tropes are evident as well. Howard Hughes is one example of the descent into immobility; the King's Two Bodies are evident in the mystification of Magic Johnson and other ailing athletes; and the gossip columns reproduce the symbolic drama of a serenely confident pageant hiding a brutal but vital world of gossip, innuendo, and cynical argument. Even the pee lackey lives among us: "Henry Kissinger, too, is fond of the constitutional, often accompanied by his dog Amelia; his bodyguard walks behind him to take care of any scooper duties."[52] Whether it is structuring mass audience perceptions of a distant elite, or regulating the most ordinary practices of that elite as they walk through the world, the courtly style is an active element in contemporary life.

Perhaps there is a correspondence between the "nonpolitical" cast of modern entertainment and its activation of courtly tropes. The style characteristic of premodern political institutions becomes palatable only when emptied of prior political doctrine, yet the social conditions of the entertainment industry reproduce many of the characteristics of an aristocracy, including the concentration of great wealth among a small class that produces and controls the society's spectacles while being defined by norms of physical appeal and sexual love. Although assertions of monarchy usually would be considered neurotic within a modern political forum, the style constitutive of courtly politics provides the symbolic resources for organizing a set of social and cultural practices having little relation to the institutional structures of modern governance. When this style shapes major media productions, it could become a source of social knowledge for the media audience, and most specifically, for that audience's predicament of comprehending the political dimension of all those practices officially deemed "nonpolitical," "social," or "personal."

It is interesting to note how the courtly style has been mastered

82

by two entertainers who have been singled out as particularly important resources for helping people make sense of their lives: Oprah Winfrey and Madonna. Each might choke at the association, yet they are two of the highest-paid entertainers in the world and they use a common repertoire. Oprah established her show through the drama of her weight loss: would she be able to lose enough to fit into a particular pair of jeans? She did, of course, to great fanfare. Subsequently, her show is anchored by running commentary on her body: its weight, parts, exercise, diet, and dress. It could be that she is providing practical advice for those many women suffering a similar fate—but who is prepared to believe, for example, that her audience will set out to lose weight by each hiring a full-time personal chef? Under the guise of offering advice, Oprah's fixation upon her body activates the central trope of the courtly style, which confers great appeal and authority on the actor while it provides the audience with a vocabulary for understanding the micropolitics of gestural empowerment in diverse social settings and other forms of courtship. Meanwhile the topical interest of the show is devoted to the negotiation of social mores and readily swerves toward examination of other people's bodily conduct, functions, experiences, and traumas. Like some other talk shows, ultimately the talk is the least of it—a discursive background of banter and liberal pieties that displaces all other forms of speech for display of the sovereign's characteristic gestures and signs of approval. As the show plays out over time, it fills out the style according to the habits of its genre: codes of public morality, social etiquette, medical privacy, and the like are temporarily overruled to create a new mode of decorum as all strive to influence the host's final stance on the question. The hierarchies implicit in fashion and entertainment are validated on stage while the gossip magazines present the complementary drama of private accusations. The host's self-control amidst the staged turmoil of animated discussions becomes a sign of legitimacy, and her longevity becomes first a sign of power and then an anxiety when the question arises of whether the show can continue without her presence.

While Oprah's self-fashioning is relatively staid, Madonna's has been legendary in her own time and provides a premier example of the courtly style in action.[53] Although she is a talented writer, choreographer, performer, and producer of pop spectacles, Madonna's public image is a continually changing story of costuming and expos-

83

KAPUŚCIŃSKI'S COURTLY STYLE

[handwritten marginalia:]
No segmenting
No No No No and sectioning
this emphasis on body three fat women
is common, Oprah's just one of on TV

silence control, inability

— he does to Oprah
what he says advertising
do to models —
Segmenting + commodifying

could've focused
on legendary entourage
or black skin

Is objectification
of body above always
courtly style?

Hariman
Devours
Oprah—using
her as part of
his own
advertising

ing her body. Her strategy as a producer has been to focus attention on her use of her body—which, unlike the typical female celebrity, frozen into a single image, becomes a vital, mutable field of social characterization, concentrating and redirecting the flow of social energy as it appropriates all other forms of feminine iconography—and its realization has depended on her distinctive capability as a performer to strike a pose. Throughout her ascendancy, she has artfully managed fixations upon her body parts—navel, breasts, etc.—while crafting a persona composed out of a *bricolage* of archetypes. These and other elements of composition are displayed clearly in her autobiographical film, *Truth or Dare.* The film follows three patterns of organization: the conventions of its genre, the concert film, which alternates between onstage and offstage scenes while following the routines of concert production and touring; the description of her as the "mother" presiding over domestic conflicts in her troupe, a variation of the "Madonna" theme and the currently ubiquitous family metaphor (which is parodied at the film's end); and the conventions of the courtly style.

Needless to say, Madonna's body provides the focal point of the film: She is the center of every spectacle and the dominant presence offstage. As we follow her from scene to scene, our attention is focused more closely on the body itself: She always is doing something explicitly physical or having her body attended to by others: She eats, drinks, exercises, and dresses or undresses, or is being massaged, adjusted, or made-up. Nor are these incidental accompaniments of the action: They are highlighted, whether by the sloppy muck of the soup she eats from an overly large tureen (as she has to stoop over the bowl and slurp while talking on the phone), or by the many remarks (comic and otherwise) that she has to "replenish my fluids," protect her voice, adjust her makeup, etc. Nor is this attention a form of erotic provocation: Actually, it becomes quite clear that the onstage lust is very much an act (for example, the dancers are gay) and her backstage world has the combination of sexual austerity and personal frustration typical of any workplace. In general, the constant focus on Madonna's body creates not lust but power: the courtly composition of power that concentrates and distributes political energy through the body of the sovereign. In any specific scene, the additional effect is to frame the dialogue gesturally and so subordinate anything that is said to the trafficking in bodies, the flow of charisma through the entourage.

This trope of sovereign embodiment is supported by many additional elements of courtly composition, some trivial or incidental but all cohering to fill out the style: Like Lady Nijō, whose tears would stain her costume, Madonna's tears stain her makeup. Like Sei Shōnagon, she recites poetry to her friends and enjoys the cult of laughter (the poem is bawdy, of course, and replete with references to the care of the poet's body). Like the Dowager Empress, she is surrounded by women and men (her dancers) who take no sexual interest in her. Like Haile Selassie, she relies on her new class of courtiers (kids, working-class family members and friends) while blending with the Hollywood aristocracy. Like Marie Antoinette, at the last she says nothing, while the film ends as her hat (crown, head) drops to the ground, the only object in the last silent frame. Throughout the film, metonymy is the dominant figure of speech—usually due to the frequent profanity, but also including several discussions of body parts and the line (in an homage to feminine cinema icons) that "Rita Hayworth gave good face." The convention of the sovereign's two bodies underlies the drama of her damaging her voice, as well as the concluding mediation on her "race against time." The film even includes discussion of the aesthetics of selfhood, including the questions of whether she exists only for the camera and which of her body parts are real (the first question is left open, and the second neatly shifted to the question of whether her pearls are real). This pattern of composition is reinforced periodically by the concert footage, which defines her as the center of the mass spectacle, and by allusion to related popular fictions—as when a tearful supplicant asks her to be the godmother of her child—and also by popular signs of courtly life—production numbers use the decor of Pharaonic Egypt and the Roman Catholic Church, and she kowtows to honor her father on stage. Even the name "Madonna" establishes one condition of monarchy—singular political identity—while activating or transposing related archetypes: Like the sacred Madonna, mother of Christ the King, she grounds transcendental kingship in a woman's body; as the profane Madonna, promoter of sexual expression, she displaces the king and offers her eroticism as a perverse form of transcendence. Perhaps what is most distinctive of Madonna's composition of her persona is not how she appropriates kingship but how she blurs the distinctions between king and queen, and courtier and courtesan. These fluid transpositions could be typical of how the courtly style operates outside of any institutional structure, and of how its separation from governmental functions has been coincident with its becoming aligned with feminine representation.[54]

Courtly appeals are not always a means of empowerment, however. In fact, as the style reaches its most extensive propagation one can discern how a process for creating sovereignty is also a process for making subordination appealing. This process also illustrates another aspect of how the premodern social formation can become reproduced within the rhetorical practices of a postmodern culture. By considering how mass media advertising relies on patterns of courtly persuasion, we can consider how it reproduces a particular social character: Fusing aesthetic perception with personal desire, emphasizing hierarchies of class and status, composed largely in a language of bodies and gestures, focused primarily on the female body, and reducing all appeal to the adornment and exposure of the feminine body part, the culture of advertising coheres in the role of the courtesan.

Once again, we are drawn to bodies arrayed and segmented for display within a space itself segmented off from other, more conventionally "political" venues. As diffuse relationships of desire and consumption are activated by focusing the spectator's attention on the alluring body and there on the particular pose or part that is designed to feature the product or represent its appeal, the entire process of representation and response is structured by the trope of metonymy. Although metonymy occurs everywhere, it becomes a particularly powerful persuasive machine within modern advertising. This enhancement occurs because of the distinctive nature of the medium: What is a relatively limited trope within verbal composition acquires enhanced powers of vividness and discrimination through the craftwork of graphic design and electronic reproduction, which in turn are disposed by their own production constraints to rely on the trope. This emphasis of a particular form of representation also fulfills an important function: Since every representational practice constitutes relations of power, the persistent focus on and segmentation of bodily images can become a tacit political language in an ostensibly nonpolitical medium. Thus, courtly roles and responses that would be considered dangerous or embarrassing in deliberations of policy provide effective means for controlling a realm of collective imagination.

When employed to arouse desire in a mass audience, such appeals can become rather strange. Open the newspaper and take another look at the lingerie ad juxtaposed with the news of the world. There she is. Part of her, anyway. The larger photo shows a woman in bra and panties, cropped off mid-thigh. Below it are several smaller photos of women's breasts, each cut off mid-trunk and at the neck. Some breasts are larger, some smaller, some fuller. . . . Some readers will focus on the bras, others on the breasts, but none will see a whole woman's body. The entire composition in my newspaper is often framed with the local department store's slogan repeated continually all around the border of the ad: "satisfaction always, satisfaction always, satisfaction always." Whether looking for a good buy or a good time, the structuring of motives is the same: in order to prepare the woman for the male's erotic approval, attention is focused on the body part while promising satisfaction of undefined, totalizing desires.

Usually the composition is a bit more mundane, but the elements of composition are the same: beauticians' and opticians' ads present disembodied heads, while hosiery ads show us feet and legs cut off mid-thigh or mid-body, and shoe catalogs show us shoes containing women's feet and legs cut off just above the ankle. Likewise, we see a woman's hands in a pair of gloves, without seeing the woman, and a woman's butt alone demonstrates the need for a winter weight-loss clinic, and a row of headless bodies on a beach evokes the lure of the Caribbean vacation, while a row of smiling heads offer testimonial to the merits of a new, improved cooking oil. Needless to say, these representations are enhanced by their general contrast with the medium's conventional portrayals of men.[55] Since all ads operate both locally and intertextually, the general grammar of this persuasive medium consists in aligning the process of consumption with attentive care for the feminine body and identifying specific products with a general, pervasive happiness. As a woman attends to her hips, nails, legs, hair, lips, eyes, eyelashes, and so forth, her body becomes invested with a considerable store of social knowledge—the retail market is inscribed upon her[56]—while she learns to live in a partitioned body. Ironically, the woman's accomplishment of self-mastery—that is, by gaining cosmetic control over her many body parts—divides and subdivides her, fragmenting her consciousness of herself.

One reason this "political semiotics of selfhood"[57] can operate so powerfully is that it occurs through highly routine persuasive practices. In each particular case (allowing for the exception of some obviously "arty" ads in upscale publications) the presentation of the body part usually is comprehended easily and a rational response to the persuasive task—we would not expect to see eyeglasses poised on feet, etc. Even these considerations seem to recede, however, in video advertising, and particularly in ads aimed at male audiences. As the beer commercial flows across the screen, hundreds of split-second images alternate in rapid succession: women's smiling faces, swirling hair, twisting hips, (guys running up the beach carrying a cooler of beers between them), a winking eye, an uncovered belly, (guys playing volleyball in the sand, leaping, diving) a row of breasts, a bare back, now a complete figure—undulating provocatively in harem dance—and then a row of laughing faces, (two guys in profile doing a high five). . . . These more extreme cases only extend the rule, however. Whether rational or imaginative, whether focusing on the product or an idealized conception of its use, whether marketing or functioning as entertainment as well, the cumulative effect of these ads is a pervasive fixation on the female body known by its parts.

But it is not the only effect: For these ads also offer, whether in whole or part, a compensatory design that allows the audience to reconstitute these images of hair, ears, lips, arms, breasts, etc. into a pleasing whole. Everyone in the audience might be learning courtly conventions, but not all are given the same roles, and the role of courtesan supplies the figure of aesthetic coherence needed to complete this rhetoric of bodily images. This role is epitomized by the professional model: Trained for service under the male gaze, she becomes an icon of appealing dress and deportment within a structure of appropriation. Her carefully crafted and controlled eroticism, her practiced combination of self-control and "natural" grace, her poise and smiles and laughter, all signify the courtly ideal of aestheticized living while suggesting the specific role of being available and prepared for pleasure. Just as the courtesan waited adjacent to the corridors of power, so the advertisement is positioned alongside other, more legitimate discourses; and as the courtesan was the feminine complement to a politics of deference and display, so the advertisement models those habits for women today.

There is a further twist as well. The courtly style now operates without the court, and advertising gives us the courtesan without the king. More specifically, the king is displaced from representation to the position of the male spectator: so it is that both women and men will scrutinize the image, the one to compete with it for the other's approval. Thus, a second displacement occurs, which is perfectly suited to the purpose of the persuasive practice: the courtesan's body becomes a substitute for the king within the realm of representation, the new receptacle for the power flowing through the social order, now entirely an order of desire and consumption. That is, within the realm of advertising, the image of a woman's body becomes the symbolic form for concentrating and distributing a great flow of social energy. This energy includes the enormous forces (and anxieties) of the retail market economy—if she is not appealing, if the subjects of the media presentation turn away indifferent, sales will drop, orders slow down, profits wither away. It also includes society's erotic energy, which has been harnessed to serve the market. She epitomizes pervasive sexual interest, and as she adorns the promotion of virtually every product—from automotive parts to cigarettes to furniture to lighting fixtures to sports equipment to vending machines—she advances the society's pervasive eroticizing of its commodities. Finally, as she smiles confidently or adorns her feet, legs, wrists, hands, hair with evermore, always new products, she even embodies the modern *mythoi* of progressive emancipation and endless prosperity. However articulated, the proliferation and partitioning of women's bodies throughout the realm of representation reproduces charismatic social relations. By responding to her appeal (buying the product, imitating her lifestyle) one receives the charismatic touch, the flow of social energy whose marvelous quality is understandable only as a gift from one greater than oneself.

Thus, the courtly style channels the circulation of desire stimulated by the powerful technologies of modern advertising. There are other affinities between the modern persuasive practice and the premodern symbolic form as well. Advertising's language of embodiment and gesture lends itself to acute perceptions of decorousness, status, and charisma, while it encourages preferences for place rather than production, ceremony rather than policy, and the striking, silent pose rather than the embarrassments of speech. To the extent that it succeeds on these terms, it inculcates the courtly style's performative conception of power and aesthetic conception of the self. Moreover, these motifs are becoming increasingly amplified. For example, the history of advertising reveals a continual displacement of speech by a rhetoric of gestures. As the verbal text continues to shrink and the advertising code becomes increasingly a coding of objects, so does the ad itself come to culminate in silence. As the body part dominates the perceptual space, and the ad persuades, it produces not comment—and certainly not discussion, analysis, and argument— but specific behavior. If society could be completely articulated by its advertising, it would be a courtly dance of harmonious consumption, a pageant of bodies moving in concert to clothe, adorn, and otherwise please themselves and others. Consumers would walk through the malls with seeming effortlessness as they easily satisfied their desires in an environment at once competitive yet rendered graceful by successful persuasion. There would be speech, of course, but it would conform to the symbolic drama of the style: either serving as a transparent medium of exchange—"Do you want that here or to go?"—or as the troublesome sign of ruthless social and political struggles occurring behind the facade of commercial appeal. This social order culminates in silence, and finds its demise in immobility. This ideal retail market risks none of the complications of verbal life, epitomized perhaps in the barter it also avoids at all costs, yet in doing so it increases the risk that the social order will calcify in silence, becoming too habituated to current social forms of consumption as more dynamic processes of exchange move elsewhere.

Style alone does not influence economic behavior, of course, and it probably is too early to chart the effects of postmodern versions of courtliness. Yet we can conclude at least that the persistent use of courtly tropes in advertising creates another of the "shifts, slippages or displacements" that have occurred in the representation of the female body in our time.[58] The political consequences of the discursive fragmentation of women have been well documented elsewhere and there is no reason to believe that visual fragmentation works otherwise.[59] The effects would be further disproportionate when the female images worked intertextually with other means of female fragmentation, while fragmented male images were relatively anomalous as a text for defining male identity.[60] Perhaps the key difference, however, is that the portrayal of the female body part overlaps with the phenomenon of the fetish.[61] Consequently, this reactivation of the courtly style has specific consequences for the politics of gender. Woman's power is first dispersed and has to be reconcentrated; man's power begins concentrated and may be dispersed. Furthermore, as fragmented bodies become common, the whole body becomes threatening, a potentially dangerous concentration of power. Thus, mass-mediated bodily empowerment is paradoxical: Each fragment is locally empowering, but the general result is to guard against undue concentration of power in the image of a whole woman. It invests the female body with charismatic power that can be activated through the simple adornment and display of a small body part, yet it also radically fragments the female body image and so disrupts any woman's formation of coherent personal identity. As with any style, however, although its operation establishes asymmetrical large-scale constraints on action, it also provides competent stylists the means for achieving temporary advantages completely contradictory to those constraints. (Remember also that in politics, "temporary" often is long enough.) Stated otherwise, the style activates a discursive structure which does not itself have strategic intentions. Women are subordinated through tropes of courtly empowerment, yet any woman can be empowered by skillful use of those tropes. Obviously, this disjunction between structural bias and strategic capability contributes to the persistence of the style.

Within this realm of representation, the persistence of the whole male body becomes a last preserve of the appearance of organically comprehensible power. This is one reason to look to the American presidency, which will serve as my last example of how the courtly style is activated in contemporary media practices. Still an office held only by men, and one where assassination remains a frequent enough specter of political trauma, the presidency is the most probable symbolic container for our courtly moments. As Michael Novak asserts, perhaps too agreeably, "whether the achievement of an elective kingship makes our nation superior is another matter; but that what we elect is a king must be grasped with sufficient seriousness."[62] Consider how important elements of the courtly style, including focusing attention on the body of the sovereign, an emphasis on gesture, and even the conditions of silence and immobility, become possible or enhanced by the circumstances of televisual production. TV stories must have pictures, and accounts of presidential action usually are presented through pictures of the president, so that increasingly the disposition of the president's body comes to stand for executive action. "Today the President traveled by helicopter to Camp David" (picture of President walking down the steps); "today the President took a power walk" (picture of President walking forcefully along a beach); "today the President's physician reported that the President lost weight during the crisis" (picture of President standing at attention on the tarmac). These and similar examples of presidents golfing, jogging, and the like demonstrate how the reactionary potential of the mass media lies not so much in propagandizing for retrograde ideologies as it lies in subtly transforming the basic context within which our civil activities occur.[63] At times we have a courtly style without a court, a pattern of motivation unchecked by traditions of its own use.

This use of the courtly style was evident during the Reagan presidency. Most commentators agree that Reagan's passage through the assassination attempt was the turning point of his first term. The absorption of concerns of political viability into questions of the disposition of the president's body became a fixture of subsequent coverage of his presidency.[64] These stories articulated the courtly style as we ordinarily experience it—in fragments. While marveling that he seemed to escape ordinary democratic political accountability, the press encouraged the electorate to fixate on the president's diet, exercise, naps, hair color, and wardrobe. This fascination with the king's body often was channeled through sustained presentation of Reagan's various body parts. As they read detailed accounts of his skin, ears, nose, intestines, and bladder, the public gazed upon a dismembered Reagan while being reassured that the sovereign was recovering nicely. Nor did the White House object—in fact, his courtiers saw Reagan through the same lens as the public. Note how courtly tropes organize speech writer Peggy Noonan's recollection of her first glimpse of the president. "I first saw him [Reagan] as a foot, a highly polished brown cordovan wagging merrily on a hassock. I spied it through the door. It was a beautiful foot, sleek. Such casual elegance and clean lines. But not a big foot, not formidable, maybe even a little . . . frail."[65] Noonan is indeed a good writer. Her metonymic description captures both aristocratic aesthetic values and a sense of the two bodies, while the image of the single body part suggests a palace at once organized around access to the body of the sovereign and alive to local, momentary, fragmentary encounters having aesthetic unity and political effect. Such a culture might contain brilliant acts of negotiation and decision, but it also could produce a peculiar sense of achievement. As Larry Speakes recalled proudly, "I remarked, 'I bet that's the first time this word's ever been mentioned in the briefing room.' Public discussion of the President's penis? Yes, it happened in the Reagan White House, on my watch."[66]

Speakes had learned to invoke one form of decorum by overruling another. By violating conventions of medical confidentiality and personal etiquette, he created a drama of courtiers circulating around the king, channeling considerations of polity through a discourse of the body politic. When the *mise en scène* of king and courtiers encompasses the practices of republican debate, there eventually is little to say and nothing to do. The president's body (part) lies before us, and political life is brought to repose in mass-mediated immobility. We create our American kings not so much by ignoring the Constitution as by displacing one set of manners with another.

But the Reagan era already is receding, and in any case it is easy to see instances of executive courtliness as rare exceptions to democratic rule, and even then trivial because only a matter of manners rather than of policy. One need not deny the truth of these considerations to recognize that they also are symptomatic of basic preferences and assumptions in modern political commentary. The courtly style is likely to appear marginal in a polity that believes it has superseded monarchy and aristocracy, and it confounds a theoretical vocabulary that separates politics from other social practices. Consequently, the courtly style is treated much like gossip, another intensively social communicative practice revolving around considerations of decorum. Gossip is an ubiquitous and often important mode of communication in any organization, yet officially unacknowledged or discredited. Likewise, whenever courtliness is discovered to be politically consequential, it has to be disavowed, redefined, or suppressed. This marginality makes the courtly style all the more available for composing the "nonpolitical" political practices of the family, office, officers' club, theater, etc. In addition, it provides a stimulating complement to more instrumental arrangements. If people cannot or will not live according to the severe dictates of legal codes, bureaucratic procedures, economic calculations, and the like, they will become attracted to alternative, more embodied means for living and working together. The courtly style provides a mode of political expression that communicates the experience of power, and it equips a group to locate, track, and contain specific forms of persuasive skill and to identify the role of customs, status, emotions, and taste in executive decision-making.

While it composes relations of power within a group, the courtly style also immobilizes the group normatively. Although it might incorporate a wide range of social activities into political awareness and expand the scope of personal indulgence allowed any political actor, it closes off deliberation about the purpose, values, and direction of the group. (As at court, such deliberations usually are compressed and translated into the process of succession, which often is too brief and inarticulate for the task at hand.) Over time, the same rhetorical designs that animate and organize become deadly constraints, constricting adaptation and innovation. The style assumes the fate of the king's body: just as every individual, no matter how powerful, is mortal, so every assertion of majesty has to succumb to the laws of symbolic form. The dialectics of nature and culture, action and ceremony, speech and silence, and the rest become displacements, for the continued artistic development of courtly tropes inevitably leads to a formally perfected version of its original act of exclusionary definition. The court begins as a separate place, set off from the ordinary world, and so it ends as a world onto itself, an all-consuming autarchy incapable of admitting to anything beyond its round of ceremonies. Ironically, the way for the art of courtly rule to overcome its strange combination of hypertrophied sociality and moral blindness would seem to lie in stylistic failure and vulgarity. These are studiously avoided, of course, and so the courtiers' skill and refinement become the cause of their undoing. The appeals to kingship, rank, decorum, ceremony, and other signs of majesty are ancient and enduring forms for social cohesion and political power, yet in every particular case they decay, becoming brittle defenses of excessive privilege to be swept away by those who have been denied.

In Oratory as in Life: Civic
Performance in Cicero's
Republican Style

icero would not have liked his reception in the twentieth
century. Although his works have received expert reconstruction, translation, and commentary, they have had no
effect on political thought. In the United States, this irony contains
another as well, for inattention to Cicero would have astonished the
founders of the American republic. As Robert Ferguson observes, Cicero was *the* classical model for the founders, their constant "reference and inspiration."[1] Times have changed, of course, but modern
neglect of Cicero is unfortunate since he still has much to teach us.
Whatever the nobility of the democratic ideal, democratic government remains an experiment, and its precariousness is evident not
only in the fragile and often failed democratic revolutions around the
world but also in the enormous social energies required for its maintenance in established states. I believe that successful democratic
polity depends in part on its practitioners' competency within a particular political style, the *republican style* that is designed to maximize the political opportunities available within electoral campaign-
ing and parliamentary deliberation.

Cicero epitomized this style and it suffuses most of his work. It
is particularly evident, however, in his letters, which are the most
extensive collection of personal correspondence to have survived
from antiquity and are distinguished further by their remarkable dis-
closiveness.[2] These personal reflections on a public life tell the story
of how Cicero strove above all else to become the embodiment of the
political culture of the Roman republic, and they provide us with a

compendium of the conventional appeals and reactions shaping that culture. Likewise, the flaws of character revealed all too clearly in the letters prove to be defects not just of the individual historical figure but of one model of political personality. By examining the characteristic intelligence displayed in this story, we can consider how the republican style can be a resource for democratic initiative in our own day while also identifying its inherent weaknesses. Along the way, I hope to challenge the traditional conception of Cicero as a second-rate intellect, hypocritical moralist, and indecisive leader[3]— that is, the stock conception today of the democratic politician.

Any political style typically will operate as a mixture of rhetorical designs, institutional customs, and philosophical arguments as these have developed in specific historical periods and cultural locales. Although no political style is limited to an explicit institutional setting, nor identical with a political theory, obviously there can be strong correspondences reflecting common origins or interests. Perhaps even more than the others, the republican style seems to be particularly imbued with a set of ideas about human nature and good government. This conception of political life celebrates self-government as the highest moral calling, insists that citizens' political activities should be motivated and guided by civic virtues, and cautions against the influences of private, especially commercial, interests.[4] These precepts in turn require that public institutions (such as the legislature), public practices (such as the practice of oratory), and public figures (such as the president) cultivate a moral sense in the citizenry that would result in decisions being made primarily with regard to the common good. The achievement of good government at any time requires active participation by individuals successfully striving to overcome their private interests through common deliberation, and the stability of the republic through time depends on its ability to cultivate individuals possessing this virtuous character.

Despite extensive study of the role of civic republicanism in American history, and acknowledgment of the importance of classical exemplars and especially of Cicero for civic republicans themselves, scholarly reconstructions of civic republicanism have scanted Cicero's own works.[5] This lack of interest is a liability, especially when discussion of civic republicanism becomes a language for contemporary political commentary. Few would deny that it has done such double duty, generally with the intent of countering either Lockean political precepts or (less often) some version of authoritarianism.[6] I submit that inattention to Cicero's own texts can lead to a flawed understanding of civic republicanism and unnecessarily utopian political theory.[7]

The historiographic problem has two sides to it. On the one hand, the tendency has been to look for a coherent set of political ideas, whether they were labeled an ideology, tradition, philosophy, vision, etc. Not surprisingly, since the subjects of the investigation generally were active political leaders, philosophical incoherence (or, more properly, variability) immediately became one of the puzzles of civic republican scholarship. John Adams had bemoaned the unintelligibility of the concept in 1807, and contemporary scholarship has seemed to result only in "'conceptual confusion.'"[8] On the other hand, the tendency has been to find, in place of immaterial ideas, a vibrant world of political speech. America's civic republicans were alive to discourse, mastered and mixed diverse political idioms for rhetorical effect, and nurtured a "cult of eloquence."[9] Although this discovery offered a way out of the first difficulty, it has only confounded the discussion of republicanism all the more, perhaps because modern historical scholarship lacked an adequate critical vocabulary for understanding what it had found.[10] Although one strength of the civic republican revival in contemporary scholarship was that it focused on pamphleteering, oratory, and other popular rhetorical practices and took them seriously—on their own terms and as significant determinants of political experience and action—the confusion that resulted came about in part because soon the republican code was being used to translate all manner of political discourses. Civic republicanism thrived on political speech, but seemed to dissolve in its own medium.[11]

There are both substantive and methodological issues here. On the one hand, one can argue about the definition of civic republicanism or about the extent to which it influenced the political decisions of the late eighteenth century or early nineteenth century. On the other hand, one can ask how to determine whether it or any political stance is present in a particular text. Obviously, the first set of questions depend on the second. It is not easy, however, to determine in general whether one should emphasize key terms or particular patterns of argument, a preponderance of cues or the values of placement and function, the control of the specific text or connection with pervasive ideological structures. These problems are compounded by the lack of simple exemplars, the complexity of most texts, and the interpretive skills of modern academic readers who can find what they are looking for just about anywhere.

These problems can be addressed in part by considering how civic republicanism is a political style and Cicero its exemplar. It still can be understood as a philosophy or constitutional doctrine or any other configuration of political principles, but with the proviso that it also is a rhetorical repertoire for activating those ideas in performance. That is, the full presentation of civic republicanism only occurs when its doctrines are filled out rhetorically, when the republican ideas are complemented by (and at some point transformed into) the rhetorical skills and sensibility of the republican style. Without the addition of these rhetorical elements, the model of civic republicanism is incomplete; obviously, when relying on this incomplete model, it becomes more difficult either to see how it functioned in any historical period (particularly since the performative dimension of political life always is difficult to retrieve) or to believe that it could be effective today. Likewise, by identifying the repertoire of persuasive appeals that constitute the republican style, one can make more reliable assessments of republican influence within a particular text, debate, sequence of events, or political culture.[12] Obviously, the first requirement for any such analysis is selecting an appropriate model. By looking to Cicero's reflections on his active life, we can identify the elements of republican composition as they were employed by its master stylist.

My reading of the letters is both selective and caught up in the concerns of the present. This is not a historical reconstruction of the author's intentions or social milieu, nor is it necessarily representative of important themes, ideas, or techniques informing his many other works. It is an interpretation that has as its object something common to both past and present, and to many, if not all, of his works. This approach to interpretation draws upon several insights from Hans-Georg Gadamer's exposition of philosophical hermeneutics, while adding an emphasis on rhetorical forms that Gadamer would leave to specific disciplinary development. Gadamer emphasizes that interpretation always requires explicit mediation between the text and its recreation in the present.[13] This mediation is exemplified by the process of translation, which inevitably involves decisions to emphasize or de-emphasize features of the original text. This process of alternately highlighting and renouncing the original text should culminate in the "fusion of horizons" where the new meaning is "not only mine or my author's, but common."[14]

The key to activating this approach to a text is imagining the question to which the meaning of the text is an answer.[15] As letter follows letter, and as Cicero comments on his reading, writing, and waiting, and as he discusses a wide array of issues and concerns, a consistent orientation begins to emerge. Cicero writes to others of his thoughts, fears, complaints, and plans so that he might answer a single, persistent question: How is Cicero to compose himself for public life? How is he to comport himself—through all of his decisions, from selecting his place of residence to choosing his allies to concluding his next speech—if he is to become the public figure he wishes to become? Through these personal reflections on public identity, he gains an internal composure as he molds the character he will use to influence others. If he succeeds in (again) successfully incarnating Cicero, leader of the republic, then he can draw on all of his powers; and he knows he holds those powers ever so precariously, for he holds them not by aristocratic rank or military prowess or financial resources, but by virtue of successful performance.

Once this question has been posed, one can address the central task of interpretation, which is to bring into language the object of the text.[16] Whatever else they are doing, Cicero's letters have to articulate the resources he can draw on to answer his central question of how he is to compose himself. In other words, the object of Cicero's letters is the repertoire of rhetorical conventions that comprise the calculations, anxieties, and character traits typifying republican politics. Despite their provisional quality and fragmentary form, the letters offer a rich text for identifying this style, for they themselves perform by highlighting and renouncing his other texts. In his praising and lampooning of his stratagems, Cicero reveals not so much his vanity and superficiality (the conventional interpretations of his testimony) as his use of the letters as a hermeneutical space: They become an explicit mediation of his other texts and so a medium of understanding. The genre of the letter is ideal for this use, for it naturally conforms to Gadamer's requirement that "every translation that takes its task seriously is at once clearer and flatter than the

99

original."[17] By interpreting Cicero as he is interpreting himself, we can discern those techniques for composing public life that he was trying to master. As he highlights and renounces to conform to the conventions of letter writing, Cicero creates the clearer and flatter space suitable for reflecting the object of his many words.

In this essay I shall focus on the letters to Atticus. The virtues of this collection include the span of events covered (from 68 to 44 B.C.E.), the coherence and acuity that come from their being addressed to a single, erudite, and beloved audience, and their availability to the contemporary public. After cataloging their general characteristics (which help distinguish them from other works by Cicero or from letters by other authors), I draw out the specific elements of the republican style. Although one could learn as much from the rest of his correspondence, Cicero's profession of his friendship with Atticus offers eloquent testimony to the special value of their letters for anyone wishing to understand the inner life of Cicero's career: "I must tell you that what I most badly need at the present time is a confidant—someone with whom I could share all that gives me any anxiety, a wise, affectionate friend to whom I could talk without pretense or evasion or concealment. . . . you whose talk and advice has so often lightened my worry and vexation of spirit, the partner in my public life and intimate of all my private concerns, the sharer of all my talk and plans" (18/1.18).[18]

Although the letters all move with the flow of events, their appeal as literature also comes from their internal modulations of topic and mood, each pattern giving essential form to the letters. The basic topics are banter, business, politics, and personal burdens. The bantering with Atticus includes the teasing characteristic of friendship, as well as puns, shared satirical sketches of their acquaintances, and so forth. These digressions serve as a dance of engagement and disengagement, appealing always to continued association. The business includes most of what Cicero labeled "private" matters: chiefly financial transactions and generally the management of his domestic economy. Atticus is both audience and agent in the frequent discussions of debts, real estate, wills, dowries, and personal possessions such as books and statuary. Politics constitutes the whole of the world standing over against private life. The category is explicit and its contents supply the bulk of the correspondence. Together, these two principles of the private and the public make up the warp and

100

woof of the letters: note their interplay (and proportions) in his yearning (from Asia) for "the world, the Forum, Rome, my house, my friends" (108/5.15). Yet a fourth topic occasionally intrudes when he is vexed or agitated or overcome with personal burdens. In that less confessional age, such matters were usually kept hidden within the category of private life: as when he begins a paragraph on his "private" troubles with a list of financial problems and then concludes enigmatically, "My other anxieties are more *sub rosa*" (74/4.2). Yet sometimes these disturbances intrude insistently into his writing, changing the letters despite his apologies for their presence. Here we find the irritations of tending to his brother Quintus, the trauma of his exile from Rome, and the devastation of losing his daughter Tullia.

This last topic also reveals the alternation of moods which provides the second pattern to the letters. Here four tones prevail: the joy of combat, angst, fretting, and anguish. The first shows itself as a mixture of excitement and self-importance and marks his active involvement in the daily intercourse of politics. Its opposite mood is angst, the sense of vague dread, constriction, and hopelessness felt whenever he became separated from public life. A third mood, perhaps easily confused with angst, lies in his incessant fretting. Here we find the ex-consul obsessively nagging Atticus for information regarding the arrival of some books, or the payment of a debt, or the end of his governorship. It reached its apogee during the civil war of 49–48 B.C.E., when Cicero scratched over any detail, no matter how small, pertaining to the repeated movement of his person from villa to villa as he balanced himself between two continually shifting coalitions. Finally, the letters at times vent the anguish experienced during those periods of personal abjection brought on him by the loss of his beloved constitution during the first triumvirate, or the loss of his political identity during exile, or the loss of his daughter in his declining years. This darkest mood represents the emotional pattern of the letters: its intensity recalls the ubiquity of the other moods and suggests that the basic action of Cicero's story is emotional movement.[19]

As Cicero's emotional changes supply the action of his story, they also suggest its literary tonality. And here Cicero disappoints many of his readers, for he is no tragedian. At his best, Cicero's vision extends no farther than a conception of the balanced life; at other times, the letters give us Cicero's heart on his sleeve. Fretting about Tullia's dowry, he says, "Oh dear, what am I to write or wish? I'll cut short, the tears have come pouring from my eyes. I leave it to you. You decide for the best. Only don't let anything harm *her* at this time. Forgive me, I beg. Tears and grief stop me from dwelling on this topic longer" (218/11.7). With such presentational artifice and emotional excesses the letters spill over into the sensibility of melodrama.

Cicero's taste for melodrama marks him both as a representative Roman and as a spokesman for the republican style. As its aristocratic critics have always commented, republican government plays itself out in a public theater designed for broad effects and capable of, at best, middlebrow artistry. By turning to Cicero, we can discern the master tropes and related sensibilities constituting this style. The republican style begins with a relish for the pleasures of composing and delivering persuasive public discourse; it includes other modes of exchange and becomes a more focused mode of action by defining consensus as the foundational means and end of governance, and it culminates in a model of leadership that features personal embodiment of the civic culture. As these tropes are augmented by related appeals and attitudes, the style coheres as an engaging program for participation in civic life. Characteristically, Cicero's letters leave little out, allowing discussion of each of these designs in turn.

The republican style begins by conflating political activity with the compositional techniques of public address. In the republican mind, persuasion is the essence of politics, rhetorical virtuosity is the surest sign of political acumen, and public speaking is the master art. Although the republican stylist might spend a lifetime writing and reading pamphlets, newspaper editorials, declarations, and other publications, all of these are understood as forms of oratory and admired for their turn of a phrase. Thus, the republican mind easily moves back and forth through a series of synecdochic relations: From all of politics to political persuasion, from all political persuasion to oratory, from all oratory to the striking use of a few words. Witness the declension in Cicero's gleeful report on his activity:

Well, then, so long as I had the Senate's authority to defend, I took so brisk and vigorous a 'part in the fray' that crowds flocked around me shouting enthusiastic applause. If ever you gave me credit for courage in public life, you would surely have admired me in that affair. When Clodius had betaken himself to speech-making at meetings and used my name to stir up ill-feeling, ye gods, what battles, what havoc I made! The onslaughts on Piso, Curio, the whole bunch! How I pilloried irresponsible age and licentious youth! Upon my sacred word, I longed to have you by, not only as an adviser to follow but as a spectator of those memorable bouts. (16/1.16)

Such equations of rhetorical skill and political effect are highlighted by the unabashed enjoyment experienced by the republican stylist in turning a phrase or scoring a point in public debate.

Ye gods, how I spread my tail in front of my new audience, Pompey! If ever the periods and *clausulae* and enthymemes and *raisonnements* came to my call, they did on that occasion. In a word, I brought the house down. Any why not, on such a theme. . . . You should know by now how I can boom away on such topics. I think you must have caught the reverberations in Epirus. (14/1.14)[20]

Politics, for the moment, has become identical with oratorical performance, and the measure of success comes from enjoyment of the means, not the result, of that performance.[21]

A modern reader might think Cicero a cynic, proven to not believe in the substance of his speech because he can identify, even mock his manipulations of form. How could he be attached to something when he can so easily lampoon its presentation? Yet notice how this passage works by joining exactly the two attitudes Gadamer identified as the key to meaningful translation: highlighting and renunciation. Cicero again brings the glorious moment of the speech into view yet simultaneously sets it behind him. The mockery at his own delight tells us that we are at the letter's moment of translation, where it articulates the object of the other text. He does not reject his words for another, opposing stance, for his renunciation exists only to establish that his technique is his subject. The object of the speech was to invent a public character and thereby a public; its success was precisely a successful selection of means. Cicero accepts that politics includes the practice of personal display for influence, and he relishes those moments when political success comes from adroit use of the techniques for catching the public eye. Nor does the act of letter-writing provide recourse to a more theoretical knowledge, for the writer quickly plunges back into the fray. This ability to abstract a situation (by defining it in terms of the formal elements of its composition) and then set aside the abstraction (and so return to the situation and act) is an essential movement in this technical intelligence.

Perhaps vanity has a place in this style, for it can highlight sheer performance. Vanity suspends awareness of the many constraints on one's actions—not least the reality of the audience's diverse reactions and contrary motivations—so that technique itself can be seen. Witness this remark:

> I cannot help mentioning that when I drew the first lot among the Consulars a full House unanimously declared that I must be kept in Rome. The same thing happened to Pompey after me, so it looked as if we two were being kept as gages one might say for the Republic. Why after all should I wait for the other people's *applaudissements* when I am so good a hand at the game myself? (19/1.19)

Again, the double movement of highlighting and renouncing his text is at work, for Cicero's vanity foregrounds his rhetorical considerations—his relationship with the parliamentary audience, accumulated capacity for influence, and republican ethos—while the mild self-deprecation of the report, achieved by identifying it as vain, sets it aside again, reminding the reader that the letters are a special place for appreciation of the performance but not its substitute.

Such descriptions of rhetorical flair focus on the movement of political energy within a persuasive process while presuming that this process will overcome all other forms of power. Sometimes this presumption is emphasized as well, as when Cicero gloats about a colleague's response to attempts at physical intimidation: "Clodius' roughs had taken possession of the gangways. The voting papers were distributed without any 'ayes'. Suddenly up springs Cato to the platform and gives Consul Piso a spectacular dressing down, if one can apply such a term to a most impressive, powerful, in fact wholesome speech" (14/1.14). Or, on another occasion, Cicero recounts for Atticus how he shored up the republic by reversing the low morale caused by a negative outcome in a popular trial. He describes how he counseled his colleagues one by one, harried his enemies with a number of measures, and brought it all together "in a set speech of impressive solemnity and also in an exchange of amenities . . . you can sample it here and there, but the rest cannot retain its force and piquancy without the thrill of battle" (16/1.16). The letter then provides details of the exchange of repartee with Clodius on the Senate floor, which continued until "the roars of applause were too much for him and he collapsed in silence." The full implication of the report is that the political stability of the republic can be and has to be maintained by rhetorical virtuosity. Indeed, when things were going well for Cicero, he experienced politics as a seamless process of oratorical artistry and political function: "You know about my arrival in Ephesus, indeed you have congratulated me on the assemblage that day, one of the most flattering experiences of my life. From there, getting wonderful welcomes in such towns as there were, I reached Laodicea on 31 July. There I spent two days with great *réclame*, and by dint of courteous speeches effaced all earlier grievances" (113/ 5.20). Obviously, some of the time such descriptions empower the political actor, providing the means to identify and mobilize effective means of persuasion, while at other times they will be delusions. Cicero did carry that day and others against Clodius—"All in all, I am teaching the ruffian manners, by quips of this sort as well as by sustained serious oratory" (21/2.1)—but only to watch his enemy drive him into exile and destroy his property because he relied too long on the "powerful bastion of general good will" (45/2.25).

This appreciation of rhetorical artistry is not confined to oratory, but extends to his other works, his actions, and ultimately to every gesture, every detail of expressive living. Of another composition, he remarks, "Now *my* book has used up Isocrates' entire perfume-cabinet along with all the little scent-boxes of his pupils, and some of Aristotle's rouge as well," and a few lines later he asks Atticus to "please see that it is made available at Athens and the other Greek towns. I think it may add some lustre to my achievements" (21/2.1). Again, self-conscious vanity is used to feature his technical artistry and its capacity for influence, and the enjoyment of the work is due more to its artistic accomplishment than to its topical significance. His tone could be more serious, however, as during the war between Caesar and Pompey, when he scrutinized his conduct for any means to escape dishonor on the one hand and death on the other. Politics had become reduced to a deadly game of managing appearances, with its topics and themes and causes all hanging on the outcome but suspended for the moment from providing any counterweight to sheer technique.

Whatever the situation, Cicero's fascination with rhetorical artistry reveals a seemingly paradoxical self who can at once be deeply committed to a cause and yet obviously acting.

> I believe it was after you left that the Clodian drama came on to the stage. I thought I saw there a chance to cut back license and teach the young folk a lesson. So I played *fortissimo*, put my whole heart and brain into the effort, not from any personal animus but in the hope, I won't say of reforming our society, but at least of healing its wounds. (18/1.18)

This blend of conviction and stage presence produces a distinctive form of political rectitude that is defined less by simple adherence to principle or necessity and more in terms of a middlebrow aesthetic standard:

> The hostility excited against me in the minds of our spoiled and licentious young men has been so mitigated by what I may call my affability that they all make me the object of their special attention. In fact, I now avoid treading on anybody's toes, though without currying popularity or sacrificing principle. My whole line of conduct is nicely balanced. . . . I think you now see a kind of outline of my way of life and behaviour. (19/1.19)

Cicero's strong sense of rhetorical technique has itself been balanced by the practice of making oneself agreeable. Any situation can be reduced to its means of persuasion, but the difficulties of tending to many audiences require a personality simultaneously stable and flexible. This practice was objectified in the classical concept of decorum, which was, for Cicero, the one all-encompassing code: "The universal rule, in oratory as in life, is to consider propriety."[22] These norms of appropriateness—for example, to occasion, subject, and character—organize all of the tasks of persuasive composition and apply not only in speech but "in actions as well as in words, in the expression of the face, in gesture and in gait,"[23] and sometimes in one's geographical position between two generals. In every case, "whatever else decorum is, it is essentially balance in one's entire way of life as well as in individual actions."[24] Within the republican style, both influence and integrity will come from balancing the tensions between assertion and deference, virtue and virtuosity, or similar elements of the art of persuasion.

Other commentators have not been so pleased with this sensibility, particularly as it is revealed so unabashedly in the letters.

Petrarch seems to be in a state of shock when he writes, upon discovering the letters, that he is "filled with shame and distress at your shortcomings; and so even as did Brutus, 'I place no trust in those arts in which you were so proficient.' "[25] This theme, which aligns his character defects with his artistic powers, has been repeated often since then by those faulting Cicero for being superficial and unprincipled. Curiously, these criticisms beg the question of whether one kind of thinking is more virtuous than another within the world of republican politics. Here Cicero's position is clear, for he masterfully portrays the folly that results from acting as if politics could be neatly made-to-order as is philosophy. Cato is his foil: "The fact remains that with all his patriotism and integrity he is sometimes a political liability. He speaks in the Senate as though he were living in Plato's republic instead of Romulus' cesspool" (21/2.1).[26] Where others find Cicero shallow, he saw himself as skillful in respect to the game he was actually playing.[27]

For those who have admired Cicero, expediency has been the lesser issue and eloquence the higher ideal. Civic humanism of the Italian Renaissance was imbued with his equation of prudent action and the well-turned phrase.[28] His rich conception of public address became the hallmark of American civic republicanism.[29] As Kenneth Cmiel observes, "Eloquent language, almost all agreed, was critical to the new regime. Republicanism was government by discussion as opposed to force of fiat. Speech was more important to a republic than to any other kind of polity."[30] Ferguson summarizes: "The republic's leaders fought constantly but not over the importance of public expression. To men of letters the message was the same regardless of party. Their place was the podium; their vehicle, the speech."[31] Whatever it might be doctrinally, civic republicanism also is a manner of thinking animated by the social practice of public debate and the performative ideals of the art of oratory. It is staged, and so grander than life; it is aesthetic, and so experienced rather than avowed; and, because it is addressed to the events of the day, it is transitory, perhaps a brilliant victory over the dull resistance of everyday routine yet always known to be passing away before it is finished.[32]

The emphasis on oratory as the master art of the republican style has several implications beyond placing the political actor on a public stage. The style is explicitly argumentative yet also imbued with the strong sense of physical impedance and acoustic resonance that comes from speaking publicly, and especially from speaking in such places as the senate chamber. "You know how I can boom away on such topics. I think you must have caught the reverberations in Epirus." As a result of this synesthesia of arguing and orating, the republican stylist is acutely aware of the gesture in the words of the text—that is, gesture becomes a metaphor for understanding the discursive performance. Cicero provides a symptomatic example of this when agonizing over the choice between Caesar and Pompey: He imagines himself being called on to speak in the Senate: "But what am I to do? I don't mean in the last resort—if war is to arbitrate, I am clear that defeat with one is better than victory with the other—I mean in the proceedings that will be set on foot when I get back to prevent his candidature *in absentia* and to make him give up his army. 'Speak, M. Tullius!' What shall I say? 'Be so kind as to wait until I see Atticus'? There's no room for fence-sitting" (124/7.1).[33] Here the complex considerations of honor, expediency, principle, loyalty, character, circumstance, and more (which fill the many letters from this period) are compressed into the single, dramatic moment of the orator slowly rising in the silent chamber tense with expectation. Note also the assumptions about public address in this passage: it provides strict accountability, is a mode of action, and is decisive. The contrast with Atticus's position as a man of letters alone, noted without rancor by Cicero, underscores the importance of oratory: it not only shapes his imagination while providing the subject and focus for their correspondence, it is the one mode of address that can seal one's fate.

The image of Cicero standing before the Senate creates sharp gestural enactment of his need to reach a decision; the decision, however, would have to be voiced. Likewise, in the oratorical sensibility, a text ultimately succeeds as an assertion of voice, with all of the implications that has for melding thought and speech. Politics comes to be understood within the republican style as a form of oral argument—of making ideas stand the test of public debate, but letting persuasive success count as the sufficient extension of the ideas. Cicero captures this sense of politics, and highlights the hermeneutical relationship between the reflective space of their correspondence and the political action it mirrors, when he says to Atticus: "Evidently it is as you say, things are as uncertain in the political field as in your letter; but it is just this diversity of talk and comment that I find so entertaining. When I read a letter of yours I feel I am in Rome, hearing one thing one minute another the next, as one does when big events are toward" (35/2.15). Republican composition thrives within an intensified orality, whether brought on by public debate amidst the press of events or through animated conversation among friends. When this is done well, there no longer is any conflict between forensic and theatrical impulses, between addressing the argument and making a good show, for the achievement of mutually satisfying public talk requires both art and analysis and is taken as a sign of both virtue and virtuosity.

The republican style also carries with it all of the experiences and anxieties characteristic of public address. These experiences include both the euphoria experienced as one speaks eloquently and effectively, and the long drop from the sense that one's words are the reality they describe to the dissipation of meaning that occurs as the audience becomes again an aggregate of individuals each obviously qualifying or disagreeing with or misunderstanding the speaker's meaning. Against these mood swings, the republican penchant for the middle way seems a compensatory fantasy of self-control. The chronic anxieties include both the fear of not pleasing one's audience and the fear of not getting to speak at all. Witness how Cicero frets: "As I write this I think my speech must just about have reached you. Dear me, how nervous I am about what you will think of it! And yet what is that to me, since it won't see the light unless the free constitution is restored?" (417/15.13a). Later he continues in the same alternation between concern about the reception of his work and desire for its circulation: "I am glad you like my work. You have quoted the very gems, and your good opinion makes them sparkle the brighter in my eyes. I was terrified of those little red wafers [the marks from Atticus's editing]! . . . I only wish I may see the day when that speech circulates freely enough even to enter Sicca's house!" (420/16.11). Perhaps the republican values of common virtue and public concord can be understood as outgrowths of its grounding in the practice of public debate, perhaps even as idealizations of audience approval and reaffirmations of a world where speeches are a form of action.

This orientation also might explain some of the well-documented republican susceptibility to paranoia.[34] To begin with, the speaker's unreciprocated dependency on the audience, coupled with the powerful mood swings produced by their approval or rejection, makes one quick to see disagreement or indifference as betrayal. Although much of the time his social intelligence is too acute for outright paranoid fantasies, Cicero's own observations could be tinged with tones of suspicion: Driven into exile by a sworn enemy he had publicly ridiculed, Cicero nevertheless would remark darkly, "I will only say this, and I think you know it is so: it was not enemies but jealous friends who ruined me" (54/3.9). More generally, if politics, now the highest calling, is to be conducted in public and as a public and while well aware of the impermanence of the public event, then private arrangements become demonic. As republican politics is thought to be an open process of persuasion among all citizens acting virtuously, the greatest threat to the republic is imagined to be a secret arrangement by a few conspirators to manipulate or circumvent agreement. In a political culture of oral argument, secrecy becomes the sign of subversion.

The republican immersion in oratory has additional implications as well. In place of comprehensive statement of one's political precepts, the republican style emphasizes a more constitutive understanding of political discourse. Cicero firmly believed that the state was grounded in specific conditions of public opinion—the authority of the Senate and the harmony of the orders—which, in turn, were maintained by dutiful observance of civic rituals and skilled performance in public debate (for example, 18/1.18); the letters repeatedly gather and assess information pertinent to those means and ends. Cicero is well aware that republican politics involves conflicts of interest between classes and groups, but he emphasizes how the political process is the means for bringing them together—the conditions for any successful negotiation have to be created in the act of negotiating. In other words, the point of persuasive discourse is more to form the virtuous civic community than to represent it.[35] "When I praise one of your friends to you, you may take it that I want you to let him know that I have done so. The other day, you remember, I wrote to you about Varro's good offices towards me, and you wrote back that you were delighted to hear of it. But I would rather you had written to *him* that I was well content with him, not that this really *was* so but that it might become so" (45/2.25). As Cicero's tone suggests, the attitude here is comic, for the political relationship constituted in speech is achieved by all pretending to be what they initially are not. In addition, it requires all manner of exertions, by the principals and a host of intermediaries, and all manner of texts, from major speeches to thank-you notes, and it can even lead to extreme physiological reactions in both speaker and audience.[36] This emphasis on the constitutive function of public address contributes to the republican sense of the precariousness of the state. Cicero not only identifies himself with the republic, he sees its health as depending directly on his proximity to Rome, ability to speak, and similar circumstances. He worries not only about the threats poised by commercial greed and military force, but also about the general quality of public debate and what it signifies about the virtue of speaker and audience alike. The republic is always at risk, always needing to be propped up from within, somewhat without regard to its enemies without—and no wonder, for it stands on something as thin as air. Consequently, the letters are an exercise in the performative discipline needed to sustain it. They keep the orator tuned for performance today as they also collect materials for future use and, given the right audience, they work directly as part of the republic's perpetual re-creation.

   Since the republic is constituted in discourse, public speech becomes defined, on the one hand, by persistent attention to ethos, and, on the other hand, by obsessive consideration of the audience. These dynamics can be unified and developed into extremely sophisticated sensibilities—for example, what Ferguson describes as an "aesthetics of cohesion"[37]—but their value to republicanism itself is measured by the extent to which they could succeed on their own terms of bonding citizens together through appeal to their civic virtue. Thus, it appears that republican anxiety about the fragility of the republic comes not just from observing the lessons of history but also as both subjective and objective result of its own stylistic habits: Because the republican stylist is so intensely social and that sociality is epitomized through oratorical performance, he or she is acutely aware of the tenuousness of one's political base. The republic that is constituted in discourse need stand no longer than the next speaker. It is even endangered by silence, for without the continuing discussion of public duties, virtue could wane, citizens become distracted, forces of change gather strength as political energies dissipate. Hence the constant talking, which in turn raises the risk of the wrong thing being said too often. Objectively, the republic that is guarded primarily by eloquence is indeed at risk. The culture of eloquence that sustains republican polity can unwisely displace more prudential considerations—of, for example, the Machiavellian correctives of force and fraud. This sense of inherent vulnerability is most familiar as the problem of transmitting civic virtue from one generation to the next. Although the problem seems solvable once we see how it requires only certain civic practices, and notably practices of eloquence (and not, for example, the civic militia Machiavelli also advocated as a mainstay of republican virtue), those practices are themselves vulnerable to cultural change. New modes of discourse and technologies of communication become particularly ominous threats to civic life, as is implicit in the contemporary denunciations of both technocratic jargon and the mass media.

Perhaps this is one reason why the republican style connects oratory with other literary and dramatic arts. Like any political style, the republican style arranges the available modes of communication into a hierarchy, and the republican hierarchy is distinguished by both its elevation of oratory and its broad valuation of all other forms of verbal artistry. (Silence, the negation of speech and the cloak of conspirators, is at the bottom of the scale.) Cicero can always understand his letters, poems, philosophical works, rhetorical treatises, and speeches as a unified whole in part because he simultaneously parses them as varied but aligned arts. Furthermore, each is always available as a resource for the others. Here the letters provide both testimony and example: We learn that Cicero discussed and composed poetry and plays as we see him allude effortlessly to a wide range of classical literature. Oratory remains the ultimate achievement, for only there are all of the human faculties activated in a performance that draws on and constitutes all other elements of collective life, but the other arts are valued as they provide both preparation for and resources to use during performance.[38] The political strategy implicit in this culture is to shore up the republic, first, by keeping everyone reading, writing, and talking, and, second, by providing for a culture of eloquence that is more versatile and so more adaptable to change because it is grounded in several verbal arts.

Cicero does not follow politics solely for its field of play, however; he also finds there better and worse decisions, justice and folly, the joys and the risks of communal living. How, then, does he discern the preferable from other courses of action? This question is answered typically by referring to his treatises to discover a political philosophy. The letters provide a different perspective, highlighting his application of the second major trope of the republican style, which is that consensus is valorized as the essential condition of successful political action. The orator's orientation toward securing agreement and praise from the audience becomes generalized, linking all public decision-making in a common process of deliberation and consent. This attitude begins with the first prerequisite of a parliamentary career, the campaign for election, which in turn schools the candidate in the appeals and demands of living by the vote: "If however you like to take a harsher view, you may assume that the exigencies of my candidature made the stumbling-block. . . . You know the game I am playing and how vital I think it not only to keep old friends but to gain new ones" (10/1.1). This attitude does not mean one merely tallies up the numbers and follows the majority, though that will do some of the time. It means more that the proper analysis of a situation requires coordination of what the others involved think is and should be the case and that a decision must maintain both the express objectives of policy and the political relations sustaining policy making.[39]

Aware that the equestrian order took it amiss, though they said nothing in public, I administered what I felt to be a highly impressive rebuke to the Senate, speaking with no little weight and fluency in a not very respectable cause. Now along come the Knights with another fancy, really almost insupportable—and I have not only borne with it but lent it my eloquence . . . The demand was disgraceful, a confession of recklessness. But there was the gravest danger of a complete break between Senate and Knights if it had been turned down altogether. Here again it was I principally who stepped into the breach. . . . I discoursed at length upon the dignity and harmony of the two orders. . . . Thus, in maintenance of my settled policy, I am defending as best I can the alliance I myself cemented. (17/1.17)

This continual definition of policy in terms of parliamentary alliances is easily criticized in general, both for deferring rational assessment of policy to a pooling of agreement and for sacrificing principle to expediency, but within the republican orbit, these outcomes are understood to be neither unacceptable in every case nor inevitable. In addition, they are balanced by the understanding that decisions are more likely to be judged acceptable and enacted by those who believe they have had a voice in the deliberative process. Thus,

113

the sufficient test of the wisdom of one's measures is found by walking them around the forum, and personal ambition (from *ambio:* to
go around, as in a canvass) need not be at odds with public accord.
This is where the republican proves to have an optimistic view of
human nature—for consensus requires that one believe in a common
ability to craft policy and a moral capacity to keep agreements.
"Worldly-wise folk tell us in all their histories and maxims, even in
their poems, to be on our guard and not to trust others. I follow the
one precept, to be on my guard, but the other, not to trust, is beyond
me" (40/2.20).

This reliance on others is evident in the intense sociality of the
letters. They are not discussions of "the good," "the just," etc. They
are discussions of Quintus and Crassus and Tiro and dozens of others. And each problem is approached in much the same way, whether
it is catching an embezzler or patching up Quintus's marriage or
choosing sides in a civil war: Cicero assays the other's views, positions his own (provisionally) within that array, and then asks Atticus
for his own and additional views as well. "On arriving at Capua
yesterday (the 25th) I met the Consuls and many members of the
Senate. . . . There is a wide variety of opinion in our debates. Most
people say . . . My own opinion is . . . I am waiting for your views
about all this" (139/7.15). Nor does awareness of the errors that can
result deter Cicero from pursuing and enjoying a world of consensus:
note the humor as he tells Atticus that "My friends' letters beckon
me to a Triumph, something I feel I ought not to neglect in view of
this second birth of mine. So you too, my dear fellow, must start
wanting it, so that I shan't look so foolish" (121/6.6).

This constant use of consensus as the foundation of political action typically is described, and faulted, as Cicero's characteristic
vacillation.

I must tell you that my decision, which seemed by now pretty well settled, is
wavering. . . . If you complain of my chopping and changing, I answer that I talk
to you as to myself. In so great a matter must not any man argue with himself
this way and that? Besides I want to draw *your* opinion—if it is still the same I
shall be the steadier, if it has changed I shall agree with you. (164/8.14)

And so he argues back and forth, with himself and others, always
trying to find the solution most satisfying to the most people. And
sometimes he is misled by his method, mistaking the applause he

records with such satisfaction for indebtedness, or ignoring the possibility that other leaders might work differently. We should recognize, however, that although vacillation is indeed characteristic not only of the man but of the republican manner of thinking, the corresponding value of consensus is more humane and humanizing than the will-to-power that can overwhelm it.

Much more could be said about Cicero's understanding of this essential norm of republican polity. I doubt more is needed, however. The values, the social practice, and the subjective process of consensus politics so thoroughly encompassed Cicero's life that their emphasis adds little to the story. Furthermore, this norm is a fixture of modern democratic government, and any differences between civic republican and other conceptions of consensus are not likely to be sticking points in negotiations of either policy or theory. For these reasons, I shall let this relatively brief account suffice, in order to turn again to more distinctive features of Cicero's republican style.

The third major trope of this style unites the others for maximum political effectivity. The self-consciousness of one's persuasive techniques and the grounding of action in consensus come together in Cicero's lifelong attempt to become the personal embodiment of republican government. We know he succeeded: witness, for example, the story of Caesar's assassination, which has Brutus turning from the dead dictator to the crowd and intoning one word: "Cicero." Whatever the truth of this story, there was no better way in the story to activate the idea of the republic than to speak the name of the man who had labored to become its signal representative. Those who read Cicero today continue to see him as he would wish: For example, Christian Habicht concludes his superb commentary on Cicero's political career with the affirmation that "Cicero had, in fact, become the idea of the Roman Republic."[40]

This apotheosis did not occur by accident. For starters, it was the point of Cicero's story of himself. According to this story (which, like any good story, is not quite in accord with the facts), he was called while still young to leave a life of study and pleasure for service to the republic, his political fortunes and those of the republic became fused forever in the white heat of the Catilinarian crisis, and at the end of his career his combat with Anthony proved once again that there was no enemy of the republic who did not also declare war on Cicero. This story was the central text in a process of rhetorical amplification that was sustained over the length of his career.[41] The defining moment in this story was his exposing and prosecuting Cataline's attempt at a *coup d'état* while Cicero was consul: Already invested with consular authority, Cicero's powerful oratory and decisive action routed the conspirators and resulted in his being hailed as the leader who had single-handedly saved the republic. Somehow in this process the separate elements of the ambitious individual, the role of elected head of state, historically determinative action to preserve the republic, and public acclaim for that action were unified into a rhetorical figure. It became something he never tired of repeating. "As for me, ever since the immortal Nones of December when I rose to what I may call a pinnacle of immortal glory, combined with unpopularity and many enmities, I continued to play my part in politics with the same disregard of self and to maintain the position and responsibilities I then assumed" (19/1.19). Although he had stepped down from the highest office, the fusion of self and polity that occurred while there was not about to be dissolved. This definition of his unique role was established through his oratory, particularly the speeches delivered during the crisis, and maintained by publication of those works along with continual repetition and allusion in others—"the whole theme which I am in the habit of embroidering in my speeches" (14/1.14).[42] His story of himself as the one individual who put everything on the line to save the republic was more than a self-serving chronicle of those events: It provided a trope for transferring the authority of the republic to the person telling the story and for activating the republican ideal when considering matters of policy. The figure even is appropriated by others as it suited their purposes. For example, Crassus

held forth on the subject in most encomiastic terms, going so far as to say that it was to me he owed his status as a Senator and a citizen, his freedom and his very life. . . . I was sitting next to Pompey and I could see he was put out, whether at Crassus gaining the credit which might have been his or to realize that my achievements are of sufficient consequence to make the Senate so willing to hear them praised. (14/1.14)

Embodiment records an achievement, and it is one, and it becomes the means for others. Indeed, it epitomizes the republican identification of politics and persuasion, for embodiment is a rhetorical ac-

complishment that in turn fuses speech and action, speaker and subject, technical artistry and political status.

Cicero's analysis of decorum can guide our reading here as well.
His anatomy of the four types of decorum, pertaining to human nature, individual character, circumstance, and, above all, one's choice
of a career, returns us to the essential question of the letters: "Primarily we must decide who we want to be, what kind of person we
want to be, and what sort of life we want to lead."[43] Each political
stance has a corresponding style of performance, and "It is the particular responsibility of the magistrate to realize that he represents
the character of the state and that he ought to maintain its dignity
and distinction."[44] Cicero's rhetorical theory also provides a clue
for tracing this figure. As Cicero remarked in *De oratore*, the non-
rational appeals should flow through the speech "like blood in our
bodies"[45]; so any strong assertion of ethos would suffuse all other
elements of public presentation. Indeed, as James May summarizes,
"The story of Cicero's oratorical and public career is, at the risk of
oversimplification, a chronicle of his struggle to establish, maintain,
reestablish, and wield that very important oratorical and political
weapon, an ethos in possession of *dignitas, existimatio,* and *aucto-
ritas.* . . . In Ciceronian oratory we find an artistic application of rhetorical ethos that far outstrips anything known in Greek oratory or
in the severely fragmented oratory of his predecessors."[46]

This observation suggests that ethos plays a particularly important role in republican discourse. The performance of the virtue appropriate to the political task at hand, which always includes the
problem of securing a consensus, is a central requirement of republican discourse, an orientation most evident in the individual's embodiment of the republic. One can trace this performative awareness
in the letters by highlighting his discussions of the glory of fame and
the horrors of exile. Fame is no incidental matter to Cicero; as Shackleton Bailey has put the point bluntly, "fame, not philanthropy or the
beauty of virtue, was Cicero's spur."[47] Unfortunately, his work *De
gloria* is lost, so we can't know the range and subtlety of his thinking
on the subject. It seems safe to say, however, that his love of fame
extended beyond the adulation of the moment to include a strong
sense of history and the higher standards that come with that. "And
what will history say of me a thousand years hence? I am far more in

117

awe of that than of the tittle-tattle of my contemporaries" (25/2.5). It is equally important to realize that his love of fame was wedded to his appreciation of the state. He reached "the pinnacle of immortal glory" while overcoming a *coup d'état,* and later he would reminisce: "There is no Republic any longer to give me joy and solace. Can I take that calmly? Why yes, I can. You see, I have the memory of the proud show she made for the short time that I was at the helm, and the thanks I got in return" (92/4.18). Cicero's rationalization betrays his method: he finds identical compensations for the temporal decline of both his government and his influence, as each achieved immortality in the same moment—that is, the moment of his consulship—and in the same way—through his "show" of republican resolve during the crisis. So, too, both his zealous administration of a virtuous governorship and his eagerness in slipping the assignment as soon as possible reveal his identification of personal integrity with personal luster. "I think the fame I'm winning for justice and integrity is likely to shine all the brighter if I lay down my office quickly" (110/5.17). Cicero strove to be more than a good man (say, an Atticus), he had to be the epitome of good government as well. Consequently, his loss of political status when driven into the exile was all the more painful. Cicero's agony at that time belies his occasional encomia to the contemplative life and shows how completely his identification with the Forum had shaped his psyche: "No man has ever lost so much or fallen into such a pit of misery. . . . I mourn the loss not only of the things and persons that were mine, but of my very self. What am I now?" (60/3.15).

As Leo Braudy observes, "for the man whose public identity was built on his way with words," fame "appears like a homegrown portent, a personal talisman to guide him safely through the world he had determined to conquer."[48] This fame is palpable evidence that one has prevailed in the difficult competition for attention within the society of speakers, it confers legitimacy automatically on speaker and subject, and, as Hannah Arendt has noted, it fulfills that "striving for immortality which originally had been the spring and center of the *vita activa.*"[49] No wonder that this quest is evident at every stage of Cicero's career, ultimately giving his life the sense of an epic narrative. He could even in his later years offer his persona as a political resource: if Caesar wishes to negotiate with the republican forces, "I conceived myself to be by nature and public image not ill fitted to help in such an undertaking" (178A/9.11A). Fame, like other elements of the republican style, is both a means for personal influence and a context for audience participation; the pursuit and acquisition of glory can even be a resource for political conciliation, something that not only motivates extraordinary action but also binds competing interests together.[50] In Braudy's words, "as far as Cicero is concerned, then, fame is basically substantial."[51]

We must also recognize, however, that this trope of personal enactment may also induce a corresponding incapacity to see impersonal determinants of political action. In the letters, despite his concern for the *concordia ordinum*, we do not see the regular attention to the causes of structural instability that we regularly find, for example, in Aristotle. Surely his typification of the *person* Anthony as the greatest threat to the republic is an example of serious blindness. J. P. V. D. Balsdon may have pointed toward the fault: "Cicero saw himself all too often in the center of the stage, when he had in fact been in the wings."[52] We could go further: as Cicero's republican style composed events on a stage, it could not account for political realities that could not be staged well.

Perhaps this propensity to view political history as a stage with popular actors is another reason why it remains difficult to see the fall of Cicero and his beloved republic as anything more than melodrama. Similarly, it becomes easy to emphasize Cicero's defects of character as the causes of his political failure.[53] This conclusion misses an opportunity to better understand Cicero's intelligence, however. As the figure of republican embodiment becomes an active means for defining and acting within a situation, it brings with it a political psychology. Republican composition occurs within a dialectic of internal dialogue and external performance. The individual oscillates between anxieties of weakness and the experience of triumphing over this incapacity by throwing oneself into public action. These anxieties are inevitable when stepping into a relatively undefined but prominent public role, such as the generic role of public speaker that is the template for republican governance. In fact, one of the tasks of republican performance is to keep these anxieties under wraps or otherwise manage them. Sometimes they do bleed into the republican's public address, which might even be a means for identification with some audiences, though also a decided weakness when opposed by the realist's toughness, the courtier's poise, or the bureaucrat's rationality. At other times, the republican stylist might craft a specific composition to displace anxiety; I would hazard that it often is done by shifting to other genres from the deliberative, such as epideictic address or Cicero's more philosophical or literary compositions. Most of the time, however, the republican orator makes a strong show that belies the self-doubt nagging its composition. Even if Cicero's speeches are symptomatic of his anxieties, they remain explicitly virtuoso performances by a master artist confident in his powers. By turning to the private record, however, we learn of the failures of nerve, moments of shame, chronic indecisiveness, self-pity (lots of self-pity), and many other accounts of personal obsessiveness that have embarrassed so many readers. (How nice it would be if he had let us keep the classical age a pantheon of heroes, so we could pretend that politics could once again become monumental.)

Yet this excessive subjectivity is also a resource for the republican style: it allows the politician a space for reconsideration, and recuperation, in the difficult task of assessing the shifting coalitions of republican politics. Thus, private and public life are not separate realms but rather different phases of an intelligence that lives for but not wholly in action with others.

My brilliant, worldly friendships may make a fine show in public, but in the home they are barren things. My house is crammed of a morning, I go down to the Forum surrounded by droves of friends, but in all the multitude I cannot find one with whom I can pass an unguarded joke or fetch a private sigh. That is why I am writing and longing for you, why I now fairly summon you home. There are many things to worry and vex me, but once I have you here to listen I feel I can pour them all away in a single walk and talk. (18/1.18)

The internal dialogue of Cicero's letters shows not just an individual who happens to be fretful, but the manner in which republican performance places special demands on an actor while also opening up a space for meditation.

Thus, the republican style joins public virtuosity with private anxiety. This fretfulness seems to be a constant, low-level accompaniment to republican political thought, its psychological background noise: "But you will say that I am manufacturing worry for myself. I can't help it. I hope it may be so, but I'm afraid of all manner of things" (114/5.21). Such fretting might be particularly appropriate to republican practice. Since psychological dialogue is particularly open to emotional and attitudinal struggles, it can help the speaker discover important means for persuasion. This psychology also provides the background for the individual's success: by finding one's nerve and crafting consent through effective persuasion, the republican actor achieves the public self that is the key to personal advancement. The republican community understands heroism not as the conquest of an alien warrior, but as the individual's triumphing over personal limitations to become the exemplar of civic virtue. (Recall Milton's encomium to Cromwell: "He first acquired the government of himself, and over himself acquired the most signal victories, so that on the first day he took the field against the external enemy, he was a veteran in arms."[54]) The full implication of this symbolic drama is that when the individual comes to embody the republic, the greatest individual success is in complete harmony with the public good.

In any case, the republican style blends personal experiences and public interests within the individual's composition of herself as a public figure. This trope of civic embodiment is a figure of completion, in several senses: It concludes the speaker's appeal for authority, it brings the other elements of republican composition together into an aesthetic whole, and it provides the audience with a coherent definition of their civic order. This achievement of aesthetic and political coherence across speaker, text, and audience reveals several additional tonalities in the republican style, each of which has a sympathetic relationship with the figure of embodiment. The first of these lesser tropes is a heroic *mythos.* The republican politician achieves greatest glory as the heroic individual seizing the moment by voicing immortal words at the height of great events. This is one reason why civic republicanism is so intuitively hostile to liberal proceduralism, by the way, for they are antithetical aesthetic attitudes: The dramatic gesture wowing the crowd or the speech turning the mob into an army of citizens is less likely to occur where polity is rationally regulated. Stated otherwise, the republican style has an aesthetic weakness for symbolic foundings, dramatic acts that transform a preconstitutive state into a republic. (As the republic itself always contends with contingency pulling it back into chaos, this attitude favors continual reprises of the constitutive act, additional performances reconstituting the elements of civic life.) This heroic attitude can explain both Cicero's peculiar sense of his own career and the general inability of modern scholarship to get a sure grasp on civic republicanism. Cicero remained ever convinced that his dramatic performances during the Catilinarian crisis were the absolute high point not only of his career, but of the history of the Republic itself, and he remained ever baffled by others, including his friends, who couldn't quite see it that way. This distortion in his otherwise often acute perceptions of political history is explained only in part by his vanity, for it also is an example of how he was captive to his political style. Since that moment had indeed been one of dramatic political action including exceptional oratorical performances all in the name of the republic, it must have been of great historical significance. Since there were no other great actors left on the stage at the end of the play, he must have been the important historical figure. For other speakers or those less caught up in Cicero's eloquence, of course, other explanations become possible. Yet civic republicanism today seems trapped in the pages of history for want of a communicative culture that allows definitive performances. Not only the disregard for oratory, but the massive omnipresence of communicative media and messages renders a heroic sensibility foolish. To play on the well-worn cliché of modern life: fifteen minutes of celebrity is little incentive for a lifetime of preparation and hardly capable of sustaining a polity when that moment is immediately swept away in a welter of messages on hundreds of channels.

Within the republican culture, however, the contrary problem arises: How to prevent the abuses of authority that can result from leaders too caught up in grand events, noble actions, and similar occasions for overbearing civic righteousness. The basic check comes not from a modern sense of rational self-reflexiveness that would ask if one really was as important as one felt, etc. The republican style instead relies on a specific sense of decorum to regulate the political actor: the code of civility. This code requires one to speak publicly with one's opponents as if one respected them. So Cicero says of someone who is working on behalf of his enemy Clodius: "There is a Tribune called C. Herennius, . . . I gave him my usual warm reception in the Senate, but he is a complete pachyderm" (18/1.18). The connection between "civic" and "civility" is as immediate within the republican style, where civility is a *sine qua non* of political life, as it is overlooked otherwise. Civility is the means and measure of a healthy polity: it allows the legislative process to encompass conflict and it is the sufficient achievement of the political education that is designed to perpetuate the republic. Such civility includes the manners of legislative address, seating, and the like, and it is defined at all points by refraining from violence, recognizing social status, observing parliamentary customs, and acting as if oneself and one's opponents always were motivated at least in part by civic virtue and the duties of public office. Obviously, from a Lockean perspective, this attitude is sheer nonsense, an elaborate but thin veil draped over the rude struggle for advantage between incommensurable interests. Within the republican style, however, it is a realistic precept: If people are to conduct public business, they must act as public figures. Rather than distinguish between competing interests, the republican first activates a distinction between public and private motives. Instead of asking for demonstration that the public motive is in fact authentic, the republican assumes that its performance is sufficient to regulate conduct. Cicero's marking of his and others' public titles and duties is not merely status consciousness but a means of constituting the republican polity amidst turmoil, and his *concordia ordinum* is not merely a mystification of an unstable coalition of incompatible interests but an idealization of his deepest sensibility.[55]

Thus, the republican style is invested heavily in the rules of decorum attending the society as a whole and its legislative institutions in particular. Interestingly, however, these rules have no necessary relationship to the topics of public debate. Even as they, like any form of decorousness, create zones of the sayable and unsayable, and do so within the ideological structuration also shaping the society, they do not make substantive specifications. (This is the point of closest contact between liberal and republican politics.) This sensibility locks the politician into the status quo but does so in order to create a space for debate about any issue whatsoever. That debate must follow the rules of the assembly, but they also are being negotiated within the process of debate. (So it is that they are codified as arcana and inseparable from memory and interpretation by elders, and some important rules always remain unwritten.) Obviously, the republican culture can appear to the radical as a very rigged game on behalf of established elites, while the republican sees it as an arena

123

that is constantly changing, with issues, personalities, and even the rules of the process continually in negotiation. Stated otherwise, civility is the postconstitutive attitude of republican governance, the regulatory norm consistent with the republican ethos and intended to maintain the republic beyond the conditions of its origin.

In contemporary politics, this emphasis on civility is evident in several areas. It is always active in the ordinary interactions of legislatures, whether in the persistence of such formalities as referring to "The Senator" from wherever, or in the day-to-day arguments and jokes about the conduct of the assembly, or in the give and take of drafting legislation. Not surprisingly, civility also has been a favorite norm of conservative political commentators.[56] This need not make the republican style a stalking horse for a particular political doctrine, however, although that is indeed possible.[57] Civility also has become an appeal within several strains of liberal democratic theory, though only occasionally with civic republican overtones.[58] Perhaps these various uses of the term suggest that "civility" can be a form of political euphemism, for example, for ignoring injustice and perpetuating authoritarian rule or for glossing over the fact of liberal cultural hegemony. Or, it also might be that the republican style is likely to be seen as *relatively* reactionary: it will appear conservative to liberals, liberal to progressives, etc. It also is likely that civility has a hollow ring and is easily suspected to be little more than a Trojan horse for an ideological advance when its use is not grounded in a familiar persuasive practice such as parliamentary debate. Conversely, for those using it as it is embedded within a culture of performance, the term (and its kin, such as "tact" and "prudence") will require little explication and be no cause for alarm. One also should consider how there could be varieties of republicanism running across the ideological spectrum, and how particular political stances might become better versions of themselves (for all of us) by developing more explicitly their republican sensibilities.[59]

The best example of a republican advocacy that has received a favorable press is that of Vaclav Havel, hero of the liberal literati, whose speeches, letters, interviews, and essays have been published widely in the United States in the past few years. Havel, distinguished as both an intellectual and a political leader, emphasizes that "'civility,'" "the general level of public manners," and "good taste" are essential elements in the democratic restoration of his country.[60]

Havel's definition of his sensibility reads like a précis of Ciceronian rhetoric:

I have discovered that good taste is more important than a postgraduate degree in political science. It is essentially a matter of form: knowing how long to speak, when to begin and when to finish, how to say something politely that your opposite number might not want to hear, how to say, always, what is most essential in a given moment, and not to speak of what is not essential or uninteresting, how to insist on your own position without offending, how to create the kind of friendly atmosphere that makes complex negotiations easier, how to keep a conversation going without prying or, on the contrary, without being aloof, how to balance serious political themes with lighter, more relaxing topics, how to plan one's journeys judiciously and how to know when it is more appropriate not to go somewhere, when to be open and when reticent, and to what degree.

But more than that, it means having a certain instinct for the time, the atmosphere of the time, the mood of the people, the nature of their worries, their frame of mind—these too can perhaps be more important than sociological surveys. An education in political science, law, economics, history, and culture is an invaluable asset to every politician, but I am still persuaded, again and again, that it is not the most important asset. Qualities like fellow-feeling, the ability to talk to others, insight, the capacity to grasp quickly not only problems but also human character, the ability to make contact, a sense of moderation; all these are immensely more important in politics.[61]

Here many of the precepts of the republican style are restated in a modern idiom, including elements such as the appreciation of rhetorical technique, the norm of consensus, attention to the presentation and discernment of character, the equation of polity with public talk, an architectonic rule of decorum, a cultivation of liberal education, and the like. (Lesser elements are evident as well, such as when Havel, like Cicero, repeatedly defines the art of politics against professional expertise.) It is interesting that Havel has not been widely accused of moral relativism and the other Ciceronian vices. In part, I suppose, *our* sense of negotiation is presumed to be morally secure, whereas the same plasticity in others appears suspect, but Havel's exemption also will come from his skillful use of the whole armamentarium of Enlightenment appeals in conjunction with his practical advice.[62] Like many political figures today, Havel does not exemplify only one style at all times. Furthermore, even taken straight, his republicanism differs from the Ciceronian model, perhaps largely

125

due to his living within a culture that suppressed public speech and so channeled democratic aspirations through other arts, notably the theater.

Whatever the ideology or cultural milieu, the republican sense of decorum is developed further through coordinate senses of ethical conduct and aesthetic representation. The republican understanding of political ethics is grounded in a narrative conception of the self. This conception of civic identity defines the individual in terms of a civic role and the correct performance of the role in terms of the traditions and prospects of the community. As Alasdair MacIntyre has remarked:

We all approach our own circumstances as bearers of a particular social identity. I am someone's son or daughter, someone else's cousin or uncle; I am a citizen of this or that city, a member of this or that guild or profession; I belong to this clan, that tribe, this nation. Hence what is good for me has to be the good for one who inhabits these roles. . . . This is in part what gives my life its own moral particularity.[63]

One's closest sense of duty and personal fulfillment comes from identification with one's role, which in turn acquires its significance from its place within the history of a community. Witness Cicero's remark to the Senate upon his return from exile: "You have restored to me the brother I so sorely missed and me to the most affectionate of brothers. You have restored their parent to my children and my children to me. You have given me back rank, status, fortune, a noble commonwealth, and source of delight second to none, my country. In a word, you have given me back myself."[64] Cicero's identity is defined by the social roles he inhabits, which include above all his membership in the political community, and their obligations and enjoyment give him his sense of moral particularity. The ties between this identity and communal narrative are confirmed a few lines later, when Cicero claims to have gained immortality. Perhaps this rapid shift from humility to conceit is possible because of the primacy of social classifications and rhetorical artistry in Cicero's sense of himself. What he is can be withdrawn by others, yet he can be anything that can be conferred if he can succeed in his appeal. Consequently, one's character is derived not from personal authenticity, but from social competence. Within the republican narrative, this competency must involve civic performances that perpetuate

126

the republic in time. Actions are judged ethical as they exemplify the civic virtues, which are assumed to maintain the republic, or as they are decisive (heroic) moments in the story of the republic's survival.[65] However they might be judged in the particular case, Cicero understood that his actions required joining virtue and its display in order to coordinate his life with the story of his polity.

This idea of ethical performance also includes a general rule of appropriateness and specific considerations of timing, both of which depend on the prior association of morality and gesture. Thus, in the republican style, ethics will of course include judgments of principle, obligation, honor, and the like, but these concepts will be epitomized by making the right gesture at the right time. The Aristotelian problem of wedding goodness to calculation to produce *eupraxis* is transformed within Cicero's sensibility, which recognizes that goodness occurs through use of gestures that are already self-limiting in performance. As Cicero reminds Atticus of their strategy for his earning glory as an honest governor, "How far from easy a thing is virtue, how difficult its simulation for any length of time!" (124/7.1). Just as the republican actor becomes a public figure through performing within the conventions of public address, so does ethical restraint develop as one adheres to the conventions of public life in order to develop and protect one's reputation. Furthermore, the gestural sense is partially metaphoric, a means for conceptualizing political action, particularly as it is expressed through persuasive speech acts. Throwing one's weight around in the Forum will have included the swagger in one's gait, but it also encompassed any other element in one's sense of political action. Performance is not a threat to ethics, as it is when the ethical sense is defined prior to the realm of appearance, because it is the mode of ethical being.[66] In Cicero's extended discussion of ethics, he grounds social convention in the control of natural bodily impulses, and his sense of decorum underscores this point, as when he observes that it applies "in actions as well as in words, in the expression of the face, in gesture and in gait."[67] To be good is to be self-controlled, which is to control the body, which is done not by suppression or sublimation but through the redirection of desire into effective use of gesture. Of course, this is a means for both overcoming personal desires and for giving lip service to one's obligations toward others. As with any question of ethics, there are no guarantees.

127

The aesthetic sense of the republican style includes an appreciation of form and function taken from public arts such as architecture and commemorative statuary. This aesthetic favors figural representation of the civic culture and artistic definition of its public space, and it is evident across its various modes of composition. Whether created through statuary, dramatization, or anecdote, the republican culture places models for imitation in a public space. Of course, the epitome of this artistry for the classical republican was the public oration. Note how Cicero laments the demise of the republic through contrasting depictions of Pompey poised in oratory:

So there is our poor friend, unused to disrepute, his whole career passed in a blaze of admiration and glory, now physically disfigured and broken in spirit, at his wit's end for what to do. . . . I could not keep back my tears when I saw him addressing a public meeting on 25 July about Bibulus' edicts. How magnificently he used to posture on that platform in other days, surrounded by an adoring people, every man wishing him well. (41/2.21)

Cicero's depiction of an orator's splendid public display memorializes his civic culture, while the change in Pompey's public figure provides his most vivid sense of republican collapse.

Republican representation is not limited to oratory, however, and includes statues and other monuments, paintings and murals, civic rituals, stories of great leaders, autobiographies, and so forth.[68] What later generations might see as granite banality or antique curiosity can be objects of deep feeling for those who dedicate them. So Cicero could ponder building a memorial at Athens (115/6.1) because of his fondness for the city, and after the loss of his daughter he became obsessed with the construction of a public shrine to honor her memory (254/12.18ff.). His most personal affections were expressed through aesthetic conventions from the public arts. In its more typical use, republican appropriation of the public arts addresses the two fundamental problems facing a republic: convening at all for debate and majority rule amidst conflict and perpetuating the republic across time. This artistry typically displays political leaders and audiences who have figured in the history of the republic, it represents civic virtues and accounts for political achievement and the common good in terms of those virtues, and it follows habits of representation that feature the whole, clothed body and standard typifications of gender (featuring male leaders such as Cato and female abstractions such as Lady Liberty). Furthermore, whether in monumental gesture or biographical anecdote, these figures often emphasize rhetorical artistry.

Whatever the signification, such memorials function as a form of *imitatio:* They are understood not so much as accounts of what happened, but as designs for imitation while preparing for events to come. Certainly that is one basis for the heavy reliance on Cicero by the civic republicans of the eighteenth and nineteenth centuries; he had styled himself to be the kind of material they needed to understand politics on their terms. On the other hand, this republican style was not carried by important arts of the ages following the collapse of the Roman Republic, including intensively literary movements such as the Second Sophistic, the many forms of religious art, or the literature of chivalry. Nor is it likely to be carried by modernist artworks placed in museums, corporate headquarters, and private homes, or by classical music reproduced in concert halls or private electronic environments, or by literature written for an audience of writers—in fact, by much of the high cultural production of the twentieth century. Perhaps more important, any representation of specific historical figures becomes less respected as political study moves away from an educational process that featured the copybook and direct imitation of the prose of great men. Likewise, in a political environment that values innovation, a political intelligence that works by variation on a set pattern will seem antiquated rather than resourceful.[69]

Thus, the republican sensibility depends on specific practices of cultural memory that are themselves of little importance within contemporary political culture. The veneration of the dead orator and recollection of great public speeches seem outdated. Civic remembrance persists, however, whether through popular icons such as JFK or Martin Luther King, Jr., or through the eulogies, testimonials, conversations, or other fragmentary yet familiar texts that help constitute political communities. Let me provide one example, one of several that could be taken from the publications I happened to receive in the mail recently. In his letter to the editors of *The New Republic*, Marshall S. Shapo of Chicago comments on a review of a biography of Allard Lowenstein by recalling "an indelible fragment of memory of Lowenstein's uncanny ability to inspire an audience":

129

Lowenstein, who I believe had been a past president of the National Student Association, was a featured speaker at its 1957 national congress in Ann Arbor, Michigan. Without remembering any specifics, I recall two things very well. One is that he was, at least for an audience of 18- to 22-year-olds, perhaps the funniest speaker I had ever heard.

The other memory, especially bright, is of a remarkable oratorical capacity joined with a ringing call to the pursuit of justice. I have heard a lot of the great speeches of the century on audio and video tape and I have been present for many fine talks from various platforms. But Lowenstein, on that informal occasion, ranked with the best of them. There was something about the pitch and the passion of his voice, and his projection of commitment, that was extraordinarily energizing.

Students of the '90s have imbibed a lot more about the ambiguities of what "justice" means than did most of the members of my college generation. But this one image of Lowenstein, from a time of grander simplicities, provides a pretty good antidote: that of an unabashed commitment to the idea that there is such a thing as social justice, that it is worth striving for and that in some significant measure it is achievable.[70]

Mr. Shapo's eloquent letter is a fine example of republican composition. It activates cultural memory in order to motivate continued aspiration to the civic ideal. It does so by celebrating a leader's oratorical virtuosity, while exemplifying a citizen's consciousness that is steeped in the enjoyment of the art of public address and knowledge of its history (qualities of mind that are not likely to result from ordinary participation in American education and popular culture). The speech is described as both a masterful, entertaining performance and an expression of deep personal commitment to a political ideal. Its eloquence is marked by both a distinctive oral quality— "the pitch and passion of his voice"—and its ability to impel the audience into principled action. The audience, itself representative of the writer's civic community, was brought to vibrant consensus as a generation committed to a just society that could be achieved by their participation in civic life. Above all, these ideals are experienced through their embodiment by the orator. The deepest source of Lowenstein's oratorical power was his ethos—his palpable commitment to justice—and his greatness as an orator consisted in his being able to bring that ideal into the world of speech, to make it materially present through his own words in an intense moment of *memory*

public life. "This one image of Lowenstein" is contrasted with the later generation's more abstract conception of " 'justice,' " now in quotes, disembodied, and known by ambiguities implicitly acquired from philosophical instruction "imbibed" as students, not in the *vita activa* of speech and action experienced as members of a National Student Association. This contrast is honed further by the writer's sense of "grander simplicities," a perfect expression of the historical sense and preferred diction of American republicanism: a process of remembrance that can do without "specifics" in order to focus on the brilliant civic moment, which is known by its artistry of plain speech raised to eloquence, at once lofty and essential.[71] In sum, the letter crafts a pattern of political experience, and represents a specific vision of virtuous polity, by concise and coherent use of many of the conventions of the republican style. A distinctive mode of political consciousness, and call to political participation, is activated by these designs that equate politics with the social relations embodied in public address, politics at its best with the artistry of a great speech, and the political ideal with the ethos of a speaker whose eloquence makes him a fitting icon of the political community. The letter and the speech it celebrates achieve a common eloquence crafting a vivid artistic representation of republican polity. Yet even this eloquence reveals the underlying anxiety that it is too much an act of recollection, that civic virtues have waned in the passage to a succeeding generation. Despite the achievements of speaker and writer, the republic requires still more words, more displays of civic virtue, more examples for imitation.

These examples can be great or small. Likewise, the republican aesthetic of figural representation and imitative response can be divided further into two different tones: one monumental and the other quotidian. The monumental figure is the one that is supposed to extend across the entire public space and through historical time. It is the "great show" that Cicero made during the Catilinarian crisis, or the declaration that his own fortune and that of the republic have been indivisible. Cicero expressed publicly his desire for such achievement in the realm of appearances with characteristic modesty:

In recognition of such great services, citizens, I shall demand of you no reward for my valour, no signal mark of distinction, no monument in my honour except that this day be remembered for all time. It is in your hearts that I wish to have set all my triumphs, all the decorations of distinction, the monuments of fame, the tokens of praise. Nothing mute can please me, nothing silent, nothing in short that can be shared with less deserving men. Your memories, citizens, will cherish my deeds, your conversation enhance them and the records of history will bring them age and strength.[72]

This passage is suffused with republican artistry: Cicero valorizes his audience of citizens while identifying himself with their republic; he explicitly evokes a monumental aesthetic to address the problem of perpetuating his reputation (and thereby providing a basis for continued reproduction of the republic through imitation of its heroes); finally, he amplifies his subject (the cultural memory of his great deeds) by suggesting that it deserves the function but exceeds the form of public statuary. Public speech still is celebrated as the premier art of republican life, the only comprehensive form of civic representation, yet its full aesthetic effect is brought out through metaphoric identification with the explicitly figural representation of a public monument.

The quotidian gesture is one that follows the republican aesthetics of representation but on a small scale in order to manage a specific situation. Here one looks to the fit between one's public figure and the immediate social scene and does so in respect to some pragmatic objective. "I think I had better *not* attend the games at Antium. It would be a bit incongruous, when I want to avoid the suspicion of any kind of pleasure seeking, to turn up suddenly as a holiday-maker amusing myself, and in so silly a fashion too" (31/2.10). Cicero realizes that in this case the scene will define the actor, and the motive attributed within the festive scene doesn't fit the ethos he is crafting for another performance. Such discriminations extend as well to minute adjustments of personal display within a scene. So Cicero can't help remarking, in a speech no less, that his performance during the Catilinarian crisis included going out in public wearing "that broad cuirass."[73] In accord with his general rule of decorum, no detail of personal expression has been overlooked; in accord with the republican aesthetic, he has taken care to embody the virtues of preparedness, courage, and resolve in his own figure. (And he enjoyed doing it—perhaps his greatest offense to a modern reader.) As Cicero strides through the crowd, the individual and the republic have been fused cosmetically: An attack on the republic would most likely begin as an attack on him, and he armors himself to guard the polity. More-over, he did this "not to protect myself—for I knew that it was Cati-line's practice to thrust at the head or neck and not at the flank or stomach—but for all loyal citizens to observe and, seeing the fear and danger in which their consul was placed, to rush to his help and de-fense." This gesture serves a remarkable number of immediate objec-tives—symbolizing the present danger, motivating citizen action, controlling the jostling crowd, intimidating his foes, and raising him above his allies—while his retelling it helps secure his place in his-tory. Perhaps an exceptional republican politician will know how to manage a crisis through figural expressions that are simultaneously quotidian and monumental. Witness, for example, Lech Walesa's adroit exploitation of his house arrest, release, travel, and the like to advance the restoration of democratic government in Poland.

There is no place, however, for simulations of republican virtue in the confines of modernist political studies, and the republican cul-ture of civic performance seems outdated in a liberal society con-sumed with the pursuit of individual happiness. Whatever its impor-tance to the founders, republicanism now seems to go against the grain, and one might well doubt the relevance of anything learned from Cicero's crafting of his republican persona. Ultimately, it forces a choice between two radically different conceptions of political identity.[74] As this choice has been articulated in recent political theory, it is a choice between, on the one hand, the modernist subject who is a rational individual possessing absolute rights and negotiat-ing relative goods,[75] and, on the other hand, a composite personality that is only provisionally intelligible because it is the consequence of various practices of collective definition.[76] As Michael Sandel has noted, either the self is "independent of the desires and ends it may have at any moment," or "certain of our roles are partly constitutive of the persons we are—as citizens of a country, or members of a movement, or partisans of a cause."[77] This debate points to a pro-found dilemma within modern political culture, which is that the liberal political system might work best when it does not acknowl-edge otherwise important and enriching dimensions of personal and collective identity. There might be significant differences in the de-gree of nonacknowledgment, depending on whether one ignores, de-nies, or suppresses what is not to be recognized, but the tension is unavoidable. Even if ordinary people are adept psychologically at shifting among and coordinating multiple roles, and if communities cultivate civic virtue and common cause among their members, these practices are not easily translated into the language of individual rights and impersonal procedures that also provides crucial protections for all. Worse, explicit affirmations of collective virtue can be exclusionary or domineering acts harmful to others, and unchecked skill in political persuasion can diminish public judgment and endanger liberty. The question then is, to what extent or on what scale can the republican style work within a liberal political culture?

Characteristically, the answer will have to include an appreciation of verbal artistry. The republican stylist today, as always, has to speak in a manner that can constitute the republican conceptions of speaker, audience, polity, and politics, and now has to do so for an audience who begin as liberal individualists. This audience assumes that their political status exists prior to any political process, and certainly independently of the process of public debate, and that government should provide an impersonal brokering of incommensurable interests while protecting personal liberties. The rhetorical task then is to find the means for translating this language of individualism into a language of civic mutuality. As that is accomplished, the full repertoire of the republican style can be put into play for the speaker's advantage and the audience's interest.

Cicero again provides a model, now in the prose style of the letters themselves.[78] I have read them as they mirror his political artistry, which would be expressed more directly in his public performances, but, of course, the relationship between public and private text is more complicated and valuable than that. The distinctive prose style of the letters provides yet another resource for republican composition—and one that is suited to the contemporary moment. That style is summarized by two remarks: First, "I must tell you that what I most badly need at the present time is a confidant—someone with whom I could share all that gives me any anxiety, a wise, affectionate friend to whom I could talk without pretense or evasion or concealment." Here the contrast between public and private life is marked by the shift from one kind of speech to another—from calculated misrepresentation to honest expression. By this testimony alone, the letters would seem to repudiate Cicero's many other words. The second remark points in the other direction, however:

"Evidently it is as you say, things are as uncertain in the political field as in your letter; but it is just this diversity of talk and comment that I find so entertaining. When I read a letter of yours I feel I am in Rome, hearing one thing one minute another the next, as one does when big events are toward." Although Cicero will turn to Atticus for respite from the strain of public life, he also delights in his interlocutor's representation of its excitement and he enjoys the challenge of sorting out the meaning of events from the welter of public discussion. Now they write to continue their participation in the events of the day and hone their judgment, which they do by reproducing the "diversity of talk" characterizing deliberative rhetoric. The connection between these passages can be grasped by recalling the hermeneutical frame of the letter: by translating public discourse into a clearer and flatter diction, the letters create a common ground between public and private realms. This sense of affinity between political forum and friendly exchange creates something that is defined exclusively by neither place. The letters are written to express private concerns, but about public matters, and to reenact public events, but for private appreciation. This sense of the confidential talk that is nonetheless diverse, interested, and accountable is captured by Gadamer's other, complementary metaphor for understanding: the letters succeed as an art form when they create a conversation between reader and writer.[79]

Thus, the republican style can function within the liberal milieu to the extent that it can include within its repertoire the artistic conventions of civic conversation. I wince as I write this, for "conversation" surely has been the most overblown metaphor within liberal apologetics of the past decade. The resonances of the term within a liberal culture are obvious, for a conversation seems the epitome of liberal society at its best: unforced mutuality between individuals, informal, personable speech, no subsequent stipulations. One chooses to enter the social contract of the conversation and can leave at any time, participates equally in creating a common language without burden of prior conventions or wider influence, and constitutes a reciprocally governed relationship while remaining free to enter into any other arrangement. The difference from the republican ideal of eloquence also should be obvious: the liberal conversation produces a relationship, not action, and promises intimacy, not glory. This communicative ideal aptly illustrates Arendt's thesis that the modern epoch has experienced a profound transformation of public culture into sociality.[80]

This idealization of the precepts of liberal society is not the only available model of conversation, however. Although a republican stylist now has to speak in respect to this ideal, there are additional dimensions of republican conversation as well. Recall both Cicero's request that his performance be remembered in the conversations of his audience and Havel's reference to the skill needed to keep a conversation going. The first example gives us an interplay between formal public address and informal public talk, while the second defines conversation as a mode of negotiation and as an art. In both cases, conversation is neither a mode of intimacy nor a model of polity, but a social practice that, if properly focused and skillfully conducted, sustains civic culture. By defining conversation as a verbal art, and one dimension of a wider realm of public discourse, the republican perspective lends additional considerations to its use. Even when it is as close as the relationship between Cicero and Atticus, conversation between friends is already neither wholly private or public: it is an intermediate discourse. The friends speak confidentially, but also play out their public roles and follow the norms of public debate. They dispense with many of the formalities of public discourse, yet they counsel each other to nurture the appropriate virtues for successful public performance. That is, good conversation fulfills the classical ideal of friendship: It is a relationship of reciprocated goodwill helping each become more virtuous, in this case, through a discourse that inculcates the virtues of republican politics. Republican conversation becomes a medium for reconciling public roles and private anxieties while it prepares the interlocutors for the challenges of performing in the give and take of political debate. This conversation not only is an intermediate discourse, but at times it also can be an intermediate step, say, a means for preparing an audience of liberal individuals to become capable of appreciating the oratory necessary for full enactment of republican life. Finally, it is mediated by its own artistry: if there is to be conversation on behalf of the republic, it will have to be capable of eloquence.

The conversation conducted in Cicero's letters with Atticus achieves this standard. The achievement comes first from managing the tensions constituting the letters as a unique form of republican discourse: The letters are a discourse strung between the two poles of private counsel and public discussion. They have the informality and confidentiality of a diary and the rationality and artistry of a debate. Furthermore, the artistry of the letters comes from successful creation within a written medium of a strong sense of orality, the sense Cicero had when he wrote to talk with Atticus and when he delighted to hear the many voices in the other's report. This orality in turn serves as both a tonality of the republican style, the sign and medium of its fascination with public speech, and as the proof that the interlocutors have indeed achieved an authentic language.

Even if communicating successfully in a liberal idiom, however, the republican stylist today faces additional problems. From the standpoint of civic republicanism, the paramount question—as always—is whether enough can be done to ensure the survival of the republic. From this perspective, it seems that republics are fragile indeed—disposed to self-destruct when young, succumb to conquest when prospering, and mutate into imperial states when powerful. In every case, once the damage is done, it is irreparable.[81] History itself is imbued with the rhetorical value of timeliness, and if republican artistry does not prevail in the crisis, it will gain nothing back from the passage of time. In the contemporary moment, republican practices are threatened by both reactionary attempts at fragmentation and appeals to liberal commonality. The first problem arises when communities are defined by norms of cultural homogeneity. In other words, the republican style has to retreat in the face of nativist enclaves and assertions of ethic identity, whether in the Balkans or Orange County. Although it seems tailored for small communities, the republican style is cosmopolitan in practice. The identification of power with eloquence supersedes any form of kinship, and the priority of civic identity encompasses all forms of organic affiliation. One can dream that its infusion into virulently homogenous communities could transform their political practices within and without, but here it seems that realism prevails, or at best a martial republicanism so distorted by the modern arms economy that it becomes a mockery of the republican ideal.

Republicanism also is likely to be undone when confronted by the egalitarian ethos of democratic societies. The basic problem is that the republican style does cultivate elitism. Strictly speaking, this is only a political elitism—recognition and reward based on

137

meritorious speech and action on behalf of the polity—but the republican affinity for established social norms and the tendency of any elite to incorporate other forms of privilege has led historically to unjust domination in the name of civic order. Although now republican practices can be free of familiar forms of prejudice—just as contemporary constitutional interpretation is not bound by Jefferson's use of slavery—the very presence of skilled insiders who have accumulated influence and advantage can be an embarrassment in a liberal democratic culture. Civic leaders can lose their legitimacy—in the minds of all concerned—simply by being labeled elitist. Ironically, this democratic bias is most harmful not to the bastions of wealth and power, but to those groups struggling to make their voices heard. Many a grassroots organization or local community has difficulty finding individuals with the skills and time needed for sound deliberation and effective advocacy; when material resources are not available and high status is suspect, there is little to offer. Although egalitarianism is an important principle of modern life, it also can be an inhibition blocking development of both participation and leadership in democratic politics.

This egalitarian attitude hardly is conducive to the quest for fame through embodiment of the republican ideal. It is reinforced by a related phenomenon, which is the mass media's current understanding of its role as the watchdog of the public interest. Although it is indeed important that the media fulfill this role through active skepticism of all official practice, there has been a shift in its focus on the character of the official. Instead of scrutinizing the performance of the official's public role (and public trust), media coverage now focuses on the character of his or her private life. Reporting on public officials has become the job of tarnishing reputations, usually by pointing to the inconsistency between public authority and personal conduct. Perhaps we should not return to the time before *New York Times v. Sullivan,* when public officials had more privacy rights than private citizens. And there is much to be said for having expanded the conception of the political to include all power relations and having expanded the conception of justice to include the fundamental relationships of private life. From the standpoint of republican practice, however, the current emphasis on personal morality involves a damaging substitution of the values of family life for the civic virtues required for political leadership. From this perspective, there is little value in electing someone whose cardinal virtues are monogamy and piety, who embodies the role of father, and who claims that he is content to be remembered only by his grandchildren. Ultimately, the republican stylist might find that there no longer are any terms within public discourse that can carry a civic consciousness.

One response to this problem is to rethink the process of composing reputation in order to raise the status of civic character. Cicero's letters epitomize the classical republican understanding that reputation was the medium in which one's principles and desires existed at all and the very means of personal integrity.[82] It was the glue that held one together within the constantly shifting alliances of electoral politics. So he would mourn during his exile: "Can I forget what I was, or fail to feel what I am and what I have lost—rank, fame, children, fortune, brother?" (55/3.10). Note how this lament is structured by the classical division between public and private realms, with the linked concepts of rank and fame serving as the sole markers of his public life. His later report continues these emphases, while noting as well their political value: "Of my general position it can so far be said that I have attained what I thought would be most difficult to recover, namely my public prestige, my standing in the Senate, and my influence among the honest men, in larger measure than I had dreamed possible. But my private affairs are in a very poor way" (73/4.1). If we were to put the whole of his calculations into a formula, it would be his advice to Atticus to have regard "to my honour, reputation, and interest" (101/5.8). Here reputation is on rightly equal terms with ethical principle and self-interest, and its artful composition provides the means for joining the other, often contrary, impulses.

Some may object that this step sends us pitching headlong down the path toward "public relations," "media events," and related horrors of the age of television. It could, but we also should consider that republican government may require some version of those practices. The question is not whether one should seek or grant public acclaim, but what kind, and how, and to what end. The republican actor has to labor at the task of creating a reputation for civic virtue, rhetorical skill, timely action, etc., and then continue to act in accord with that reputation. No doubt there are strong inducements to deception here, but sometimes the difference between appearance and reality doesn't matter if it motivates the right action, and the demands of continued attention to one's reputation also can regulate conduct: "How far from easy a thing is virtue, how difficult its simulation for any length of time!" Furthermore, the Ciceronian example pushes us to an additional consideration, which is that the cynical obsession with image-making increasingly characteristic of modern electoral politics is itself caused in part by an inferior sense of reputation. That is, Cicero's sense of reputation has no counterpart in contemporary political culture because he simultaneously is articulating a sense of shame. For all his attention to expediency, when push came to shove Cicero worried as much or more about the ignobility of his position as he did about his security.[83] Reputation might empower or constrain initiative, provide a context for action or create the risk of humiliation, but it remains a key element in republican understanding of political authority.

The good news is that we don't have to start from scratch. Although the republican period is long gone, the republican style is alive and well. Its legitimacy need not rely on the shaky premise that it once was singular and sovereign, and its effectiveness probably lies more in interplay with other styles and more modern precepts than it does in achievement of any neoclassical purity.[84] If it cannot provide a wholly credible political philosophy for a late-modern political order, neither should it be judged solely on the terms of individualistic or proceduralistic alternatives. By understanding republican politics as a discursive practice having its own rhetorical norms and aesthetic coherence, we can nurture it as a means for improving public life while still recognizing that it must incorporate a wide range of ideological positions. The beauty of the republican style is evident all around us, usually in the ordinary practices of self-governance that characterize the thousands of school boards, church boards, unions, party organizations, and other political groups that make up the fabric of a modern democratic society. For awhile, anyway, the republican style even can be found in the presidency: William Jefferson Clinton provides a case study in its weaknesses and its strengths. At its best, it gives us a capacity for incorporating a wide range of ideas and peoples into an exciting process of collective decision making. For it to work well, however, it requires not just verbal competency but appreciation of the art of public address. In the present day, that might be its greatest vulnerability.

140

5

A Boarder in One's Own Home: Franz Kafka's Parables of the Bureaucratic Style

But do we have the doctrine which Kafka's parables interpret and which K.'s postures and the gestures of his animals clarify? It does not exist; all we can say is that here and there we have an allusion to it. . . . In every case it is a question of how life and work are organized in human society. [1]

Kafka's *Trial* has become the great parable of modern life. The story portrays an individual trying, and failing, to comprehend and influence a bureaucratic apparatus that destroys him. This structure is what Max Weber saw as the "iron cage" imprisoning all values and aspirations and what Jürgen Habermas identifies as the "system" relentlessly appropriating the "lifeworld."[2] Yet prophecy can be misleading even when true. The idea that bureaucracy conquers a more authentic mode of living has become a commonplace of modern self-reflection, but it doesn't always square with common experience. Although bureaucracy is synonymous in modern thought with impersonality and alienation—as anyone can understand when suffering the imposition of a rule by an unsympathetic official—it also is the scene where millions of people argue, negotiate, manipulate, cooperate, and otherwise interact with one another each day. Although bureaucratic fatality has to be confronted, the task remains of accounting for our everyday experience of a social order that is a largely unarresting complex of daily habits such as paying bills, writing memos, filling out forms, and coordinating schedules. By identifying the elements of a *bureaucratic style* of political action—that is, the set of communicative conventions uniquely constitutive of office culture—perhaps one can learn what forever eluded Kafka's K.: the knowledge of how to live well within a bureaucratic world.[3]

My approach begins with a substitution: I place *The Castle* in front of *The Trial*. Usually read as a somewhat more theological version of *The Trial*, I read it as a more detailed examination of the ordinary, artful practices of everyday life that are unnoticed because obvious in bureaucratic cultures.[4] By drawing on the work of Kafka's contemporary, Max Weber, Kafka's observations can be organized into a catalog of those conventions of speech and conduct that make bureaucratic practices intelligible and appealing. (If these conventions are presented in somewhat tedious detail, just consider the subject.) This bureaucratic style culminates in the symbolic drama of a system engulfing the lifeworld. This is the drama of assimilation into the social structure of modernity, where all individuals assume a composite identity which denominates them as both persons and functionaries, residents of local cultures and participants in totalizing systems of communication and control. I conclude by addressing the question raised by *The Trial*, and left unanswered by *The Castle*: How, in a wholly organized world, can one become capable of action?

Any pretext for understanding bureaucracy would have to explore this theme of alienation, as Kafka certainly does. It is important to reflect on how he does it. If asked to imitate Kafka's style, few of us would do better than an undergraduate student at UCLA, who wrote:

The older woman shuffled around the kitchen muttering. The man washed his hands, sat down at the table, and picked up the paper. He read until the two women had finished putting the food on the table. The three sat down. They exchanged idle chatter about the day's events. The older woman said something in a foreign language which made the others laugh.[5]

This passage was not written for a literature class, however. The students had been assigned the task "of spending from fifteen minutes to an hour in their homes viewing its activities while assuming that they were boarders in the household."[6] The result was an ethnomethodological account of the routine behavior in the household. Ethnomethodology is the phenomenological inquiry developed by sociologist Harold Garfinkel, in which "persons, relationships, and activities" are "described without respect for their history, for the place of the scene in a set of developing life circumstances, or for the scenes as texture of relevant events for the parties themselves."[7] The purpose of this inquiry is to identify the "seen but unnoticed" background constituting the "organized, artful practices of everyday life."[8] This awareness is achieved by an intentional act of alienation, a bracketing of our insiders' information about our social habitat to make the familiar appear strange. "Descriptions might be thought of as those of a keyhole observer, . . . as if the writer had witnessed the scenes under a mild amnesia for his commonsense knowledge of social structures."[9]

Garfinkel's observer is like K. in *The Castle*, whose only view of the great official Klamm is through a small peephole.[10] As an outsider, K. can see only the surfaces of the bureaucratic order he seeks.[11] He cannot adequately recover the commonsense understandings that constitute the meaningfulness, and rationalize the excesses, of the social practices he is attempting to master. Kafka's reader, however, is put into the contrary position: By making what is already known appear strange, Kafka equips us to better understand our own social behavior. Kafka's fictions portray a reality we already know too well—so well that we no longer reflect on how it is a tissue of unstated understandings and acquired tastes. Although many critics have suggested that Kafka's fiction is highly abstract or spiritual or otherworldly, I read it as resolutely committed to the discovery of the known world.

Kafka himself lived much of his adult life as a boarder, and his major characters can find themselves in the same position.[12] *The Trial* begins with K. waiting to be brought his breakfast by his landlady's cook; Gregor's transformation in *Metamorphosis* also turns him into a boarder among his family; and K.'s condition as a boarder in *The Castle* is emphasized repeatedly. His initial stay at the inn involves difficult negotiations with the landlord and landlady that emphasize his separation from the villagers around him, who appear before him as an indigenous and largely uninterpreted behavioral field surrounding, and perhaps limiting, all of his actions. Despite his protests, his assistants live in the same room with him, even when he and Frieda attempt to set up housekeeping together. His living with Frieda involves a series of increasingly more humiliating arrangements as boarders, from the inn to a busy schoolhouse to her

143

mother's lodgings in a poorer inn. The result of these circumstances is an acute sense of alienation, which includes an awareness of what those not alienated overlook. This awareness features an uncomfortable attentiveness to "how habitual movements were being made"[13] and the realization that much of what seems intelligible to others is objectively absent.

This sensibility is evoked through a specific technique. As Walter Benjamin has suggested, Kafka's ability to make the known world strange comes from his focus on gesture. "Kafka could understand things only in the form of a *gestus*," a term implying the gestures of an orator, while focusing our attention on the manner in which every action is itself acted.[14] Benjamin's insight was in response to the difficult problem of identifying the subject of Kafka's art. Any discourse has to be about something, yet the critic's most challenging task often is determining exactly what that is. In Kafka's case, the problem is compounded since his work strikes many readers as both exceedingly realistic and highly abstract (or even mystical); hence, the tendency to veer into what Benjamin called either "natural" (psychoanalytic) or "supernatural" (theological) explanations of his work.[15] Each approach overstates the case, however. The distinctive effect of Kafka's writing comes from the fact that although he always points toward invisible meanings reverberating beyond the horizon, "the gesture remains the decisive thing, the center of the event."[16] Kafka gives us a world where humanity "is on the stage from the very beginning"[17] and meaning is always something created through the fitting together of stance and scene. "Only then will one recognize with certainty that Kafka's entire work constitutes a code of gestures which surely had no definite symbolic meaning for the author from the outset; rather, the author tried to derive such a meaning from them in ever-changing contexts and experimental groupings."[18]

This focus on gesture combines two elements of representation: a physical movement and simultaneous interpretation in terms of its capacity to evoke or define a scene. Most important, this interpretation itself always has a double character: it is itself unstable while implying that a stable reference is possible. Note how K.'s initial exchange with the warders in *The Trial* foregrounds their staging of his arrest and K.'s concern with the appropriateness of his gestures: "'I shall neither stay here nor let you address me until you have introduced yourself.' 'I meant well enough,' said the stranger, and then of his own accord threw the door open. In the next room, which K. entered more slowly than he had intended, everything looked at first glance almost as it had the evening before."[19] Note how the phrase, "which K. entered more slowly than he had intended," defines K. motivationally: he is not only observing his gestural performance but calculating its effect, while nonetheless already acting not entirely in accord with his own script (as he begins to act more like the guilty man he is defined to be by the situation). Furthermore, the tension of the scene is concentrated in the contrast between the forceful gesture of the warder opening the door and K.'s subjectively intensified report of his own cautious movement through the doorway. This contrast perfectly replicates the double character of the gesture: it implies that the scene is constituted by a stable code even as its meaning is continually shifting.

K.'s perceptions are those of someone entirely habituated to seeing the world from the perspective of a boarder. His consciousness is concentrated on the anxious interpretation of a gestic theater; he contends with a constantly changing play of signs in the hope of discovering a reliable script. He sees what others in the scene overlook, because he lacks their commonsense understanding of what they are doing, and he searches for rules where they rely upon habits. Kafka's fiction is realistic because it portrays essential gestures of modern living, and it is abstract because it portrays them devoid of historical decor and conventional interpretation. Kafka is the premier ethnomethodologist: "He divests the human gesture of its traditional supports and then has a subject for reflection without end."[20]

This reflection can include a profound ambivalence about its subject. If Kafka's *Trial* is a tragedy, then *The Castle* is its return as comedy.[21] Despite the many similarities between the two stories, their differences highlight this important shift in orientation. In *The Trial*, K. is someone convinced of his innocence and his integrity; late in the story, in what seems to be his last chance at reversing his impending conviction by the court, he meets a court functionary, the priest, who first berates him regarding his incompetence and then engages him in a Talmudic discussion on the nature of the Law; finally, he is executed "like a dog," his last moment an experience of extreme shame. In *The Castle*, K. is a con artist susceptible to others' seductions;[22] late in the story, at what seems the long-awaited opportunity for him to appeal for admission to the Castle, he witnesses the bureaucrats' actual manner of handling the files, which is a madcap, slapstick routine, full of doors slamming, papers flying, and grown men bellowing as they dodge in and out of identical rooms lining a corridor; finally, K's fate is left undecided as his deception is revealed, seemingly without penalty, and he faces a bewildering array of choices about where, and how, and with whom he might live.[23]

Thus, in *The Castle* we confront the structures of modern life in a context not of fatality, but of folly. As K. remarks, with insufficient irony, " 'It only amuses me, . . . because it gives me an insight into the ludicrous bungling that in certain circumstances may decide the life of a human being' " (p. 82). This is what Kenneth Burke calls a "downward transcendence": we find the means of escape from our condition not by looking to some higher principle of order, but by identifying with the socially embarrassing practices that sustain it. *The Castle* reveals what was present but subordinate in *The Trial:* a world not of Law, but lawyers; not the power to kill, but the practice of keeping people waiting.

One consequence of this comic perspective is that the bureaucratic system infiltrating the village cannot be set neatly into a drama of good and evil. It rules the village, but many villagers seem uninterested in it and unharmed by it. If at first it seems enervating or destructive, as when K. encounters the woman in white and hears the story of Amelia's family, it later appears invigorating or benign, as when the assistant ages upon losing his appointment and we learn how Amelia's family sealed their own fate. The Castle is not heaven, but neither is the village; and if Klamm is frightening, it is not because K. is honorable. In short, even if the Castle represents a universal condition of modern life, it does not represent a simple moral choice.

The Castle presents modern bureaucracy not as a totalitarian police state, but as a comedy of manners. Consequently, the rhetorical force of *The Castle* comes in great part from constant attribution of great authority to obviously flawed and probably useless officials. No matter how much the principles of bureaucratic order are betrayed by its practice, the villagers' reverence is never interrupted.[24] K. does the same. Although Frieda is able to silence Klamm immediately, K. persists in imagining that the official's power encompasses everything in the village. And he assumes the Castle is even more impressive: " 'Only think, up there you have all the inextricable complications of a great authority—I imagined that I had an approximate conception of its nature before I came here, but how childish my ideas were!' " (p. 241). K.'s own intricate analyses and arguments also make clear the source of this veneration: his need to live in a rational world. What was his tragic flaw in *The Trial* here is his comic failing: He wants to master the organization by drawing entirely on his powers of reason. Consequently, he has to assume that it is powerful because rational. He epitomizes Weber's pronouncement that, "The purely bureaucratic type of administrative organization . . . is, from a purely technical point of view, capable of attaining the highest degree of efficiency and is in this sense formally the most rational known means of exercising authority over human beings."[25] K. is a Machiavel, but without any sense of external constraint or chance; a figure of the Enlightenment, but without any memory of irrationality. K. appeals to modern readers not only because he is an individual struggling against a social apparatus, but also because of his confidence in rationality, which allows him to rationalize his submission to his desires, not least his desire for power.

This condition has to include its own denial. K. presents himself, particularly upon his entry into the village, as someone who is highly skeptical of institutional authority and obviously capable of making up his own mind. Yet his attribution of authority is most pronounced when he is pretending to be the free thinker: "If they expected to cow him by their lofty superiority in recognizing him as Land-Surveyor, they were mistaken; it made his skin prickle a little, that was all" (p. 8). This combination of attributing godlike power to institutional authorities, while professing one's ability to see authority for what it really is, becomes a key link between Kafka's work and his readers. The other characters in the story make unwarranted attributions of great authority to ordinary people and events, and K. does so while thinking he is too smart for that. The reader at once believes that great authority exists and that he or she is capable of escaping its domination by acquiring knowledge of the sort K. is always seeking, knowledge of how it works, knowledge a book such as *The Castle* might provide. Under the illusion of critique, the reader reinscribes the terms of bureaucratic legitimacy. If the officials appear laughable because they are inefficient and prevaricating, it is only because one has assumed the legitimacy of the corresponding norms of efficiency and precision. We laugh at them, but the joke finally is on us.

Kafka's text obviously does more than merely document bureaucratic practices, but its many designs and effects all serve the difficult task of facing what is actually there. As far as the reader of *The Castle* can tell, a bureaucracy controls a village without providing any service or exerting control over essential resources or using force. One wonders, how does the Castle command the villagers' obedience and reverence? What are the characteristic manners, modes of manipulation, or persuasive appeals embedded within bureaucratic organization? I believe the social order portrayed in *The Castle* corresponds to Weber's account of the structure of bureaucratic organization in uncanny scope and detail, and Kafka's precise use of disorientation isolates the ordinary, artful practices activating bureaucratic consciousness.[26] This correspondence ranges from the story's deep structure of system dominating lifeworld, to the standard institutional norms that Kafka exploits for comic effect, to minor details of institutional decor.[27] I shall emphasize how *The Castle* isolates the persuasive designs Weber identified as the basic forms of rationally regulated association. These conventions for projecting bureaucratic authority include jurisdictional autonomy, a hierarchy of offices, the ethos of the official, and the priority of writing. Kafka's comic exaggeration of each of these conventions reveals how they operate as a familiar style of communication regulating modern life.

It is not surprising that bureaucracies are thought to be impersonal, for they begin with the assertion of jurisdictional autonomy— that is, the insistence that some office is the necessary and sufficient authority for any class of organizational decisions.[28] The office is organized to perform a set of routine activities according to standard procedures, and those activities are defined as official duties for the organization. The procedures are articulated as rules and applied uniformly to determine both the employment of the officials and their authority over others, while the same pattern of definition also generates larger organizational units such as the section or division and authorizes the organization in respect to other institutions. In brief, bureaucracy makes the office the primary unit of authority, and a bureaucracy is a polity of offices. Relationships are first and foremost among offices, with officials acting as their emissaries and persons having only incidental status. For example, when Olga tells of her plan to infiltrate the Castle, she distinguishes between "'an actual official employee'" and "'a private and semiofficial one, he has nei-

ther rights nor duties—and the worst is not to have any duties'"
(p. 287). This social order is perfectly summarized in an exchange
between K. and the official Momus: "'You only think of yourselves.
I would never and will never answer merely because of someone's
office, neither then nor now.' Momus replied: 'Of whom, then,
should we think? Who else is there here?'" (p. 314).

   K. likes to think of himself as a sovereign individual who should
be expected to negotiate only with a peer, and it will be easy for many
readers to see this exchange as a celebration of individualism.[29] As K.
remarks, "'I fancy that two things must be distinguished here: first,
what is transacted in the offices and can be construed again officially
this way or that, and, secondly, my own actual person, me myself,
situated outside of the offices and threatened by their encroach-
ments, which are so meaningless that I can't even yet believe in the
seriousness of the danger'" (p. 85). Ordinary bureaucratic practices
reflect this tension between jurisdictional norms and personal identity. Relationships between officials, or between officials and nonof-
ficials, are determined to be legitimate by the regulations defining
the offices and their clientele. Likewise, any nonjurisdictional relationships (such as friendship among officials) are suspect; they imply
a deviation from rational procedure and the potential subversion of
authority. Although one can quickly think of many examples of how
people in organizations work otherwise, it is just as easy to identify
the many jokes, gossip, games, and fantasies that accompany these
other arrangements and mark them as deviant. Personal arrangements might be necessary, enjoyable, even more rational than working according to official protocols,[30] but they cannot be normative.
Personalizing of the workplace occurs, but always in dialectical
tension with the primacy of office.

   This tension in turn accounts for and informs an additional characteristic of jurisdictional definition: the dependency on formally
designated procedures. When politics is jurisdictional, rules become
the signs of power. Although perhaps any culture can be described as
operating according to a set of rules, bureaucratic culture is one in
which rules are explicitly cited as the legitimate means of social exchange. K.'s exchanges with Momus underscore the role that rules
play in the organization. Momus is Klamm's secretary for the village—actually, there are additional jurisdictional nuances to his appointment—and he has come to interview K. Again, K. is in the

position of a boarder: He has returned to the inn where he had peered at Klamm and made love with Frieda. When he tries to do things his own way by refusing the interview, we discover that he has committed a serious social error. The rest of the chapter consists of the landlady and Momus explaining to K. why his conduct was a breach of their social order; their explanation identifies the usually unstated commonsense understanding of that order. The gist of their explanation is that the interview can only be understood according to its procedures rather than for any other purpose. K. states that he is willing to submit immediately if it will lead him to Klamm, but he is told, "'that doesn't follow at all. It's simply a matter of keeping an adequate record of this afternoon's happenings for Klamm's village register. The record is already complete, there are only two or three omissions that you must fill in for the sake of order; there's no other object in view and no other object can be achieved'" (p. 148). In fact, as the landlady elaborates, Klamm will never read the protocol, and, although Momus is merely a functionary, he should be treated as the very epitome of Klamm's power.

Just as this scene captures the absurdity of bureaucratic authority, it also distills its essence. Whereas K. wants to find another, prior, more primitive basis for authority, he is confronted with the fact that the authority lies in the organization itself—that is, in its formal, impersonal, procedures. As the landlady says of Momus: "'I'm speaking of him not as an independent person, but as he is when he has Klamm's assent, as at present; then he's an instrument in the hand of Klamm, and woe to anybody who doesn't obey him'" (p. 151). The landlady's account is not quite so absurd if one sees how it has changed Klamm into the spirit of organization itself; Klamm represents the organization's ability to be everywhere at once, knowing more than any of its parts. Bureaucratic authority is generated by the arrangement of offices and mastery of protocol, not by personal possession of independent means of reward or punishment. Thus, when acting according to the bureaucratic style, one thinks of terms of appointments, procedural stipulations and conundrums, the nuances of overlapping jurisdictions and jurisdictional lacunae, and so forth and so on. These negotiations in turn lead to the next form of bureaucratic appeal: the image of hierarchy.

K. needs to make sense of his relationship with the Castle, and it is not enough to imagine the Castle as a collection of offices de-

150

fined by their rules. The divisions of the social order into areas of jurisdiction, and of individual identity into personal and official capacities, are organized further by a pyramidal structure of command and accountability.[31] Although the arrangement of the official work areas in the village seems completely haphazard, K. and everyone around him continually look for lines of superordination that would establish the officials' authority and define their responsibilities. It becomes clear, moreover, that this seemingly static principle of social order generates a complicated set of motives. The bureaucratic hierarchy that Weber outlines as a structure of assurances—a means of supervision establishing the accountability of any official—becomes both a source of cosmic power and a condition of hopelessness.[32]

As his encounter with Momus comes to a close, K. drifts into a moment of reverie, recalling how the landlady had once compared Klamm to an eagle:

He thought of Klamm's remoteness, of his impregnable dwelling, of his silence, broken perhaps only by cries such as K. had never yet heard, of his downward-pressing gaze, which could never be proved or disproved, of his wheelings, which could never be disturbed by anything that K. did down below, which far above he followed at the behest of incomprehensible laws and which only for instants were visible. (p. 151)

K. has given himself over to a fantasy of power. It is the fantasy of the *Übermensch*, the sole remaining figure of personal authority, high atop a hierarchy of offices and guided only by the ultimate rules, those cosmic laws that ordinary mortals cannot see. His fantasy of Klamm exemplifies what Kenneth Burke calls "the entelechial tendency" shaping any image of hierarchy: "the treatment of the 'top' or 'culminating' stage as the 'image' that best represents the entire 'idea.'"[33] As K.'s fantasy illustrates, it also offers the vision of being connected with sources of power far distant from the middling decor and mundane routines of office life. The cheap materials of cinderblock walls, Styrofoam cups, and brown interoffice envelopes become signs of a vast administrative network connected to an ultimate source of power.

This peculiar motivation is balanced, but hardly eliminated, by its inevitable contrast with the mundane circumstances in which it works. "All these things Klamm and the eagle had in common. But

151

assuredly these had nothing to do with the protocol, over which just now Momus was crumbling a roll dusted with salt, which he was eating with beer to help it out, in the process all the papers becoming covered with salt and caraway seeds" (p. 151). Here is a corresponding downward transcendence, as the deadly protocol is treated like a disposable table napkin and the commanding official shown to be an ordinary slob. It is precisely this contrast, however, that is essential to the persistence of hierarchical attributions. By highlighting the individual's inferior stature, the text reinscribes the image of an impersonal structure of ascending positions. As Burke discerns, "the very dinginess of the officialdom as *persons* absurdly suggests the omnipresence of the mystery that infuses their *office.*"[34] The most shabby and compromised figures are thought to be marked by signs of a higher-order system of awesome power and rational operation.

Ordinary bureaucratic life oscillates between these two motives, between total devotion to the institutional structure and the daily reductions of institutional protocols to ordinary informalities. No wonder there is a very fine line between hardheaded accounts of organizational control and full-blown paranoid fantasies of organizational conspiracy. The bureaucratic organization generates power through a system, but we cannot see systems; so it is that K. can admire the "autonomy of the service, which one divined to be peculiarly effective precisely where it was not visibly present" (p. 74). The arc up to Klamm's celestial vantage and back down to the dim interior of the inn illustrates how the image of hierarchy represents a transcendent system for concentrating, distributing, and regulating authority which cannot be invalidated by actual practice.

This sense of permanence need not translate into a sense of assurance, however. Hierarchy also represents a process of endless deferral. Even those who are able to apply for official appointment—a position seemingly well beyond K.'s reach—face so many steps that they end up waiting in vain until they die (pp. 287–88). In order to inquire about the position of the official first handling his case, Schwarzer, K. asks the landlord if the picture of an authority on the wall is of the Castellan who Schwarzer claimed as his father. " 'No, no,' said the landlord, drawing K. a little toward him and whispering in his ear: 'Schwarzer exaggerated yesterday; his father is only an under-castellan, and one of the lowest, too' " (p. 10). The first official has been set within an upward enfilade of officials, but not with the

152

result of diminishing his authority: "'The villain!' said K. with a laugh. But the landlord instead of laughing said: 'Even his father is powerful.' 'Get along with you,' said K., 'you think everyone powerful. Me too, perhaps?' 'No,' he replied, timidly yet seriously, 'I don't think you powerful'" (p. 10). The distinction between person and office becomes magnified by the latter's definition within an ascending hierarchy. No longer does an assertive individual face a prevaricating official; instead, a solitary figure looks upwards toward a towering succession of offices. K.'s frustration often arises from this predicament: although connection with the lowest part of the system would provide at least potential access to the supreme authority he seeks, he is continually informed that the system actually extends far, far upward from any position he might obtain. A great vault over these obstacles would not mean much either, for the possibility of endless deferral is generated by the formal design of the hierarchy itself, which is to increase attentiveness by multiplying its structure, as branches of a fractal design can reproduce themselves indefinitely by splitting into ever smaller extensions of a basic pattern.

Thus, the bureaucratic hierarchy that is rationalized as a structure of accountability becomes a condition of hopelessness. K. learns that there are hierarchies within hierarchies: his case is "'a very unimportant case—one might almost say the least important among the unimportant'" (p. 90); and he discovers, again as evidence of his own unimportance, that there even is a hierarchy of inns. The basic problem facing K. is illustrated whenever he attempts to walk toward the Castle: he becomes bogged down in snow that seems to increase exponentially as he moves through it, or he finds that his walking toward the Castle leads him ever farther away from it.[35] The question is, how can one make any progress through the endless extensions of organizational structure? This is the deeper assurance that anyone within the system has to have. One answer comes from the next element of the bureaucratic style: the persona of the official.

Much as we like to think of an organization as having a human face, we expect the people working in it to be fully dedicated to fulfilling their organizational functions. All Kafka has to do to suggest the illegitimacy of the system is portray its officials as incompetent, lazy, distracted by their desires, or otherwise living for themselves rather than for the organization. The conclusion typically drawn is not that the worker is a genuine and interesting person, for the modern reader is thoroughly habituated to the ethos of the speaker created in the act of bureaucratic communication. Despite the displacement of person by office, the character of the official remains important, and bureaucratic character is developed not only through the suppression of obvious signs of personality, but also by signifying the attributes Weber identified as specialized training, maximized labor, and procedural rectitude.[36] By restructuring Weber's criteria as elements of ethos, I have drawn on classical rhetorical theory to define them as they would be encountered (together) in ordinary bureaucratic communication. Stated otherwise, the elements that Weber identified as rules also can be identified as means of persuasion—that is, prominent, recurrent, formal patterns of discourse having proven capability to influence decisions among competent interlocutors—and these patterns can combine into additional figures, such as the speaker's persona. When the characteristics cohere as a persona, they provide a basis for coordinating the other elements of the bureaucratic style. When effective, they function in place of the act of commanding others and do so, perhaps, with less individual accountability. They also can be used to justify the official's lack of personality and excuse willful abuse of bureaucratic authority.

Kafka's portrayals of the officials of the Castle isolate the elements of bureaucratic character by exaggerating both their observance and their violations. The villagers praise the officials' highly specialized competencies, unstinting dedication to their work, and zealous attention to procedural details while also reporting actual conduct that contrasts wildly with these norms. Any sense of discrepancy is either unnoticed or rationalized away by appeal to the same norms. For example, after Olga has claimed that the officials couldn't stop for her father because they are busy studying the documents crammed into their carriages, K. corrects her, stating that he looked inside a carriage and found it carried nothing other than the passenger. "'That's possible,' said Olga, 'but then it's even worse, for that means that the official's business is so important that the papers are too precious or too numerous to be taken with him, and those officials go at a gallop'" (p. 280).

This persona, which is formed by education, expertise, and work, is taken to the extreme in the figure of Sordini, an official described by the Mayor as someone "'famed for his conscientiousness . . . it is incomprehensible to me, though I am one of the initiated, why a man of his capacities is left in an almost subordinate position' " (p. 81).[37] On discovering an inconsistency in the organizational record involving the Mayor, Sordini swings into action. Refusing to rely on the Mayor's personal assurances, who nonetheless considers it "'right and proper, an official must behave like that,' " he begins a voluminous correspondence. The Mayor hasn't a chance, for "'whenever Sordini has in his hands even the slightest hold against anyone, he has as good as won, for then his vigilance, energy, and alertness are actually increased' " (p. 85). If there is any hope, it would lie only in that Sordini has so much to do:

"I have never managed yet to come within sight of him. He can't get down here, he's so overwhelmed with work; from the descriptions I've heard of his room, every wall is covered with pillars of documents tied together, piled on top of one another; those are only the documents that Sordini is working on at the time, and as bundles of papers are continually being taken away and brought in, and all in great haste, those columns are always falling on the floor, and it's just those perpetual crashes, following fast on one another, that have come to distinguish Sordini's workroom. Yes, Sordini is a worker, and he gives the same scrupulous care to the smallest case as to the greatest." (pp. 85–86)

This last scene perfectly captures the internal economy of the bureaucratic character. The image of Sordini's workroom is a picture of the displacement of personality by organizational function. The organization commands his full working capacity. He is not seen, not even heard, only imagined within a room which we do not enter, and from which we hear only the sounds of bundled files thudding to the floor. Personal bias, favor, or vengefulness all are controlled by the fact that the official's authority stems not only from his position in the hierarchy, but also from his training, knowledge of the rules, and complete dedication of his labor to the organization.[38] The implication is that if officials are distant, dangerously insulated from the world they regulate, and exempt from ordinary means of public accountability, they nonetheless are so completely tied to the organization, and particularly to its use of rational procedures, that their behavior is predictable and their power moderated. In other words, within bureaucratic culture, it is assumed that bureaucratic authority is justified by the prior disciplining of the official. If we imagine a last gestural moment of Sordini sitting engrossed in his work, oblivious to the towers of documents crashing around him, we see someone who has been wholly formed by his training. He is someone already regulated by the expertise he is capable of using to rule others. If the scene itself is crazy, it is not because he is unpredictable. This internal economy of means, whereby the same organizational procedures control both ruled and rulers, produces an additional sense of legitimacy: The attribution of power made to the organization by its clients seems to be matched by the dedication of its workers.

Or so it seems to the villagers. One could ask whether the Castle needed any other means for controlling the village, as so much is achieved and excused by reference to the character of its officials. Olga can excuse their inattention to her father's supplication, because "'officials are highly educated, but one-sided; in his own department an official can grasp whole trains of thought from a single word, but let him have something from another department explained to him by the hour, he may nod politely, but he won't understand a word of it'" (p. 278). The official Bürgel can justify inattention to clients, because "'we secretaries are, it is true, by no means jealous of each other with regard to work, as everyone carries far too great a burden of work, a burden that is piled on him truly without stint, but in dealing with the applicants we simply must not tolerate any interference with our sphere of competence'" (p. 344). The irony in these testimonials, which celebrate the capabilities of officials who are producing nothing, should not be misleading. These descriptions illustrate how closely and consistently the signs of training, labor, and procedure defining bureaucratic ethos fit together and also how important they are to accounting for official conduct.

This is not the only means by which bureaucratic authority is established, however. Sordini's workshop also exemplifies the last, and most significant, element of the bureaucratic style. As his diligence becomes defined by the documents piling up around him, Sordini becomes the bureaucratic organization's archetypal figure: the scribe, someone who produces and manages the written text. As Weber observed,

Administrative acts, decisions, and rules are formulated and recorded in writing, even in cases where oral discussion is the rule or is even mandatory. This applies at least to preliminary discussions and proposals, to final decisions, and to all sorts of orders and rules. The combination of written documents and a continuous operation by officials constitutes the "office" (*Bureau*) which is the central focus of all types of modern organized action. . . . The management of the modern office is based upon written documents (the "files"), which are preserved in their original or draft form, and upon a staff of subaltern officials and scribes of all sorts.[39]

Whatever the absurdity of the scene, the piles of documents and continual activity of the assistants scurrying in and out of Sordini's workroom perfectly illustrate Weber's definition of the office. In the same way, Kafka's other portrayals of the Castle officials and their documents reveal how bureaucratic organizations are cultures organized around the social practice of writing. Knowledge is indeed power in bureaucratic life, but the key to knowledge is the production, control, and interpretation of written documents. Consequently, bureaucratic politics become negotiations for advantage that are conducted through a set of communicative conventions that characterize the practice of writing. The bureaucratic style optimizes a politics of documentation.

Although K. does not make it to the Castle, he does come to learn something about how it works. Sordini, a "correspondent" in search of a missing document, begins a "voluminous correspondence" to rectify the organizational record, adding to the piles of official paper that dominate his office. His story is told by the Mayor, whose own office is awash in documents: "The papers now covered half the floor. 'A great deal of work is got through here,' said the Mayor nodding his head, 'and that's only a small fraction of it. I've put away the most important pile in the shed, but the great mass of it has simply gone astray. Who could keep it all together? But there are piles and piles more in the shed'" (p. 78). Although the Mayor is not a member of the Castle bureaucracy, his intermediate position between Castle and village is well documented. The same holds for the teacher, who handles any writing the Mayor needs done, and whose own place also has "a great pile of papers" (p. 91). In these and other cases, K. always sees officials defined in terms of their documents, agents defined by the agency of reading and writing texts.

As one moves into and up the Castle hierarchy, this correspondence of bureaucratic authority and documentation becomes more extensive and more subtle in its operation. Note how Momus is introduced:

Pepi . . . hurried to and fro, fetching beer and then pen and ink, for the gentleman had already spread out papers in from of him, was comparing dates which he looked up now in this paper, then again in a paper at the other end of the table, and was preparing to write. . . . "The Land-Surveyor at last," said the gentleman at K.'s entrance, looking up briefly, then burying himself again in his papers. (pp. 140–41)[40]

Momus demonstrates the well-known administrative tactic of keeping the person in one's presence waiting on the completion of a written task; he also embodies a pattern of definition shaping attributions of authority throughout the organization. K. begins to catch on: "'There's a great deal of writing there,' said K. glancing at the papers from where he was standing" (p. 143), and it seems he notices how awed the others are when Momus announces that he is Klamm's village secretary. (To underscore the point, Momus, "as if he had said more than his judgment sanctioned, and as if he were resolved to escape at least from any aftereffects of the solemn import implicit in his own words, buried himself in his papers and began to write, so that nothing was heard in the room but the scratching of his pen" (p. 144).) Yet K. refuses the interview, persisting in his conviction that he should be able to converse with Klamm. The attempts to dissuade him make the situation perfectly clear: Speaking to Klamm is impossible; the organization requires that his speech be transcribed into a written document (the "protocol"); this transcription is done solely for the purpose of completing the organizational record; his only hope for recognition within the organization lies with the document. Momus's authority is defined by his gestures, which are the gestures of a scribe, and K.'s relationship with the organization is to be secured by a written document or not at all.

This equation of written communication with organizational access and control operates within the Castle as well. There we see the officials lined up behind a long "standing-desk," upon which "there are great books lying open, side by side, and officials stand by most of them reading. They don't always stick to the same book, yet it isn't the books that they change, but their places" (p. 233). The activity of even the higher officials is organized around the written texts: The books are the focal point of organizational action, the referents of official propositions, the signifieds of organizational speech. Even the layout of the room emphasizes the equation between written text and official power: the area behind the standing-desk is constricted, squeezing even the officials, whereas the area in front of it, for those

158

awaiting official action, is spacious, illustrating their distance from the texts. To complete the picture, scribes sit at tables close in front of the standing-desk, ready to write the officials' memoranda, which will serve as the sole connection between the organization and its clients. Nor is this lost on those waiting and watching:

"Nevertheless Barnabas fancied, so he has told me, that he could clearly see how great were the power and knowledge even of those very questionable officials into whose room he is allowed. How fast they dictated, with half-shut eyes and brief gestures, quelling the surly servants merely by raising a finger, and making them smile with happiness even when they were checked; or perhaps finding an important passage in one of the books and becoming quite absorbed in it, while the others would crowd round as near as the cramped space would allow them, and crane their necks to see it." (p. 294)

The gestures here focus all attention on the officials' proximity to and use of their documents, and the attribution of authority (by characters and reader alike) follows from their identification of documentation with bureaucratic control. Even the great Klamm is so defined: in the Castle he is seen checking something in a book, or sitting and reading, or polishing his eyeglasses.
These gestures identify both the nature and tone of bureaucratic authority: the organization is constituted as a written culture, and power flows through the culture not by oral commands, but by writing and reading. The priority of the written text is further evident in its close relationship with other principles of bureaucratic organization. By highlighting the official's fixation on their documents, Kafka also illustrates both how the documents are valued because they are inscribed with such bureaucratic principles as impersonality and hierarchy and also how these foundational principles of bureaucratic polity are the result of the practice of writing.
Despite his desire to speak with Klamm face to face, K. can't make too much of his letter from Klamm. He even goes so far as putting it on the wall of his room (p. 33). The letter itself is a compendium of bureaucratic conventions.

"My dear Sir, As you know, you have been engaged for the Count's service. Your immediate superior is the Mayor of the village, who will give you all particulars about your work and the terms of your employment, and to whom you are responsible. I myself, however, will try not to lose sight of you. Barnabas, the bearer of this letter, will report to you from time to time to learn your wishes and communicate them to me. You will find me always ready to oblige you, in so far as that is possible. I desire my workers to be contented." (p. 30)

As K. recognizes, this letter presents a structure of political relations. K. is changed from a person to someone defined within a hierarchy, and the hierarchy, more than the author of the letter, becomes the dominant authority within the letter. Moreover, this hierarchy is actively at work against K.: It expands between him and Klamm, presenting first the Mayor, then a messenger, and implicitly a host of other intermediaries and obstacles (who probably will cause Klamm to lose sight of him). As the letter places K. in a hierarchy, it also alters his status: there is a long fall from the opening "Dear Sir" to becoming one of Klamm's workers. The letter transforms him from someone worthy of being addressed by Klamm to a minor functionary. These shifts from person to office and from autonomy to hierarchy are evident in Klamm's own signature: "The signature was illegible, but stamped beside it was 'Chief of Department X'" (p. 30). In addition, these elements of bureaucratic authority are made more powerful, and more worrisome, by being identified as elements of accountability. The structure is a structure of oversight, a means for aligning authority and responsibility while assessing productivity, and it is a structure of anxieties, for the most equivocal statements occur precisely as accountability is being defined. Klamm allows that good work could go unnoticed and that K. could be given duties but not the means to accomplish them. Finally, Klamm's simple phrase, "from time to time," is an ominous portent of the endless deferral that K. will begin to experience as the story develops. By the close of this short letter, the endemic problems of bureaucratic work become the dominant context for K.'s quest.

The letter acknowledges no single detail of K.'s circumstances and specifies only the organizational structure, not the actual work to be done. It inscribes a social form but not its content; its characteristic features include the impersonality, abstraction, and temporal openness of writing itself. In short, it reveals the equation of bureaucratic order with the conventions of the printed word. Likewise, all of the written documents in Kafka's story illustrate the role writing plays in organizational politics. The other letters, protocols, documents, and books that rationalize life in the village are objects of great interest and veneration, signs of authority and the means for regulating social life, and they exemplify the generative principles of bureaucratic polity itself. Control of the texts in every way is the fulcrum of organizational politics, and the designs of the texts provide the intelligibility of organizational behavior.

Since bureaucratic authority depends on the practice of writing, one imperative of bureaucratic control is to keep writing the dominant mode of communication within its domain. Thus, the bureaucratic style includes yet another hierarchy: a hierarchy of modes of communication, which subordinates speech to writing, with a language of gestures in the intermediate position. The basic opposition between the two major modes (of speech and writing) is essentialized in the relationship between K. and Klamm. K. never writes, and the focal point of his quest is an audience with Klamm so that the two can speak to each other. Klamm is identified with the artifacts of reading and writing, and he responds to K. by sending him letters which emphasize K.'s subordination. Although Klamm initially is heard, and his power signified by a "deep, authoritative voice," that voice is also "impersonal." Speech remains an agency of power, but particularly so if it already is marked with the features of writing. Eventually Klamm acquires the characteristics of writing itself: he becomes ever more distant, extended across the organization without specific time or locale, a text or principle of authority itself not subject to influence.

The subordination of speech to writing extends well beyond their relationship, moreover. The Mayor tells K. that he has overvalued his telephone conversation with the Castle and says that the phone could be compared to a music box. There is, in fact, no fixed connection anywhere in the phone system with the Castle, and the lines are constantly humming with the sounds of thousands of calls being made while most of the phones are purposefully left off the hook by the clerks (pp. 93–94). In the Castle, the real work consists of the handling of documents, and when that work is described, the written texts are produced within a context of whispers and silence. Barnabas admits that he wouldn't dare to speak there (p. 292) and reports how the dictating by the officials always is done in a particular manner:

"There's no express command given by the official, nor is the dictation given in a loud voice, one could hardly tell that it was being given at all, the official just seems to go on reading as before, only whispering as he reads, and the clerk hears the whisper. Often it's so low that the clerk can't hear it at all in his seat, and then he has to jump up, catch what's being dictated, sit down again quickly and make a note of it, then jump up once more, and so on. What a strange business! It's almost incomprehensible." (p. 233)

The writing of the texts is intimately tied to the reading of prior texts, with speech only a momentary means of transmission from one document to another. This speech is barely audible, entirely evanescent, and merely a process of transmission. Meaning lies in the printed words, which speech can only carry for the moment. Speech is restrained, repressed, kept closely under the control of those reading and writing, perhaps because it has the capacity to disseminate the words to the audience of clients waiting before them, loosening bureaucratic control over the texts and their interpretation.

The clerks' jumping up and down at the behest of dictation provides gestural representation of the political relations inscribed in the bureaucratic practice. Organizational rule is not a dictatorship, but rule by dictation, and the organizational worker is commanded by a process of composition that begins and ends with printed documents and only incidentally involves association with those waiting outside. The clerks' gestures also activate this pattern of authority; just as speech is subordinated to writing, so does the bureaucratic polity elevate gestures to a specific communicative function within the organization. Barnabas knows as much, for he is always attempting to discern the gestural characteristics of the Castle officials—"a particular way of nodding the head, for instance, or even an unbuttoned waistcoat" (p. 232). In each of the accounts of the work at the standing-desk, the officials are presented according to a formula of description that identifies them with reading and writing, reduces any oral speech, and highlights their gestural enactment of the preferred practices: "How fast they dictated, with half-shut eyes and brief gestures, quelling the surly servants merely by raising a finger, and making them smile with happiness even when they were checked." The importance of these gestures is summarized in an account of K.'s encounter with an official in the courtyard of an inn: "'Come with me,' said the gentleman, not really as a command, for the command lay not in the words, but in a slight, studiedly indifferent gesture of the hand which accompanied them" (p. 137). Speech lacks the power to command, but gesture has become a sign of authority. The official's control of his body mimes his transformation from person into official, while his use of gesture acts to keep speech subordinate when documentation is not available, and it provides the ready performance of relations of superordination which are not fully articulated until one is actually engaged in the practice of reading a document. Thus, those interested in gaining access to the Castle school themselves in learning this sign language, the intermediate medium for discerning official intention. As the gestures are most evident during the actual process of composition—that is, the process of decision making—they offer a momentary aperture into organizational power, a clue that one might use to make a suggestion, however small, that could redirect the flow of institutional authority to one's advantage.

Or so it appears to the outsiders. Inside of the organization, there is another side to this negotiation between the different modes of communication. In this case, the struggle for control of documents is decisive, and acts of speech or gesture are but provisional means and rude signs in the constant scramble to triumph over one's adversaries. Kafka captures this internal competition with his hilarious burlesque of the distribution of the files. As K. wanders through an inn at the start of the workday, he looks down a corridor lined with doors and sees "a little cart pushed by a servant, containing files. A second servant walked beside it, with a catalogue in his hand, obviously comparing the numbers on the doors with those on the files. The little cart stopped outside most of the doors, usually then, too, the door would open and the appropriate files would be handed into the room, sometimes, however, only a small sheet of paper" (p. 356). Sometimes the officials within don't answer, so that the files are piled up outside of their doors; other times, the officials complain that they have not received the correct files, some of which turn out to have already been distributed to other officials. "The further it progressed, the less smoothly it went; either the catalogue was not quite correct or the files were not always clearly identifiable for the servants, or the gentlemen were raising objections for other reasons; at any rate it would happen that some of the distributions, had to be withdrawn" (pp. 357–58). Officials do not give up their documents easily, however, so the servants have to run back and forth, begging here and reassuring there, even tricking their superiors by baiting

163

them with other files, and soon the corridor is awash with papers scattered about as the cart rolls back and forth across them. The officials themselves become similarly uncomposed; all pretense of official decorum disappears as they fight for the files:

> The impatient official was often made still more impatient by the attempts to appease him, he could no longer endure listening to the servant's empty words, he did not want consolation, he wanted files; such a gentleman once poured the contents of a whole washbasin through the gap at the top onto the servant. (p. 358)

The epitome of bureaucratic activity—the distribution of written, rationally ordered documents—is revealed to be a chaotic brawl, and the impersonal, dispassionate persona of the official is shown to cloak the raw motives of political conquest. Of course, this parody of the inner workings of the organization only works because we assume that a methodical, silent distribution would be the sign of an organization in good working order.

This competition for the files further highlights the relation between speech and writing in the organization. Although organizational life is replete with spoken negotiations, they are conducted with continual deference to the practices of documentation. The written text is the absent signifier dominating any conversation, and speech waxes and wanes in proportion to the presence of writing. As the officials are awakening, the corridor fills with sounds like children at a picnic, or a hen-roost at daybreak, all signs of the life-world. As the files appear, the officials become quiet. The initial negotiations with the servants are conducted in whispers and are accompanied by gestures that communicate clearly the priority of the written:

> If the gentleman concerned deigned to enter into negotiations at all, there were matter-of-fact discussions during which the servant referred to his catalogue, the gentleman to his notes and to precisely those files that he was supposed to return, which for the time being, however, he clutched tightly in his hand, so that scarcely a corner of them remained visible to the servant's longing eyes. (p. 358)

As the procedure unravels, it becomes a cacophony of sound: officials slam doors, howl with rage, shout out file numbers, and sob, and finally one of them presses unrelentingly on a loud electric bell. The breakdown of bureaucratic order follows a declension from checking a catalogue in silence through raucous speech to uninterrupted noise.

Thus, the scene reveals the principle of order at stake: as speech articulates and displaces sound to organize community life, so writing articulates and displaces speech to organize it bureaucratically. Written texts can't speak for themselves, however, so bureaucratic negotiation contains an inevitable disorderliness.

Furthermore, even when writing has been established as the dominant mode of communication, the bureaucrat is not automatically the master writer. Although the official learns to control decision making by marking his or her statements with the sign of the written text, there remain various negotiations within writing itself, including questions of what kind of writing will be authoritative and who will stand as an authoritative interpreter of the written text. This is itself a matter of artful balance: if everyone writes and reads with equal authority, then the organization loses its advantage; if no one else writes or reads, it limits its scope. The successful interpenetration of all other social relations by the organization requires a general field of literacy, while officials maintain control over others, and compete among themselves, by becoming adept in standard maneuvers of interpretation. So it is that every bureaucratic culture coalesces around several *topoi* of textual interpretation. These are conventions of reading developed to allow sufficient control and adaptation of written materials for the purpose of using them to regulate others over extended periods of time and amidst changing circumstances. Although usually developed in regard to the specific subject of the organization's work and its history, they also function as standard models for manipulating terms on any subject.

Some of the commonplaces of written culture have been evident already: Momus's subordination of speech to writing was accompanied by an equal insistence on following correct (written) form. The full significance and essential habits of bureaucratic reading can be summarized briefly by following the several interpretations of Klamm's first letter to K. The letter is given three readings; it becomes the premier hermeneutical object in the text. The first reading is K.'s own. He emphasizes that the letter positions him within a structure of subordination and concludes that the "inconsistencies" in the letter must be due to rational choice by the author rather than, as the narrator hints, due to indecision (p. 31). In addition, he matches the nuances of the letter with the subtleties of his own circumstances and so concludes that those choices reflect close attention to his own intentions. K. reads the letter as the sort of direct communication that would be more likely to occur in a face-to-face encounter, while also assuming that its content is as fixed in the text as the printed words themselves and representative of stable authorial intention. He is not a skilled bureaucrat, however.

The second reading of the letter is provided by the Mayor. The Mayor begins by identifying the genre of the letter and does this by distinguishing between official and private correspondences. The letter is a private one, but it also is "'all about state service in general'" and "'officially and expressly'" makes K. one of the Mayor's subordinates. So it is and is not an official letter; "'To anyone who knows how to read official communications, and consequently knows still better how to read unofficial letters, all this is only too clear'" (p. 92). The Mayor is identifying inconsistencies of a different nature: he is suggesting how to read between the lines. Bureaucratic reading depends on distinguishing between degrees of official determination of the document and on the negotiation between the fixed meaning of the written text and the negotiable meaning of its interpretation. All subsequent interpretations (save by K.) involve these intertwined *topoi* of distinguishing between official and unofficial and between literal and interpretive meanings. (Consider how readily these *topoi* are activated by our common phrase, "off the record.") K. reacts in exasperation: "'you interpret the letter so well that nothing remains of it but a signature on a blank sheet of paper'" (p. 92). The Mayor demurs: his reading is quite respectful of the letter, and he reiterates the importance of knowing what kind of letter it is.

These habits of interpretation are amplified and augmented in the third reading of the letter, by Olga, who would do very well in an academic department today. Like the Mayor, Olga stresses the ambiguity between the letter's status as an official document and as a personal correspondence, and she further devalues any consideration of K.'s circumstances. The only real significance of the letter lay, first, in its being a letter from the Castle, and second, in referring K. to the Mayor. Beyond that, she observes how its meaning also turns on the sense of context. The letter would mean one thing to Barnabas, another to Olga, another to the author, and yet another to the addressee. Whereas K. had begun by reading the letter in solitude and concluding he knew what it meant, Olga suggests that its meaning is turning continually on readers' negotiations with one another according to the commonplaces for interpreting a written text. The letter does not provide an account of a set of circumstances—K.'s status in the village—or communicate an intention—K.'s commission as a land surveyor—so much as it constructs a set of conventions for negotiating those issues. In other words, the letter is about itself: it communicates the techniques for its interpretation. These interpretive devices include the distinctions between the correct and incorrect written form, official and unofficial warrant, literal and interpretative meaning, and text and context. At any given moment, successful application of these commonplaces can provide interpretative control of the document, but there is no guarantee beyond that. "And to hold to the mean, without exaggeration on either side—in other words, to estimate the just value of those letters—is impossible, they themselves change in value perpetually, the reflections they give rise to are endless, and chance determines where one stops reflecting, and so even our estimate of them is a matter of chance" (p. 297).

Olga sees a written text that, while still venerated, is wide open to interpretation, and she sees the Castle as a place of endless reinterpretation of its own documents. The practice of writing creates the necessity of its interpretation and the autonomy of the interpretative act from the communicative text.[41] Therefore, bureaucratic culture becomes a hermeneutical space and one of a particular sort. Because it is an instantiation of the practice of writing, and oriented toward meeting continuing demands of ordinary living,[42] the bureaucracy exists in a continual tension between the fixity of the written text and the multiplicity of its readings, both of which are repeatedly reaffirmed. Interpretation of the document is a necessity of bureaucratic life and its locus of control; no wonder it is also the source of many of its ongoing anxieties. The organization operates within a continual deconstruction, simultaneously asserting the fixity of its rules and the legitimacy of their interpretation, the primacy of its documents and the limited value of their literal meaning, the omnipresence of its formal structure and its constitution as an endless series of supplements, always promising, and deferring, the original meaning, the direct intention, the clear command.

Perhaps this is why critics have been able to disagree passionately about whether Kafka is primarily a commentator on the modern political condition or a thoroughly modernist artist making a self-reflexive literary text.[43] Kafka is indeed a writer writing about writing and a writer of political sensibility: that sensibility includes his artistic portrayal of how writing structures polity. The relationship between Castle and village turns on the manner in which an organic community of people speaking together can be changed and controlled by their incorporation into a culture of writing. As he reduces bureaucratic domination to its gestures of writing and filing documents, Kafka opens up the question of how meaning is created and controlled within a rational structure. This question in turn raises the issue of how the bureaucratic style operates as a process of assimilation.

Any style can be understood at several levels of analysis. It can consist of a compendium of techniques and rules of composition in a particular medium, and also carry a history of the art and conception of its ideal accomplishment, and also invoke a drama of human endeavor. Modernist architecture, for example, rules out imitation of other styles, emphasizes the progressive synthesis of form and function, and symbolizes the ascendancy of modern, industrial society. Postmodern architecture includes ironic appropriation of other styles, emphasizes eclectic synthesis of the building and its environment, and symbolizes a society simultaneously progressive and regressive. Political styles offer similarly complex extensions of themselves. They provide the "recipe knowledge" for effective participation in a particular political locale, arguments for the superiority of their characteristic ideals of polity, and dramas of the human condition. The bureaucratic style, for example, features the character of the official, progressive achievement of rational (rather than willful) governance, and a conception of personal identity as a drama of assimilation into a culture of procedural rationality.

This is, of course, the predicament of K., who lives among the villagers while holding a provisional legitimacy conferred by the Castle and carries a gnawing sense of alienation and the anxiousness it perpetuates.[44] K. hopes that he can blend in with the villagers enough that they "would begin to talk to him once he was their fellow citizen, if not exactly their friend," but he worries "that some day or other, in spite of the amiability of the authorities and the scrupulous fulfillment of all his exaggeratedly light duties, he might— deceived by the apparent favor shown him—conduct himself so imprudently as to get a fall" (p. 75). He is already too infused with organizational ambition and rationality to want to become a villager, yet he finds little reward or security in his organizational role. His identity is defined not by one culture or another, but in the thousand minute, daily negotiations between them—choices often unconscious and always consequential.

Once begun, this drama of assimilation structures the consciousness of everyday life. One's identity becomes composite, a constantly shifting mixture of two seemingly incommensurable cultures. This process works on not only the individual but also the society as a whole. As modern bureaucracy requires and rewards the individual's assimilation into its culture of impersonal, rationalized work, it facilitates the incorporation of peoples into the larger culture of modernity. The normal operation (primary discipline) of a bureaucracy habituates all involved to the transformation of a past life of historied, enculturated, parochial customs into a present routine of impersonal, rational procedures. As this mechanism for the composition of identity operates routinely and ubiquitously, it provides proven substitutes for those wishing to suppress their "original" affiliation and also sufficient protection for those wishing to work within and benefit from the dominant culture while reserving a private life not subject to public scrutiny. The ordinary office worker is a model of this composite personality: she is at once a person and a persona: a clerk sitting at a gray, metal desk, upon which rests a color picture of her family. Bureaucracy is the medium within which assimilation into modernity occurs and one reason it becomes possible, desirable, and inevitable.

This is one reason why bureaucratic politics are more than just a bad day at the office. The extension of bureaucratic organization into all aspects of modern life incorporates everyone into its drama of assimilation. Everyone becomes a composite personality made up of an inheritance from the lifeworld—which might include everything from a love of *bocci* to the experience of child abuse—and an organizational identity—which might confer everything from richly rewarding work to carpal tunnel syndrome. Daily life becomes a negotiation between the mores of the family, neighborhood, church, or community, and the procedures of the office, organization, or government. The conventions of bureaucratic life structure these negotiations, which then turn on such acts as choosing between speech and writing, identifying oneself in terms of either expertise, discipline, and dedication or other forms of character, honoring or ignoring organizational hierarchy, and recognizing either jurisdictions and their rules or persons and their relationships.

These bureaucratically induced and managed patterns of assimilation are never complete, never finished, and rarely a choice between two wholly separate conditions. The integration of organizational persona and individual personality occurs seamlessly but provisionally. Often it is not clear, and not important, whether our actions are more motivated by bureaucratic imperatives or the material needs of everyday life, as the two are already artfully interwoven. The depth of the relationship between the organizational culture and the culture it absorbs is suggested by the fact that K., in *The Trial* as well as in *The Castle*, never can find the point where the one world ends and the other begins. As he goes deeper into the anterooms of the court lodged within the slums, or deeper into the corridors of the organization lodged within the inns, he finds only that the two cultures are as intimate as ever. "Never yet had K. seen vocation and life so interlaced as here, so interlaced that sometimes one might think that they had exchanged places" (p. 75).[45] Ultimately, we have to conclude that there is no "real" point of contact, and no simple interiority and exteriority, but a complex process of perpetual transformation between two sides of being human. The personal and the impersonal, the material and the formal, the natural and the artificial, the spoken and the written word are all elements of the same condition of symbolic action.

This condition has become characteristic of modern life. Modern consciousness is self-aware, rational, and universalizing, yet no lived experience can consist wholly of those qualities. Consequently, the modern person is always going to live at one remove from his or her organic community. It is not that one wishes to be so; often there is a deep yearning for reunion with a premodern condition, whether expressed in individual fantasies or in collective ideals. The problem is that one can't return. Although its effects can be ameliorated, modern consciousness can't be jettisoned. (This is why it is useless, incidentally, to define bureaucracy as an unmitigated evil.) Thus, modern identity requires a bifocal perspective: One lives both in a private, personal, intimate, organic place and in a public, impersonal, functional, institutional space, each of which have their own rewards and dangers, neither of which suffice to define who one is. We live as Castle bureaucrats in the village and as villagers in the Castle. A

great deal of technological and commercial enterprise serves to reduce the friction between these two planes of existence, but this enterprise is itself only possible because of the demarcation. Wherever we are, and however comfortable, we live as boarders in our
own home.

The deep structure of this drama becomes articulated through a
grammar, which operates in two ways: first, it provides a set of equations for transposing social practices, and, second, it makes those
transpositions a chain of supplements. The equations are derived
from the basic axioms of bureaucratic organization: offices = procedures = rules = expertise = documents . . . For the most part, the
relations are transitive as well. Assimilation can begin at any point
in the equation and then move along its axis: A job applicant passes
an entrance exam (correct use of procedure), which leads to a training
program (to learn the rules), which leads to a position (in an office),
etc. Or a citizen goes to a government office, to obtain a form, to
follow the rules, to receive a service, etc. By following these equations, one's experience becomes structured by bureaucratic categories and one assumes the composite identity typical of modern life.

These equations have additional significance, moreover, which
they obtain by being set over other terms. As Chaim Perelman has
suggested, discourses operate argumentatively in part by constructing "philosophical pairs" of terms, which then define (dialectically)
the structure of the reality that is the subject of the discourse.[46] So
we might set "culture" over "nature," or "human" over "animal," or
"rational" over "imaginative," etc. In the bureaucratic culture's ongoing drama of assimilation, this operation generates paired equations, which in turn establish the one order as more real, more enduring, than the other: for example, the equation "organization = rules
= writing . . ." is set over "individual = desires = speech . . ." Not
surprisingly, some of these pairings lead straight into the constitution of modernity and also structure the study of modern organizations: Weber's own work, for example, is grounded unequivocally on
the priority of "the bureaucratic = the modern = the written = the
efficient" over "the traditional = the premodern = the spoken = the
inefficient." Likewise, we are accustomed to setting "the bureaucratic = the rational = the state = rule of law" over "the political
= the emotional = the ethnic community = rule of custom" and,
therefore, exempting bureaucratic culture from political commen-

dangers, neither of which suffice to define who one is. We live as Castle bureaucrats in the village and as villagers in the Castle. A great deal of technological and commercial enterprise serves to reduce the friction between these two planes of existence, but this enterprise is itself only possible because of the demarcation. Wherever we are, and however comfortable, we live as boarders in our own home.

The deep structure of this drama becomes articulated through a grammar, which operates in two ways: first, it provides a set of equations for transposing social practices, and, second, it makes those transpositions a chain of supplements. The equations are derived from the basic axioms of bureaucratic organization: offices = procedures = rules = expertise = documents . . . For the most part, the relations are transitive as well. Assimilation can begin at any point in the equation and then move along its axis: A job applicant passes an entrance exam (correct use of procedure), which leads to a training program (to learn the rules), which leads to a position (in an office), etc. Or a citizen goes to a government office, to obtain a form, to follow the rules, to receive a service, etc. By following these equations, one's experience becomes structured by bureaucratic categories and one assumes the composite identity typical of modern life.

These equations have additional significance, moreover, which they obtain by being set over other terms. As Chaim Perelman has suggested, discourses operate argumentatively in part by constructing "philosophical pairs" of terms, which then define (dialectically) the structure of the reality that is the subject of the discourse.[46] So we might set "culture" over "nature," or "human" over "animal," or "rational" over "imaginative," etc. In the bureaucratic culture's ongoing drama of assimilation, this operation generates paired equations, which in turn establish the one order as more real, more enduring, than the other: for example, the equation "organization = rules = writing . . ." is set over "individual = desires = speech . . ." Not surprisingly, some of these pairings lead straight into the constitution of modernity and also structure the study of modern organizations: Weber's own work, for example, is grounded unequivocally on the priority of "the bureaucratic = the modern = the written = the efficient" over "the traditional = the premodern = the spoken = the inefficient." Likewise, we are accustomed to setting "the bureaucratic = the rational = the state = rule of law" over "the political tary, or assuming that institutional politics are a temporary corruption of rational procedures.

These equations operate through an additional mechanism as well. Bureaucratic order is articulated according to the grammatical operation of supplementarity. Here I obviously am drawing on Jacques Derrida's examination of Jean-Jacques Rousseau's writing about writing. Derrida criticizes the idea that the written text communicates the presence of an original act of speaking. Instead, he argues that meaning resides in the supplement: The presence of the spoken word is not pre-given, but implied by the act of writing that defers it. Furthermore, there is no escape from this condition: If presented with speech, it would become a supplement to thought, which would come to be a supplement to direct, unmediated knowledge of the world, etc. In brief, "Immediacy is derived."[47]

Derrida also identifies a connection in Rousseau between writing and erotic life. This seemingly exotic observation provides a clear connection to *The Castle*, for K.'s relationships with women are acts of supplementarity. He takes Frieda as his lover because she already is Klamm's mistress, and he abides with Olga because of her brother's commission as a messenger. The relationship with Frieda is particularly poignant, for it reveals the futility, and cost, of K.'s quest for contact with the Castle.[48] Frieda at once presents and defers the essence of the Castle, and as Frieda supplements Klamm, he supplements the higher authorities, who supplement the hierarchy itself, which supplements the "cosmic laws" . . . At this point, it is easy to see why *The Castle* usually is read theologically: The chain of supplements seems to lead straight to God. But the theological reading is a "metaphysics of presence," for God, too, is presented through deferral, and we are left only with the chain of supplements, the traces of bureaucratic life.[49]

Any bureaucracy appears as a supplement in both senses that Derrida identifies: it augments, expands, adds to the fullness of what is already present in the world, and it also intervenes, interferes, stands between, and defers the satisfactions it promises.[50] Both legitimation and critique of bureaucratic authority rest upon the two sides of this relationship. Bureaucracies are defended when they are perceived to augment previously constituted communities and satisfy material needs, and they are faulted when they are perceived as deferring important social resources. Even the dialectic of system and lifeworld is a form of the supplement: The lifeworld stands for the immediacy that is deferred, the presence of organic, authentic community that must be displaced by the inscription of bureaucratic organization. Within a local environment, the success or failure of bureaucratic operations can depend on the acceptance of the supplemental relationship being proffered. K., for example, is strung along successfully by the occasional letters from Klamm: each activates the presence it defers and functions to keep K. oriented toward the organization that is largely indifferent toward him.

We should not underestimate the power of these conventions. Once it gets a toehold, the bureaucratic style can absorb all others.[51] It is capable of transforming—(re)writing—all other visions of polity into versions of itself. This imperial tendency then raises the question of how to live within a bureaucratic order. (This essay is not the place to discuss what can come from optimizing the criteria of the administrative sciences such as efficiency.[52]) Let me suggest that the key to good bureaucratic polity lies in four things. First, as with any political system, good governance requires self-reflexive mastery of its rhetorical conventions; this account of the bureaucratic style attempts to contribute to that end. Second, good bureaucratic polity turns on understanding the two sides of supplementarity. The attempt to augment collective living will also defer some of its goods, and the representation of the deferred reality will then become one means of sustaining the system of deferral. This paradoxical condition of bureaucratic action contains its own ethic, however: an ethic of play. By playing with the terms of organizational definition, actors create local opportunities for modifying the system to meet genuine needs and recognize differences considered important for maintaining identity and dignity. Bureaucrats already know as much: Note how offices are decorated with many small satires on organizational life (albeit, invariably in posted, written form): for example, two characters rolling with laughter, as the sign says, "'You said you want it when?!'" Such jokes are more than an antidote to the characteristic seriousness of bureaucratic domination, they feature and comment on the characteristic problems of supplementarity.

Third, bureaucratic polity is better off if infused with a democratic ethos. If nothing else, this would counterbalance the tendency of the bureaucratic style to construct identity without any reference to a public sphere. Once assimilated into bureaucratic culture, one can experience a relatively satisfying sense of identity based on mastery of the transitions between private life and official employment. There is little room for, or need of, participation in a public realm where one is neither left to oneself nor recognized according to one's expertise and institutional authority.[53] Although neither bureaucracy nor democracy will allow a pure form of the other, which perhaps is for the best, each can benefit from entanglement with the other. Weber knew as much:

Germany continued to maintain a military and civilian bureaucracy superior to all others in the world in terms of integrity, education, conscientiousness and intelligence. . . . What was lacking was the *direction* of the state by a *politician*—not by a political genius, to be expected only once every few centuries, not even by a great political talent, but simply by a politician.[54]

Weber's statement moves outside of the dialectic of charismatic leadership and its routinization to incorporate practices of governance that are characteristically democratic. His "politician" would be someone capable of judgment without deference to hierarchy, someone more disposed to value collective experience than to equate facts with documents, someone capable of taking risks in public and of motivating a public by appeal to broadly based needs and aspirations, and someone capable of negotiating among disparate interests to establish consensus.[55] His emphasis on the ordinary example of these qualities doesn't make them less of an idealization, of course, but it might be a necessary ideal for correcting an already dominant equation of power with expertise.

Finally, the ubiquity of bureaucratic power suggests an additional problem and its paradoxical solution. As the system predominates, the question arises of how any action is possible in a wholly organized world. It would seem that the only comprehensible acts would be those that perpetuate and expand organizational culture and that all distribution of goods would become predictable. Would not this paralyze the individual seeking to change the system? To discern Kafka's answer to this question, we must return to *The Trial* and its context of fatality. Near the end of the book, K. has a conversation with a priest.[56] At first, it appears that the conversation constitutes a model of how the court could work humanely. The conversation begins with the priest offering K. a handshake—in contrast to K.'s obviously manipulative and abortive attempts at handshakes earlier (pp. 14–15, 20)—and continues as a debate about the parable of the doorkeeper. The parable tells of a man from the country who comes to the court, only to be told by a doorkeeper that he cannot enter at the moment. He tries repeatedly without success to persuade the official, even to the point of appealing to the fleas in the man's collar for help. Finally, he dies exhausted, still not admitted. The story is about the Law and has the essential characteristic of the Law—it is "unalterable" (p. 217)—yet it is shown also to be the subject of numerous and carefully argued interpretations. The conversation between the priest and K. is both a highly rational discourse and the most humane relationship in the book. More important, it offers K. the possibility of an active, even refutative inquiry into his moral life—the one thing he has refused to do. So it would seem that this Talmudic conversation exemplifies Benjamin's insight that Kafka "sacrificed truth for the sake of clinging to its transmissibility"[57] and would be Kafka's model of rational speech. But there are reasons for looking further, if only because he stresses that the priest is the property of the court; from a moral perspective, he is not free, and from a political perspective, he is not credible.

I believe that Kafka is offering a further ideal, characteristically paradoxical, and one whose unformed nature is suggested by its having only an incipient gesture. Kafka intimates that action requires a higher form of ignorance. K. admits to his ignorance of the Law, and he is regularly confronted with his ignorance of the court he scrutinizes, but K. is not a role model. He is, however, a lesser version of what he might become, just as the court he sees is the lesser version of the one that set out to correct him. In a similar vein, the art of rhetoric is identified typically with the ignorance of its speakers and audiences, yet skillful persuasion often is based on a more selective form of ignorance, the willed inattention to details that hinder advancement toward right living. Moreover, this decision to act, for the moment, without regard to knowledge or protocol, can be the crucial element in mustering the courage to change a society structured by institutional authority rationalized by expertise. Procedural rationality too often results in the inflexibility and impersonality of judgment characterizing both K. and the court at their worst; political freedom then can be achieved only by refusing to be limited by what one knows. If this higher ignorance is to have a gesture, it can be as simple an act as walking. In the case of the man from the country, the only real option he had was to walk through the door, a gesture not realized in the story. In the case of K., it's harder to say, but Kafka does hint several times that he could have walked away from the court into another life. The action capable of challenging the authority constricting both court and defendants could only occur if one was willing to act in ignorance of what was to come. One source of K.'s shame is that he settles for acquiring a petty knowledge always insufficient to unlock an open door. So it is that any account of bureaucratic life should not be limited to improving the normal performance of one's duties. If we are to compose ourselves within a bureaucratic style, it should be with the aim of moving toward a better life.

6

Conclusion

In the spirit of the commonplace that politics is an art, I have featured four master styles of political practice. The four styles were located in four "mirror texts"—that is, pretexts of a certain sort. These texts provided not the mirror of nature, but something closer to the hallway mirror that reflects, frames, and creates a moment for critical assessment of the figure standing in front of it, looking herself over, before she steps out for the evening. Each of the four texts is less extensive than its object of interpretation, which is a coherent repertoire of compositional techniques that will be active in any number of locales, applied to many different tasks, and modified through improvisation.

Since my approach runs the risk of identifying itself too much with its focal texts, this last chapter will present a general statement about the kind of social theory implicated in rhetorical study as I understand it. This statement looks back to classical rhetoric, and particularly to the concept of decorum, in order to identify several strong affinities between the traditional art and modern interpretive social science. These belated arguments may strike some readers as unnecessary, but they at least have the virtue of being brief. This theoretical background is then augmented by a review of other related programs of inquiry, some of which already have been put to some use in the preceding chapters and each of which can provide a wider context and more varied lines of development for the analysis of political style. Finally, I close by returning to the four texts I have featured to see how they can continue to provoke and guide interpretation.

The patron saint of this project has been Kenneth Burke, who advised that "whatever poetry may be, criticism had best be comic."[1] This interpretative attitude involves both openness to novelty—that is, to what might lie outside current conceptions of aesthetic order—and recognition that we are better able to understand symbolic action, and to avoid evil, if we can accept human foolishness.[2] Burke's work is the basis for the theory of symbolic action broadly construed as dramatism, which can be summarized by the following axioms.[3] All action is structured according to the essential ingredients of drama. Meaning is created through staged performances of conflict and resolution before an audience. Power is constituted by the persuasive communication of principles of order amidst changing situations. Persuasion is the strategic enactment of motives in discourse to induce cooperation. Discourses both structure our perceptions and are structured by the situations in which they are used. The rhetorical critic attempts to identify how discourse is impelling thought and action and focuses on the designs shaping specific texts in order to discover patterns of motivation that can operate throughout society, often in a wide range of media, genres, and practices. Thus, while appreciating the craftwork of the individual text, the critic nonetheless is oriented toward "a general body of identifications that owe their convincingness much more to trivial repetition and dull daily reinforcement than to exceptional rhetorical skill."[4] This critical task is compounded by the fact that texts (even the social text) often are fragmentary and their more important designs tacit.[5]

Burke's "sociological criticism" suggests how political events can turn on matters of artistic composition and aesthetic perception. As people use discourses strategically to fashion "equipment for living," they also become shaped by their designs, seeing the world as they would compose it and responding according to the formal pressures of their compositions.[6] These habits might work to their disadvantage, but there is no escape that does not depend on finding yet another design attractive enough to prove appealing. In every case, the individual agent cannot act without using and being used by conventions of address and interpretation developed socially, that is, by others and with others and with regard to others and without prior regard to the personal circumstances of the speaker. Thus, the basic

178

interpretive task is to develop "maximum awareness of the complex forensic material accumulated in sophisticated social structures."[7]

This perspective does not avoid well-known analytical problems in the human sciences, however. On the one hand, when charting general patterns of identification, it is subject to the criticisms of any structuralism, not least of all, the objection that the analysis is indifferent to specific experiences. On the other hand, when uncoiling the motivational dynamics of a particular text, the analysis can be discounted as merely ad hoc description (however thick, ethnographically sensitive, or well written) of a unique event. Yet we should not be too quick to assess any version of rhetorical criticism solely in terms of the arguments of structuralist and poststructuralist theory. Although today many social theorists are likely to be suspicious of Burke's emphasis on the abstract, structural, and unifying features of discourse, they should not overlook his attempt to explain how motivations were simultaneously conventional and particular and the result of not only the discursive activation of deep patterns of meaning but also the situational transformation, synthesis, or subversion of those patterns.[8] Similarly, the analysis of political style has to identify its subject both as a relatively stable and comprehensive pattern of motivation embedded in specific social practices and as a dynamic process that is inherently unstable and unsettling because it generates at the intersection of poetics and politics. This might be summarized in several ways—for example, as "structuration"[9]—but the general term (and theoretical affiliation) is unimportant. What is important is discovering how little props up any political order and how that much is often sufficient for powerful constitutions of human activity.

In any case, both structuralist and poststructuralist projects of any sort ultimately come up against a vexing empirical problem as well, for the discovery of social reality requires examination of what is unseen because obvious. To the extent that political life is styled, it will be a life lived on the surface of things. Therefore, stylistic analysis should contribute to the task of understanding how it is that specific surfaces are seen or not seen at all and often will require that one uncover what is in full view. Although this problem seems incongruous after an age of enlightenment, it was a problem to which classical thinkers had devised a solution. In the spirit of Allan Megill's suggestion that postmodern theory might advance by attend-

179

ing to "premodern" texts and traditions, and in particular to the tradition of rhetoric,[10] we ought to consider how that tradition provides a carefully wrought background for understanding political style. Certainly there are other places for conducting postmodern inquiry, and my approach does not presume that classical texts alone are even adequate for understanding and engaging the world of the present. If postmodern theory is to succeed on its own terms, however, it will have to develop a compelling reconfiguration of aesthetics, rhetoric, and politics. Classical rhetoric provides one model, however limited, of how that could be done.

The sensibility of classical rhetoric that I want to emphasize was most evident in its concept of decorum (*to prepon, decorum, quid deceat*). Decorum articulated the rules governing the selection of diction appropriate to one's subject or situation.[11] This stable discursive code specified, for example, that dramatic characters should not speak urbanely if they are rustics, poets should not use pedestrian words for heroic subjects, and orators should not discuss weighty matters in an offhand manner. The lineaments of this concept are presented in the classical handbooks, which suggest two dimensions of the concept corresponding to the alternative perspectives available in any explicitly identified social code: a relatively uniform, commonsense, commonplace system of instructions and a more complicated awareness of those instructions as somewhat arbitrary markers of a constantly shifting field of social relations. Decorum operated at both levels, as a set of conventions and as a theory of conventions. In either case, such conventions blended significant aspects of rhetorical practice, social awareness, and political structure into an aesthetic sensibility that could be applied uniformly to literary texts, rhetorical performances, and official conduct.

Much of the time, the system was there, ready to be drawn upon enthymematically by those social actors accustomed to the advantages of the social order. Yet against this backdrop we also have to consider Cicero's statement that "in an oration, as in life, nothing is harder than to determine what is appropriate."[12] If the rules of decorum seemed to construct "a closed system,"[13] they also contained internal tensions that could open possibilities for new thought about communication. First, there were problems of representation; signs could be faked so that one could simulate rank and feign deference—and instruction always was undertaken with the expectation that one could advance beyond ordinary expectations—but that artistry could be discovered.[14] Second, there were problems of function; specific effects of some genres (such as demonstrative oratory, comedy, and tragedy) were achieved by violating the rules of decorum, although audiences rewarded some violations while rejecting others.[15] Finally, there were problems of praxis; for example, Quintilian recognized how Socrates made the less effective defense at his trial for impiety by choosing to be appropriate to his character rather than to his situation.[16] In sum, "decorum" articulated not so much a set of rules as a process of invention. This process included both the major stylistic code for verbal composition and the social knowledge required for political success, and it equipped the classical thinker to discern, evaluate, and appropriate elements of artistry across a wide spectrum of human activity.

There is another reason for considering the classical account of decorum as a model for a contemporary theory of political style: That model was itself a response to foundational questions in the human sciences that continue to challenge modern inquiry. We can learn from the classical model today not so much by reactivating it as by using it to highlight pertinent resources in contemporary scholarship. Several programs of inquiry have circled around ordinary communicative artistry, despite the indifference to the subject in the human sciences generally. The most comprehensive of these is the strong strain of social theory that began with the work of Max Weber and Georg Simmel, received significant restatement by Alfred Schutz, was augmented by George Herbert Mead, and which influenced Kenneth Burke and informs several contemporary research programs. Although this school of thought is very much part of the modern project—not least in its theoretical curiosity and ambition—it is also somewhat of a countermovement, which, if it had reached full velocity, could have exploded the entire system of the social sciences. By briefly considering how classical rhetoric corresponds with the analytical interests of modern interpretive social theory, we can suggest how any theory of political style might negotiate specific questions regarding the relationship between the subjective and objective definitions of social experience, the intelligibility and rationality of social practices, and the analytical character of social theory.

The classical ideas of decorum cohered easily with discussions

181

of verbal style (*lexis, elocutio*) and with the complete lexicon of rhetorical studies generally. This is important in two aspects. First, it suggests a comprehensive approach to a host of practical and theoretical problems, including the tasks of winning a legal case, or an election, or a literary contest, and accounting for better and worse arguments, or differences among genres of discourse, or among dialects, and negotiating the political institutions of the various Greek city-states, etc. All of these questions could be answered, in part, through the analysis of verbal technique. In short, the art of rhetoric functioned as a "cultural hermeneutics," a theoretical vocabulary (however incomplete) used to identify how diverse texts, acts, and actors are determined by their processes of composition and interpretation.[17]

Second, the idea of studying decorum in order to understand and act to advantage within a social situation was, like rhetorical studies generally, an essentially pragmatic approach to the major philosophical questions raised by the Sophists as they also were establishing rhetoric as the preeminent educational enterprise. These questions are recognizable today as the major issues of twentieth-century social theory: What is the object of study in the human sciences? How can it be known? How should one act with that knowledge?[18]

One could without too much exaggeration say that the human sciences began with Protagoras's statement that the individual is the measure of all things (*pantōn krēmatōn metron estin anthrōpos*).[19] With this battle cry, he announced the separation of the human sciences from the study of the physical world and did so by focusing on the human being's account of the world. The world exists independently of us—this is not philosophical idealism—but it only exists to us, and we only act within it, as we interpret it. Moreover, each experience is unique, determined by the inevitably singular standpoint of each subject. What makes this assertion particularly interesting, however, is its relationship to the project of understanding human communication. A paradox develops: Protagoras's radical subjectivism would seem to preclude his prized art of rhetoric. Certainly, communication could not be the exact transfer of individual meanings, as the interlocutors could never escape the differences in standpoint, for example, of speaker and auditor. The solution to this problem was not the formulation of logically consistent definitions of consciousness and communication. Instead, the art of rhetoric became the study of common knowledge (*doxa*), forms of practical reasoning (*enthumēmata, topoi,* etc.), forms of social and verbal display (*to prepon* and *lexis*), and the like. In the vocabulary of interpretive social theory, rhetorical study was focused on ordinary intersubjective processes and commonly appropriated interpretive constructs.[20]

This account of the discursive means for making meaning had to be commensurate with ordinary actors' understanding of their own communicative practices. The study of communication was not a phenomenological exploration of a state of consciousness, as in the act of speaking or listening or deciding; rather it was an inventory of the forms of ordinary communicative practice as its practitioners could recognize and manipulate them. Rather than treat the gap between individual experiences and social practices as a philosophical problem, the art of rhetoric offered individual actors the means to orient self toward other through discourse on a practical, continuing, contingent, open-ended basis.

This approach to the problem of intersubjectivity is pragmatic in two other senses as well: it is directed toward solving actual problems (or, equipping individuals to act advantageously or responsibly), and it involves a radical attentiveness to agency.[21] Rhetoric's orientation as a practical art is well known, although the relation between this orientation and its particular emphasis on agency might not be evident. Again, we begin with the paradox of unique individuals producing agreement. Effective persuasion requires understanding how other people will act, even though their actions result from their unique and unknowable interpretations of the world. The solution to this problem is to base the understanding of action upon knowledge of the social practice of communication, which in turn requires an analysis of its forms, techniques, rules, and the like. As Aristotle put it, rhetoric produces not simply persuasion, but an account of how particular means of persuasion could work or be rendered ineffective according to the circumstances of the case (*Rhetoric* 1355b.10). We cannot know exactly how a message is formed or received, nor would one want to, unless one is interested in understanding thereafter only that single moment. Although persuasive discourse is used to gain advantage and is addressed to someone, the individual speaker and auditor quickly are bracketed to focus attention on the available means of persuasion and alternative possibilities for design, all of which can be common knowledge. This is the source of its objectivity: Like any science, rhetoric theorizes not about individuals, but about the relationship between standard techniques and typical reactions (1356b.30). In summary, the rhetorician's cataloging of proofs, commonplaces, and tropes in reference to basic social situations was an attempt to explain the structure of indirect social experience in a manner consistent with ordinary understanding. It allowed the classical theorist to still be connected to the dynamics of personal interest and response while providing an objective account of action—an explanation of the production of meaning that could be validated without reference to individual subjective experience.[22]

Thus, we can observe that classical rhetoric produced a particular kind of understanding that corresponds to ideal type analysis as it was introduced by Max Weber and refined by Alfred Schutz, Karl Mannheim, and others. The key to this mode of understanding is that it presumes the concreteness of anonymous formulations. It is as true to say that young men are rash (*Rhetoric,* 1389a) as it is to say that Polus is rash. In fact, the first claim is more reliable than the second: The first identifies an objectified structure of understanding that any competent interlocutor can recognize. As Schutz states, "The more anonymous the personal ideal type . . . , the greater is the use made of objective meaning-contexts instead of subjective ones."[23] "Young men are rash" is one of the means with which one thinks, at least somewhat independently of one's standpoint. "Polus is rash" is a statement that has to include an account of Polus's self-understanding, which is at some point incontestable. In like manner, the statement, "The grand style is appropriate to high officials or important subjects," is a statement that can provide an objective basis for an explanation of the meaning of an official's speech, whereas the statement "the grand style is appropriate to Pericles" is less useful (though still relevant, especially if understood as a pregiven personal type).[24] Therefore, the analysis of a persuasive message requires an initial inventory of its use of *typical* social forms. And to identify a text in terms of its typical forms is to typify the text, to bring it out of sheer particularity into a realm of public meaning. By identifying the stylistic devices in a text, one identifies its meaning in terms of familiar communicative practices, and to identify those devices is to interpret the text in like manner, namely, by considering how it can or cannot function in accord with particular motives, thoughts, and the like by virtue of being an example of one type of text.

184

In addition, classical rhetoric presumed a double hermeneutic: After the determination of the type (that is, the typification of the text), it still had to be interpreted in respect to the circumstances of the particular communicative act. As before, this second stage of the classical model is tightly coordinated with the ordinary interpretive practices of the lifeworld. The recognition of speakers, subjects, occasions, audiences, and styles all involve use of the interpretive constructs of the communicators themselves (although additional categorization and analysis can follow). Even so, the knowledge of types does not suffice to direct interpretation of their use. (In Mannheim's formulation: ideal type analysis consists of two levels of explanation: the identification of the types and then a history of their actual usage.[25]) The techniques of persuasion can be effective because not observed, or despite being observed, or because observed and admired. The forms of speech acquire a history of usage and idiomatic inflection within any particular community. The strategic effect can result from reassuring use of the familiar or from innovation. . . . As Isocrates summarized: "But I marvel when I observe these men setting themselves up as instructors of youth who cannot see that they are applying the analogy of an art with hard and fast rules to a creative process."[26] Modern social theory has yet to overcome this problem, which is captured in the famous image of the Parsonian actors all arrayed on the stage, but immobile.[27]

This problem of accounting for artistry threatened the basic legitimacy of rhetorical study (which was not escaping suspicion anyway). The function of the classical handbooks was to maximize the accessibility and intelligibility of the various persuasive techniques, yet their best use could not be determined by inventory alone. Nor could the list of forms be supplemented with a catalog of "rules of usage," for such rules would necessarily be indeterminate, contingent, modifiable during use, and usually tacit. (Consider: once specified as a rule, the decision process is focalized and reified and therefore less capable of working automatically or adaptively.) The most significant classical response to this problem was to position rhetorical study at the limits of explanation in the human sciences. Aristotle's formulation is well known, though too often neglected: The first condition of rationality in the human sciences consists of identifying the appropriate standard for evaluating a particular claim; therefore, one should not expect apodeictic proofs from a rhetor.[28]

Isocrates' formulation is less well known today, and it presents a more pessimistic sense of constraint: "For since it is not in the nature of man to attain a science by the possession of which we can know positively what we should do or what we should say, in the next resort I hold that man to be wise who is able by his powers of conjecture to arrive generally at the best course."[29] As elaborated recently by Hans Blumenberg, the human being "needs rhetoric as the art of appearance" because of our *cognitive deficiency*. Unable to know the truth, the human being survives by developing its peculiar relation to reality, which is "indirect, circumstantial, delayed, selective, and above all 'metaphorical.' "[30]

Thus, the classical accounts of rhetoric, and particularly of stylistics and of decorum, might be read as provisional solutions to perennial problems. As these accounts are situated in respect to foundational dilemmas of the human sciences, their limitations are not excused but their analytical strengths can be appreciated. The handbooks were indeed prescientific compendia of commonplace observations, but they also were elements of a comprehensive cultural hermeneutics that was available for the understanding of social practices and civic discourses. When style was celebrated as the supreme accomplishment of skilled speakers, it was because they had mastered in their own discourses the fundamental conditions of language in use: they had tapped a tacit economy of signs to effectively organize a potentially boundless and ineffable realm of experience. In addition, the speaker's artistry consisted of the same hermeneutical operations as those used to explain the persuasive effect: application of universal patterns in a particular case and activating one set of possible interpretations rather than another in order to obtain agreement about the intelligibility of an action.

In sum, although classical rhetoric and modern interpretive social theory are indeed worlds apart, they also have significant analogies. Each attempts to account for the interior life of the human world while presuming the inaccessibility of subjective experience; each attempts to explain the means of interpretation used by ordinary actors and requires that explanation be commensurable with its object; each features the anonymous, typical, formal features of understanding in order to advance understanding of more specific, local, and dynamic conditions; each emphasizes the sufficient rationality of actions that are provisional, indirect, abbreviated, open to other interpretations, and the like. These similarities can give special direction to an account of how political actors stylize their conduct in our world. On the one hand, unrestrained by modern conceptions of artistic (and political) autonomy, the classical model directs our attention toward the role of artifice in the composition of ordinary political experience. On the other hand, unhampered by the classical fixation on the education of the orator, the modern context encourages more comprehensive explanations of social reality once we have developed appropriate analytical constructs. By identifying various political styles, I have tried to provide some of the initial typifications that could be used to better understand how political events are meaningful, accomplished, and decisive.

The correspondences between classical rhetoric and modern interpretive social theory should be evident in the following extended definition of political style as: (1) a set of rules for speech and conduct guiding the alignment of signs and situations, or texts and acts, or behavior and place; (2) informing practices of communication and display; (3) operating through a repertoire of rhetorical conventions depending on aesthetic reactions; and (4) determining individual identity, providing social cohesion, and distributing power. Like any other element of political life, the particular rules and the degree to which these rules are determinative of political outcomes will vary across and within particular cultures and events.

It is encouraging to note that this expansive concept of style has been persistently available as a minor theme in twentieth-century social and political theory. Weber's use of the term is representative when he suggests that a comprehensive social theory needs to include at some point an account of how common living coheres into different styles. His usage captures the fusion of aesthetic and social codes suggested by the contemporary term "lifestyle," and his discussion indicates that inquiry would have to move beyond the economic and institutional matrices that occupy much of his own work.[31] This nascent recognition of the interpenetration of aesthetic and social codes (or, in the Aristotelian scheme, productive and practical arts), wends through subsequent theory as well. Sometimes it has been grounded in the discussions of the role of art, as in Georg Simmel, John Dewey, or George Herbert Mead. Simmel recognized that art exemplifies the intersubjective character of all communication forms.[32] Dewey's emphasis on the relationship between personal experience and communal practice was summarized in his declaration that "all communication is like art."[33] Mead captured their interest in the confluence of (democratic) aesthetic sensibilities and political ideals with the image of the statesman whose "attitude is aesthetic": He "stops in his common labor and effort to feel the surety of his colleagues, the loyalty of his supporters, the response of his public, to enjoy the community of life in the family, or profession, or party, or church, or country, to taste in Whitmanesque manner the commonality of existence."[34]

These intimations have sounded again in more recent social theory. Although the preceding essays have suggested how an analysis of each political style can draw on and perhaps contribute to specific research programs, several bear special mention here for the particularly rich contexts they provide for the project as a whole. Harold Garfinkel's ethnomethodology provides a strong theoretical background and innovative methodological work that suggests just how insightful an analysis of style can be. Although Garfinkel's vocabulary features cognition and moral sense more than political or aesthetic variables, his analysis of the "organized, artful practices" of everyday life is a model for the analysis of how action is stylized.[35] Similarly, Erving Goffman has provided highly detailed examinations of the forms, functions, and occasions directing face-to-face interaction.[36] Goffman finds the universe in a grain of sand, for ordinary interactions prove to be intricately organized and dynamic patterns of social structure and performative skill. The various forms of practice theory provide a similar focus on the activities, awarenesses, and localized decisions that make up the texture of everyday life, while paying special attention to the political character of mundane decision making and the tactical sensibilities informing action by people in subordinate positions.[37] The basic intuition of this perspective has been stated succinctly by Michel de Certeau, who invokes the Sophists' discovery of rhetoric as the original attempt to theorize ordinary practice and who posits "styles of action" that each operate as a "way of walking" through a social terrain.[38]

An interest in the relationship between aesthetic and political qualities of action is even more evident in recent formulations of social dramas and social texts. Although it includes scrutiny of quotidian interactions, a resurgence of dramatistic analysis, particularly in anthropology, has highlighted the importance of major symbols and ceremonies as determinants of collective life.[39] The richness of this perspective is evident from Clifford Geertz's account of the aesthetic orientation of Balinese society, which illustrates how political power can issue from collective processes of composition and interpretation epitomized in social ceremonies.[40] The attempt to understand society as a text offers a related perspective, which is receiving extensive development in the work of Richard Harvey Brown.[41] From this perspective, society is maintained and modified by practices of composition. Because we act through discourses and according to discursive constraints, social understanding requires skilled interpretation of how we speak, write, and act accordingly. Brown's concept of "the political semiotics of selfhood" could serve as one definition of political style, and his work emphasizes the importance of recovering "literary" sensibilities for both social analysis and political judgment.[42]

If nothing else, these investigations of social texts, dramas, and practices have established that the conventional, modernist account of power is, at best, a partial explanation of important phenomena. Instead of defining power as the possession of individuals who efficiently employ force or control a coercive apparatus, these alternative accounts demonstrate how power is a property of social relationships constituted by symbolic acts and subject to changes in interpretation. S. R. F. Price has put the matter succinctly: "The 'efficient' is no less a construct than the 'dignified'; the 'dignified' no less an expression of power than the 'efficient.' "[43]

This perspective is hardly the common sense of political science, however. There have been a few attempts in Anglo-American political theory to recognize connections between polity, taste, and practical wisdom, but, although they cover a fairly broad ideological spectrum, they often are treated as idiosyncratic. Hannah Arendt's theory of the *vita activa* is an important attempt to restructure political inquiry by linking the success or failure of political affairs and the character of political institutions with the dynamics of personal conduct oriented toward the cultivation of appearances.[44] Michael Oakeshott's use of his distinction between technical and practical knowledge also provides a potential point of departure for the analysis of political style, as does the celebration of democratic political sensibility by other British writers such as Bernard Crick and Henry Fairlie.[45] More recently, Ronald Beiner has emphasized the relationship between taste and political intelligence,[46] and Peter Euben has emphasized the profound interrelationship between politics and tragic drama in both the classical polis and contemporary literature.[47]

The more influential political theory has come from the reconsideration of the relationship between art and politics conducted by the Frankfurt School, which has received new impetus from recent work by Terry Eagleton.[48] This approach explicitly attacks the idea of an apolitical aesthetic realm and argues for an art capable of political intervention. Yet even here, in work well disposed to challenge established assumptions about practical experience, a thoroughly modernist conception of aesthetic autonomy persists. The standards of judgment are derived from the fine arts and against the influence of popular arts such as advertising, and the argument ultimately concludes that art can contribute to emancipation only through an act of negation achieved by intensifying the autonomy of the artwork.[49] This claim relies on a radical separation of artistic production and political practice; consequently, critical theory cannot understand events that are simultaneously practical and productive.

In addition, several other research programs have demonstrated the role of style in quite varied locales of political decision making. The work of the Birmingham School in cultural studies, represented best by Dick Hebdige's study of the conjuncture of style and subculture, has stimulated considerable analysis of the political significance of stylistic decisions in popular culture (more precisely, in the relationships between hegemonic mass media and marketing enterprises and the many subcultures of consumption that constitute popular culture).[50] The study of political communication, particularly in the United States, has included a strong emphasis on the use of political symbols and often relies on the theoretical framework of dramatism. This work has identified the role of political language, imagery, and settings in determining both opportunities for individual success and constraints on collective decision making, particularly within established practices such as electoral campaigns.[51] Both of these programs, however, have become tied to a fascination with the power of the mass media, at the expense of appreciating either ordinary interpersonal experiences or carefully written texts that are not driven by mass communication practices.

Other research programs in American political studies also reveal both the significance of political style and the difficulties of incorporating it into a comprehensive account of political behavior. Presidential studies frequently identify how an awareness of rhetorical practices and aesthetic judgments is a constant in executive campaigns and governance, but the studies themselves have difficulty formulating these considerations as anything other than ad hoc descriptions of individual personalities.[52] The study of congressional politics also has included clear demonstrations of the importance, for example, of a "home style" to electoral relations, and of rules of appropriateness in committee deliberations.[53] Unfortunately, these studies have been limited by their close identification with specific institutional forums. Finally, public opinion research has demonstrated that the general public cares more about considerations of style than policy and more about general patterns of social identification than about individual personalities.[54] These are important findings, but they also are limited by their methodology, for the determination of specific stylistic preferences and functions would have to include close analysis of public texts and other social practices.

But every analysis is limited by its methodology, and by time and chance as well. The four essays in this volume have identified four master styles of political action, each style presented as an ideal type articulated through the critical vocabulary of rhetorical studies, along with some illustration of how it can be applied to contemporary phenomena. There is much more to be done, of course. I hope analysis in terms of these and other styles can guide the interpretation of specific events. Such interpretation would have to look for both general patterns and local modifications, and ought to consider how specific styles could be competing, complementing one another, or blending together. The full value of this approach will require identifying how these designs were imbricated with other forms of argument and assent and demonstrating their interaction with other structures of motivation and constraint. Any such list of methodological criteria can be daunting and particularly so when discussing matters of style, for stylistic commentary typically is incidental, condensed, more a form of showing than telling, and highly contextual. It could well be that we also need to identify how it is that people move in and out of aesthetic awareness: The key to political success might be knowing (however intuitively) when to be aesthetically sensitive and when to be relatively anesthetized, and knowing when to activate a political style and when to keep it under wraps. Perhaps stylistic commentary itself needs to be well timed, and perhaps its value will deteriorate rapidly if continued too long. Of course, there will be times when any stylistic commentary will be inadequate right from the start, because the events at hand are largely the result of other influences on the political process. Some of the time, however, it will provide the best means for understanding the actions, inhibitions, and pleasures of participation for those involved in important events.

My reading of the four texts has relied on a single critical vocabulary and primarily for the purpose of discriminating the separate styles rather than to develop a schema for their comparison. For example, I have noted how each style creates a hierarchy of various modes of communication, but I have not considered how these hierarchies might account for the affinities and reactivities between the various styles. In like manner, as I have focused on ethos, gesture, and other related concerns, I have neglected direct comparison along these lines. I believe that it could be crucial for the interpretation of specific events to consider these and other bases for compatibility or incompatibility among the styles, however. I also have scanted both philosophical and institutional complements of each style, as well as the explicitly argumentative designs that have been a preoccupation of rhetorical studies both traditionally and in the modern period, even though these factors certainly are important in many particular cases. In any case, I grant that my emphases could be extended further but perhaps also challenged as an approach to the texts and the styles which they mirror.

There is good reason to return to the texts that I have featured. Although these four texts do not circumscribe the full range of their objects, they each nonetheless are more than just another instance of the style at work. Each is not a political discourse per se, but a commentary on political discourse—an attempt to grasp the essence of what it portrays, whether to instruct a prince, record a dying culture, converse with a friend, or transmute life into art. Whatever its orientation, each is an exceptionally powerful condensation of a particular style of political practice. Each also reveals not only an array of techniques that are proven designs for the composition of power, but also the profound complexity, ambiguity, and contradiction in the political motives, experiences, and effects that are composed.

Rather than fuse each text with the interpretation I have provided, I would rather keep them open for additional reflection.

For example, Machiavelli's presentation of the realist style can lead to other deconstructive moments, each of which reveals another dimension of that style's appeal. By examining the affinity between the realist style and the imperial state, we reach the irony that the realist has a virtually unrestricted license for rationalizing imprudent acts by the powerful. By recognizing that this style easily acquires deep substantive development—whether in the doctrines of international relations or "the way we do business here," wherever "here" is—we reach the irony that Machiavelli's emphasis on innovation becomes a design for conservative politics. This problem has two related corollaries which already have some currency in political theory and the philosophy of history: First, as the realist style constitutes the world it would describe, it locks us into our lesser selves. In pointing out that ethical virtue is not necessary, the realist makes it less possible. Second, there might be a further implication of Blumenberg's argument about reoccupation, even if one rejects that model of historical change: Perhaps the realist style is a defective modernity. This last suggestion becomes more plausible when one considers again the barrenness of the world of *The Prince*. Once transposed into the topographical scene and an ethos of self-control, there is no pleasure in the little things. Although Machiavelli's evocation of the pleasure in sheer power could well be an aesthetic discovery, it comes at great cost.

The Emperor, particularly when placed in the context of Ethiopia's subsequent miseries, poses the irritating question of whether that court, for all of its corruption, and perhaps because of its corruption, was better than the more modern government that followed. This argument can be transposed to other realms as well. Rather than displacement of the public sphere or regression from governmental rationality to sovereign willfulness, perhaps courtliness provides a "realistic" vocabulary for understanding complex social experiences that persist despite the routinization of modern life. Although it appears foolish, perhaps it provides reassuring social forms while offering the possibility of some charismatic presence that would be a welcome disruption in a high modernist world. At the same time, Kapuściński's text also reveals other aspects of this style that are indeed dangerous. In the mass media, it nurtures a personal conception of power that disables practical reasoning regarding matters of policy, and in any particular setting it can become a virtually closed system that results in cult pathologies and is more susceptible to revolution than reform.

Cicero's letters present more aspects of republican identity than I could develop. One has to acknowledge that what Cicero presumed to be a great strength—his copiousness and multifacetedness—today could be a weakness. His many different capabilities—as lawyer, poet, translator, administrator, etc.—are so many vulnerabilities in a culture of experts. The letters reveal another problem with the republican style as well, which is that it exhausts its practitioners. Cicero's occasional pining for an academic retreat from public affairs rightly invites skepticism, but it also is a symptom of the fatigue of living a largely public life. Left to itself, without involvement in other styles and institutions, the republican life is likely to end in solitude, for removal from public life is at once the greatest punishment and the only opportunity for rest, the consequence of failure and success alike. Finally, we have to consider the ultimate irony, which is that the republican style falters precisely because it cannot be communicated as widely and as persuasively as the others. For all of Cicero's many delights in the art of politics as he knew it, it remained an insiders' game. The enjoyments of republican politics all come from participation, and any attempt to broaden its appeal can seem like an empty promise.

It is a truism of Kafka scholarship that his texts defy comprehensive interpretation. Certainly there is more that could be said about his images of bureaucratic order. Perhaps the first correction to my analysis would be to restore more fully the context of fatality. The bureaucratic style can induce cooperation because it allows tinkering with procedural details while always deferring more systemic change. Furthermore, it might well be that all local choices are balanced out in the long run in accord with the principle of maintaining and extending the system. Kafka's genius stems in part from his unflinching conjunction of both local comedy and cosmic fatality, the possibility of freedom and the absolute indifference of nature to anything human. The bureaucratic style is at once the most familiar to us moderns, and the most dangerous, as it aligns itself with those forms of rationality that make no allowance whatsoever for other values. In this case, as with each of the others, there are no easy choices.

Whatever their different objects, these texts also provide a common lesson. They illustrate how living with power is inevitable, and even desirable, but always limiting. There is no escape from power, for it permeates all interactions, but there is no salvation through power, for power is always already fragmented. Just as there is no one style, there is no one form of power. Moreover, politics is not just a way of acting in the world, but also a way a thinking about the world, and one that leads not to certainty but rather to indeterminacy, perplexity, and anxiety. Hence, power is always incomplete, self-frustrating, and the study of power is a study both of the richness of ordinary experiences and the limitations of extraordinary achievements. The full extension of this line of argument is simple: To the extent that the ubiquitous human activity of politics is an art, there is no one way of being human.

Thus, we come full circle, returning to the Sophists' discovery that human nature is variable because artificial, yet the only standard available for understanding political conduct. No wonder they were preoccupied with style. I hope the preceding chapters have been true to this preoccupation. By understanding how matters of style are crucial to the practice of politics, we discover not sham, but design, not decoration, but a world of meaning.

195

notes

Chapter One: Introduction

1. Thomas Cole, *The Origins of Rhetoric in Ancient Greece* (Baltimore: Johns Hopkins University Press, 1991); George A. Kennedy, *The Art of Persuasion in Greece* (Princeton: Princeton University Press, 1963), *The Art of Rhetoric in the Roman World, 300* B.C.– A.D. *300* (Princeton: Princeton University Press, 1972), *Classical Rhetoric and Its Christian and Secular Tradition from Ancient to Modern Times* (Chapel Hill: University of North Carolina Press, 1980), *Greek Rhetoric under Christian Emperors* (Princeton: Princeton University Press, 1983); James J. Murphy, *Rhetoric in the Middle Ages: A History of Rhetorical Theory from St. Augustine to the Renaissance* (Berkeley: University of California Press, 1974) and *Renaissance Eloquence: Studies in the Theory and Practice of Renaissance Rhetoric,* edited by Murphy (Berkeley: University of California Press, 1983); Thomas M. Conley, *Rhetoric in the European Tradition* (New York: Longman Publishing, 1990); Samuel Ijsseling, *Rhetoric and Philosophy in Conflict: An Historical Survey* (The Hague: Martinus Nijhoff, 1976); Paul Oskar Kristeller, "Philosophy and Rhetoric from Antiquity to the Renaissance," in *Renaissance Thought and Its Sources,* edited by Michael Mooney (New York: Columbia University Press, 1979), pp. 211–59; Tzvetan Todorov, "The Splendor and Misery of Rhetoric" and "The End of Rhetoric," in *Theories of the Symbol,* translated by Catherine Porter (Ithaca: Cornell University Press, 1982), pp. 61–83 and 84–110; Roland Barthes, "The Old Rhetoric: an aide-mémoire," in *The Semiotic Challenge,* translated by Richard Howard (New York: Wang and Hill, 1988), pp. 3–94; John Poulakos, "Toward a Sophistic Definition of Rhetoric," *Philosophy and Rhetoric* 16 (1983): 35–48; Brian Vickers, *In Defense of Rhetoric* (Oxford: Clarendon Press, 1988) and "Rhetorical and Anti-Rhetorical Tropes: On Writing the History of *elocutio,*" *Comparative Criticism* 3 (1981): 105–32; W. Ross Winterowd, "The Purification of Literature and Rhetoric," *College English* 49 (1987): 257–73.

2. For example, "Mind, knowledge, truth; action, power, conviction: *elocutio* provided the passage from potentiality to realization, via the control of language and the force of feeling. If *elocutio* was the hinge around which the whole of Renaissance moral

and civic philosophy turned, then it can only be fully understood by reference to life" (Vickers, "Rhetorical and Anti-Rhetorical Tropes," p. 129).

3. For the record, although the postmodern necessarily perpetuates some elements of modernity, I do not subscribe to the belief "that modernity is for us an unsurpassable horizon in a cognitive, aesthetic and moral-political sense," or to its corollary "that the critique of the modern, inasmuch as it knows its own parameters, can only aim at expanding the interior space of modernity, not at surpassing it" (Albrecht Wellmer, *The Persistence of Modernity: Essays on Aesthetics, Ethics, and Postmodernism,* translated by David Midgley [Cambridge: MIT Press, 1991], p. xii). This belief in modernity's endlessness is an important article of faith for many of those defending modernism. For the most part, it seems that the issue is more a matter of assertion than argument and more an expression of attitude than a choice of analytical tools. I see no reason to put the more general question ahead of more specific ventures, such as my own, that are willing to set out for that horizon.

4. Stuart Ewen, *All Consuming Images: The Politics of Style in Contemporary Culture* (New York: Basic Books, 1988), pp. 2–3.

5. This modern account is not exclusively modern, of course. The distinction between style and content is stated matter-of-factly in Aristotle's *Rhetoric* (1403b.15). Perhaps modernity has accounted for style by amplifying a particular discourse on style. It is not the only discourse available, however; one alternative—the language of decorum—also is available in the *Rhetoric.* Other discourses on style can be found in the arts, the design sciences, popular culture, and postmodern theory. Ewen's *All Consuming Images* can be read as an attempt to capture the contemporary popular discourse(s) on style and also as a synopsis of modernist ideas of style. For criticism within analytical philosophy of the style-substance distinction, see Nelson Goodman, "The Status of Style," *Critical Inquiry* 1 (1975): 799–811.

6. William Strunk and E. B. White, *The Elements of Style,* 3d ed. (New York: Macmillan, 1979); Joseph M. Williams, *Style* (Chicago: University of Chicago Press, 1990; textbook, 3d ed: Glenview, IL: Scott, Foresman, 1989); "Style," *Princeton Encyclopedia of Poetry and Poetics,* enlarged ed. (Princeton: Princeton University Press, 1974).

7. The essays in Berel Lang, ed., *The Concept of Style,* revised and expanded ed. (Ithaca: Cornell University Press, 1987), identify common elements of style while looking toward, but not reaching, "those attempts to establish a role for style that refer it well beyond the artworld or even the conventional domain of rhetoric, the two sources that have historically provided the objects of stylistic analysis" (p. 16).

8. For example, see Edward P. J. Corbett, *Classical Rhetoric for the Modern Student,* 3d ed. (New York: Oxford University Press, 1990), and Vickers, *In Defense of Rhetoric.* There are recent exceptions, however. Thomas Farrell claims that a strong conception of praxis is available to rhetorical theory if we define rhetoric less as a practical activity and more as a paradoxical activity that results from a dialectical tension between its ethical and aesthetic norms ("Rhetorical Resemblance: Paradoxes of a Practical Art," *Quarterly Journal of Speech* 72 [1986]: 1–19); see also, *Norms of Rhetorical Culture* (New Haven: Yale University Press, 1993). For a related argument regarding the tension between "cognitive" and "performative" conceptions of practical wisdom, see my essay, "Prudence/Performance," *Rhetoric Society Quarterly* 21 (1991): 26–35. Michael Leff argues that the conventional schism between argument and style inhibits full consideration

198

of the rhetorical text as a mode of action, and he suggests that the concept of decorum could provide a bridge between the two modes ("The Habitation of Rhetoric," *Argument and Critical Practices: Proceedings of the Fifth SCA/AFA Conference on Argumentation,* edited by Joseph Wenzel [Annandale, VA: Speech Communication Association, 1987]). See also Thomas Rosteck and Michael Leff, "Piety, Propriety, and Perspective: An Interpretation and Application of Key Terms in Kenneth Burke's *Permanence and Change,"* *Western Journal of Speech Communication* 53 (1989): 327–341. Edwin Black provides a number of critical studies that explore the relationship between style, ideology, and motivation; see, for example, *Rhetorical Questions: Studies of Public Discourse* (Chicago: University of Chicago Press, 1992). Karlyn Kohrs Campbell identifies a "feminine style" in women's public address: *Man Cannot Speak for Her: A Critical Study of Early Feminist Rhetoric,* vol. 1 (New York: Praeger, 1989). See also Bonnie J. Dow and Mari Boor Tonn, "'Feminine Style' and Political Judgment in the Rhetoric of Ann Richards," *Quarterly Journal of Speech* 79 (1993): 286–302. John S. Nelson and Allan Megill have remarked that "part of the revival of rhetoric results from its reconnection with poetics" ("Rhetoric of Inquiry: Projects and Prospects," *Quarterly Journal of Speech* 72 [1986]: 32). This would not have surprised Herbert A. Wichelns, who defined rhetoric as the art "at the boundaries of politics and literature" ("The Literary Criticism of Oratory," in *Studies in Rhetoric and Public Speaking in Honor of James Albert Winans,* edited by A. M. Drummond, pp. 181–216 [New York: Russell & Russell, 1925]).

9. Allan Megill, "What Does the Term 'Postmodern' Mean?" *Annals of Scholarship* 6 (1989): 131. In this context, several discourses on style compete without any one of them serving as an all-encompassing rule. "Style" still can refer to the aesthetic dimension of avowedly artistic products. More commonly, however, it also can refer to a social code—for example, "the L.A. style"—or to a political practice—for example, "the Chicago style." For an exemplary study of how social groups create political meaning through stylistic invention, see Dick Hebdige, *Subculture: The Meaning of Style* (New York: Methuen, 1979).

10. For example, Ewen warns of the political dangers for a culture that increasingly substitutes style for substance (*All Consuming Images,* pp. 259ff.). This association of political aesthetics with fascism has become a commonplace of left-wing cultural analysis. As far as I can tell, the common source is Walter Benjamin's "The Work of Art in an Age of Mechanical Reproduction," *Illuminations,* edited by Hannah Arendt, translated by Harry Zohn (New York: Schocken Books, 1968). For other examples, see also Jean Baudrillard, *For a Critique of the Political Economy of the Sign,* translated by Charles Levin (St. Louis: Telos Press, 1981); Arthur Kroker and David Cook, *The Postmodern Scene: Excremental Culture and Hyper-Aesthetics* (New York: St. Martin's Press, 1986).

11. Victoria Kahn, *Rhetoric, Prudence, and Skepticism in the Renaissance* (Ithaca: Cornell University Press, 1985), p. 24; see also p. 190: "In fact, the invention of a political science *depends* on the exclusion of the humanist notion of rhetoric and the consequent redefinition of aesthetic experience as the most apolitical (i.e., disinterested) of experiences." Timothy Engstrom's account of the "politics of separation" in the history of philosophy neatly captures the process Kahn is describing: see his "Philosophy's Anxiety of Rhetoric: Contemporary Revisions of a Politics of Separation," *Rhetorica* 7 (1989): 209–238. For the related argument in ethics, see Alasdair MacIntyre, *After Virtue: A Study in Moral Theory,* 2d ed., (Notre Dame, IN: University of Notre Dame Press, 1984).

12. Josef Chytry, *The Aesthetic State: A Quest in Modern German Thought* (Berkeley: University of California Press, 1989). Likewise, the Frankfurt School attempt to rejoin art and politics can be seen as both a courageous effort to grapple with a powerful and dangerous separation between aesthetics and politics that already characterizes modern cultural production—especially in the arts—and as the rather hidebound application of modern categories of analysis that are never likely to provide a strong account of practices that are simultaneously practical and productive, artistic and political. For an excellent critique of Habermas's theory of communication from this perspective, see John Durham Peters, "Distrust of Representation: Habermas on the Public Sphere," *Media, Culture and Society* 15 (1993): 541–71.

13. Dorothy Ross, *The Origins of American Social Science* (Cambridge: Cambridge University Press, 1991); Edward A. Purcell, Jr., *The Crisis of Democratic Theory: Scientific Naturalism and the Problem of Value* (Lexington: The University Press of Kentucky, 1973); David M. Ricci, *The Tragedy of Political Science: Politics, Scholarship, and Democracy* (New Haven: Yale University Press, 1984); John G. Gunnell, *Between Philosophy and Politics: The Alienation of Political Theory* (Amherst: University of Massachusetts Press, 1986); Peter Novick, *That Noble Dream: The "Objectivity Question" and the American Historical Profession* (Cambridge: University of Cambridge Press, 1988); Thomas Haskell, *The Emergence of Professional Social Science: The American Social Science Association and the Nineteenth-Century Crisis of Authority* (Urbana: University of Illinois Press, 1977); Burton J. Bledstein, *The Culture of Professionalism: The Middle Class and the Development of Higher Education in America* (New York: W. W. Norton, 1976).

14. Fredric Jameson, "Interview," *Diacritics* 12 (1982): 75.

Chapter Two: Machiavelli's Realist Style

1. Lord Acton, "Introduction" to L. A. Burd, *Il Principe* (Oxford: Clarendon, 1891), p. xl; Max Lerner, "Introduction" to *The Prince and the Discourses* (New York: Modern Library, 1950), p. xlii; Felix Raab, *The English Face of Machiavelli: A Changing Interpretation, 1500–1700* (London: Routledge, 1964), p. 1. Even those maintaining their scholarly circumspection admit to "the beginning of a new stage—one might say, of the modern stage—in the development of political thought" (Felix Gilbert, *Machiavelli and Guicciardini: Politics and History in Sixteenth Century Florence* [Princeton: Princeton University Press, 1965], p. 153).

2. John H. Geerken, "Machiavelli Studies Since 1969," *Journal of the History of Ideas* 37 (1976): 351. For other review articles, see Eric W. Cochrane, "Machiavelli: 1940–1960," *Journal of Modern History* 33 (1961): 113–36; Felix Gilbert, "Machiavelli in Modern Historical Scholarship," *Italian Quarterly* 14 (1970): 9–26; Richard C. Clark, "Machiavelli: Bibliographical Spectrum," *Review of National Literatures* 1 (1970): 93–135. The contrast between the simplicity of the text and the welter of interpretations animates reviews at least since Burd (*Il Principe*, p. 12). Isaiah Berlin addresses the hermeneutical question extensively in his superb essay, "The Originality of Machiavelli," in *Studies on Machiavelli*, edited by Myron P. Gilmore, pp. 149–206 (Florence: G. C. Sansoni, 1972). For a recent, highly accessible account, see Athanasios Moulakas, "Which Machiavelli?" *Perspectives on Political Science* 22 (1993): 84–89.

3. Nor does the work suffer from the recurring claim that it was a ruse. For the most recent presentation of this argument, written apparently without regard to its his-

tory, see Mary Dietz, "Trapping the Prince: Machiavelli and the Politics of Deception," *American Political Science Review* 80 (1986): 779–99, and the subsequent discussion in volume 81: 1277–88. Even if it were true, of course, this argument falls into the intentional fallacy.

4. The most influential statement of this position has been by Felix Gilbert, "The Humanist Concept of the Prince and *The Prince* of Machiavelli," *Journal of Modern History* 11 (1939): 449–83.

5. As Anthony Parel announced, Machiavelli "brought to the field of political enquiry the scientific spirit of detachment, which like a steel frame holds together his doctrines and gives them durability" (Anthony Parel, ed., *The Political Calculus: Essays on Machiavelli's Philosophy* [Toronto: University of Toronto Press, 1972], p. 3). Parel subsequently has developed a different understanding of Machiavelli, which is presented in *The Machiavellian Cosmos* (New Haven: Yale University Press, 1992). I have used the earlier quote because it expresses perfectly an attitude that was representative of its time and continues to prevail. See the reviews in Cochrane, "Machiavelli," pp. 119ff., and Clark, "Machiavelli," pp. 103ff. Influential statements have included Herbert Butterfield, *The Statecraft of Machiavelli* (London: Bell, 1940), and Ernst Cassirer, *The Myth of the State* (New Haven: Yale University Press, 1946).

6. For extended development of this perspective, with emphasis on the role of status in discourse theory, see Robert Hariman, "Status, Marginality, and Rhetorical Theory," *Quarterly Journal of Speech* 72 (1986): 38–54. For another synopsis of this trope's operation within the tradition of rhetoric, see Roger Moss, The Case *for* Sophistry," in *Rhetoric Revalued,* edited by Brian Vickers, pp. 206–24 (Binghamton: State University of New York Press, 1982).

7. For reviews of Renaissance rhetoric, see Nancy Struever, *The Language of History in the Renaissance: Rhetoric and Historical Consciousness in Florentine Humanism* (Princeton: Princeton University Press, 1970); Jerrold Seigal, *Rhetoric and Philosophy in Renaissance Humanism* (Princeton: Princeton University Press, 1968); James J. Murphy, ed., *Renaissance Eloquence* (Berkeley: University of California Press, 1983); Brian Vickers, "On the Practicalities of Renaissance Rhetoric," in *Rhetoric Revalued,* pp. 133–42; Hanna H. Gray, "Renaissance Humanism: The Pursuit of Eloquence," *Journal of the History of Ideas* 24 (1963): 497–514. For a sense of counterpoint, see the debate between Seigel and Hans Baron in *Past and Present,* vols. 34 and 36. For a defense of genre criticism, see Quentin Skinner, "Some Problems in the Analysis of Political Thought and Action," *Political Theory* 2 (1974): 277–303. Skinner illustrates his approach in "Sir Thomas More's *Utopia* and the Language of Renaissance Humanism," in *The Languages of Political Theory in Early Modern Europe,* edited by Anthony Pagden, pp. 123–57 (Cambridge: Cambridge University Press, 1987). My criticism goes beyond Skinner's focus on the specific period of composition to identify how Machiavelli's text provides a model for composing political experience that can be (and has been) imitated in widely differing contexts. This approach has some similarities with J. G. A. Pocock's studies of the continuing influence and alteration of political discourses. He summarizes the pertinent methodological assumptions in "Custom & Grace, Form & Matter: An approach to Machiavelli's Concept of Innovation," in *Machiavelli and the Nature of Political Thought,* edited by Martin Fleisher, pp. 153–55 (New York: Atheneum, 1972). According to this model of interpretation, Machiavelli's innovation is achieved by reworking the received language of political thought;

the effects of his craftwork exceed his intentions; his text has shaped its history of interpretation; it also can have had many other and diverse effects; analysis should establish
a possible relationship between his text and the literary context of his time and demonstrate actual usage of his technique subsequently. There are many differences between
Pocock's project and my own, of course. For one, I don't pretend to the achievement of
*The Machiavellian Moment: Florentine Political Thought and the Atlantic Republican Tra-
dition* (Princeton: Princeton University Press, 1975). There are substantive disagreements
as well; most pertinent is that I see a realist where he sees a republican. I discuss the
relationship between these positions at the close of this essay. Briefly, there is no question that Machiavelli was a dedicated civic republican and that he was enormously important to the development of that strain of political thought in Britain. He also was the
author of modern political realism, however, and whatever the possibilities for their con-
gruence in particular persons or periods, today realism and republicanism operate often
as distinct political styles that often are competing for influence and ultimately are
incompatible.

8. Lester K. Born, "Introduction" to Desiderius Erasmus, *The Education of a Christian Prince,* edited by Lester K. Born (New York: W. W. Norton, 1968), p. 45.

9. Born, "Introduction," p. 125. M. L. W. Laistner's description of the genre carries
the same implication: "They contrast the good and the bad ruler; in enumerating the
virtues that make up the good ruler and the duties that devolve upon him, if he is to
remain a just king, they reproduce examples from the Bible and citations from earlier
writers of authority" (*Thought and Letters in Western Europe:* A.D. *500 to 900,* rev. ed.
[Ithaca: Cornell University Press, 1957], p. 317).

10. The first two systematic accounts of *The Prince's* relationship to this genre
appeared simultaneously in 1938 and 1939. Allan Gilbert provided a comprehensive comparison of the text in respect to many similar works that appeared before and after 1513.
He conceived of the genre as relatively uniform across historical time, attempted to establish only a probable context for reading rather than demonstrate direct influence on
Machiavelli's composition, and argued that *The Prince* so essentially conforms to the
genre that it remains the "best representative" of the type. By contrast, Felix Gilbert's
analysis emphasized the changes occurring within the literature during the Renaissance to
demonstrate both that the humanists had direct influence on Machiavelli and that he consciously repudiated the fundamental tenet of both medieval and Renaissance writers that
the virtues were necessary for political success. Despite these differences, they were
remarkably uniform in their approaches to defining the genre and Machiavelli's placement
within it. See Allan H. Gilbert, *Machiavelli's Prince and Its Forerunners* (Durham: Duke
University Press, 1938), p. 232; F. Gilbert, "The Humanist Concept of the Prince."

11. This project begins with F. Gilbert's essay, while Quentin Skinner's analysis
has set the standard. Skinner follows the common tendencies of the essays by A. Gilbert
and F. Gilbert while also refining the latter's argument that Machiavelli was influenced by
civic humanism. Skinner emphasizes the development from early quattrocento ideas of
living for glory while struggling against *fortuna* by means of *virtu,* which is developed via
the right education, to the later quattrocento ideas that security is the primary purpose of
government and that the leader's virtue will of necessity be different and more heroic
than the ordinary citizen's. He also defined Machiavelli's innovation against the genre,
paying special attention to the two references in *The Prince* to other writers. See Quentin

Skinner, *The Foundations of Modern Political Thought*, 2 vols. (Cambridge: Cambridge University Press, 1978), I:118–22 and I:123–28. Marcia L. Colish presents an interesting case for Machiavelli's dependency on the culture of humanism in her thoughtful article, "Cicero's *De Officiis* and Machiavelli's *Prince*," *Sixteenth Century Journal* 9 (1978): 81–93. For earlier review of the question of his relationship with humanism, see Cochrane, "Machiavelli," pp. 126ff. A useful summary of Machiavelli's break with the ethical precepts of Ciceronian humanism is provided in the introductory essay in Quentin Skinner and Russell Price, eds., *The Prince* (Cambridge: Cambridge University Press, 1988), p. xv ff.

12. F. Gilbert, *Machiavelli and Guicciardini*, p. 154; Skinner, *Foundations*, I:129 and I:131–38.

13. *The Prince*, translated by Luigi Ricci, from Max Lerner, ed., *The Prince and the Discourses*, p. 56. Subsequent quotations are from this edition unless otherwise noted and are cited in the text with parenthetical page references.

14. J. H. Hexter, "*Il Principe* and *Lo Stato*," *Studies in the Renaissance* 4 (1957): 113–38; "Persistently and dominantly he had in mind political command over men" (p. 126). Revised essay printed in J. H. Hexter, *The Vision of Politics on the Eve of the Reformation: More, Machiavelli, Seyssel* (New York: Basic Books, 1973), pp. 150–78.

15. Machiavelli's epistemic pretensions also might be less responsible than those of his genre, for the *speculum* metaphor could carry a profound understanding of the process by which we negotiate between the real, the apparent, and the ideal; see Marianne Shapiro, "Mirror and Portrait: The Structure of *Il libro del Cortegiano*," *Journal of Medieval and Renaissance Studies* 5 (1975): 41–44.

16. Aristotle, *Rhetoric* 1404b.18, translated by W. Rhys Roberts (New York: Modern Library, 1954).

17. Baldesar Castiglione, *The Book of the Courtier*, translated by George Bull (Harmondsworth: Penguin, 1976), pp. 69–70.

18. Struever provides this appraisal of the role of decorum in the Renaissance humanists' appropriation of classical sensibilities: "Of all the rhetorical canons, the principle of decorum is probably the most crucial, since it predicates the synthesis of the other criteria of expression. . . . Since the Humanists' critical apparatus was rhetorical analysis, the concept of decorum became the framework of their attempts to establish internal coherence in their texts" (*The Language of History*, pp. 67–68). Furthermore, in a world circumscribed by texts, the means of coherence within texts become the means for finding coherence in the world; see Cicero, *Orator* 71.

19. See Colish, "Cicero's *De Officiis* and Machiavelli's *Prince*," and Cochrane, "Machiavelli," pp. 126ff.

20. Allan Gilbert, ed. and trans., *The Letters of Machiavelli* (Chicago: University of Chicago Press, 1961), no. 137, pp. 139–44. For a recent example of the conventional use of the letter:

203

> E in quest' ultima immagine non è difficile riconoscere il motivo reso celebre dal Machiavelli nella famosa lettera a Francesco Vettori del 10 dicembre 1513, che ha fissato in termini indimenticabili il concetto umanistica della cultura come società ideale che si struttura nella comunicazione, nel linguaggio, nel discorso. (Eugenio Garin, "Retorica e 'Studia humanitatis' nella cultura del Quattrocento," in Vickers, *Rhetoric Revalued*, p. 226)

Colish also uses it to sound the tones of Renaissance humanism. Her last paragraph begins:

> One would like to think that, as evening fell and Machiavelli shook the dust and grime from his clothes, . . . when he put on his curial robes and retired to commune with the ancients . . . a copy of *De officiis* [was] at hand. ("Cicero's *De Officiis*," p. 93)

Perhaps contemporary scholars are wrapping Machiavelli in classical textuality to restrain his power.

21. Burd, *Il Principe*, p. 171, and frequently noted by others as well.

22. Isocrates, *Nicocles* 6–7, translated by George Norlin, *Isocrates I*, Loeb Classical Library (Cambridge: Harvard University Press, 1926). I have substituted "humanity" for "man."

23. For another suggestion of this theme, see Thomas M. Greene, "The End of Discourse in Machiavelli's 'Prince,'" *Yale French Studies* 67 (1984), and reprinted in Patricia Parker and David Quint, eds., *Literary Theory/Renaissance Texts* (Baltimore: Johns Hopkins University Press, 1986), pp. 63–77. "The dedicatory epistle repudiates rhetoric; the clipped opening chapter repudiates the graces of humanist elegance; from the beginning, the book refuses to be literature, . . . *The Prince* signals its willed estrangement from the cultural processes it claims to analyze. . . . Machiavelli's authorial stance as his book opens seems to reject that *textual* conclusiveness and to promise only whatever *analytic* conclusiveness can be wrung from the perennially continuous" (p. 64). Despite the parallel assertions, Greene's study differs from mine at several important points: He focuses on the text's designs for closure, and without reference to the genre, ignores the significance of the attack for political thought, and argues that Machiavelli successfully restores the received textuality in the last chapter. This last point requires a brief rejoinder. First, Greene's reading of the last chapter is completely speculative. Second, to the extent that this is a matter of logic, once the text's double movement between asserting and denying its authority has begun, no instance of assertion can stop entirely the contrary denial; by the end of the Dedication the damage has been done. Third, given the explicitly hortative purpose of the last chapter, the recourse to a more explicit textuality can be explained more simply as Machiavelli's use of the conventional means for moving his audience to action; furthermore, the relationship between writer and text remains instrumental, for textual resources are appropriated to achieve the end of persuading others rather than to reflect upon the character of one's own text. Finally, the last chapter usually has been regarded as both a failed attempt at persuasion and a stylistic aberration; either response strengthens the idea that Machiavelli's previous designs against discourse are stronger than the final exhortation. For yet another similar observation, see Timothy J. Reiss, *The Discourse of Modernism* (Ithaca: Cornell University Press, 1982): "That dedications are a commonplace may well be, but what is important here is that the text is not so much a meditation (though it is also that) as a value in its own right: The system now seems to replace what it ostensibly relates. With Machiavelli we are already passing into a new class of textuality" (p. 112). Finally, for an argument that the text is validated primarily not by reference to events but by its own discursive structure, see Michael McCanles, *The Discourse of Il Principe* (Malibu: Undena Publications, 1983).

24. For further discussion of the strategy, see Chaim Perelman and L. Olbrechts-Tyteca, *The New Rhetoric: A Treatise on Argumentation*, translated by John Wilkinson

and Purcell Weaver (Notre Dame: University of Notre Dame Press, 1969), pp. 450–59. Note also Hans Blumenberg's comment regarding Hobbes:

> The example of Hobbes shows that in the modern age anti-rhetoric has become one of the most important expedients of rhetorical art, by means of which to lay claim to the rigor or [*sic*] realism, which alone promises to be a match for the seriousness of man's position (in this case, his position in his "state of nature"). ("An Anthropological Approach to the Contemporary Significance of Rhetoric," in *After Philosophy: End or Transformation?* edited by Kenneth Baynes, James Bohman, and Thomas McCarthy [Cambridge: Harvard University Press, 1987], p. 454)

For further discussion of Hobbes's use of rhetoric against its tradition, see Victoria Kahn, *Rhetoric, Prudence, and Skepticism in the Renaissance* (Ithaca: Cornell University Press, 1985). There are other examples as well of the change that is being charted here, such as the campaign of the Royal Society against elaborate speech. In the words of Thomas Sprat: "Who can behold, without indignation, how many mists and uncertainties, these specious Tropes and Figures have brought to our Knowledge? . . . the only Remedy, that can be found for this extravagance: . . . has been, a constant Resolution, to reject all the amplifications, digressions, and swellings of style." See *History of the Royal Society* (1667), facsimile edition, edited by Jackson I. Cope and Harold Whitmore Jones (St. Louis: Washington University Press, 1958). For Descartes's use of the maneuver, see Gerald L. Bruns, "A Grammarian's Guide to the *Discourse on Method*," in his *Inventions: Writing, Textuality, and Understanding in Literary History* (New Haven: Yale University Press, 1982). For a succinct comparison of Machiavelli and Descartes as authors of modernity, see Eugene Garver, *Machiavelli and the History of Prudence* (Madison: University of Wisconsin Press, 1987), pp. 3–5. For discussion of how Kant, Locke, and Shelley relied on the denigration of rhetoric to compose modern philosophy and modern poetics, see Hariman, "Status, Marginality, and Rhetorical Theory," pp. 40–44. For more general discussion of the Enlightenment and Romantic displacements of rhetoric, see John Bender and David E. Wellbery, *The Ends of Rhetoric: History, Theory, Practice* (Stanford: Stanford University Press, 1990), pp. 3–39. My claim is not that Machiavelli was more original than similar early modern denigrators of rhetoric, only that he used that attitude to craft an influential style for the composition of political experience, which in turn exemplifies how modernity was invented in part through a revaluation of the arts of language, beginning with a subordination of rhetoric.

25. Isocrates, *Antidosis* 70. Translated by George Norlin, *Isocrates II*, Loeb Classical Library (Cambridge: Harvard University Press, 1929).

26. Isocrates, *Nicocles* 10.

27. Struever, *The Language of History*, p. 63.

28. Delio Cantimori, "Rhetoric and Politics in Italian Humanism," *Journal of the Warburg and Courtauld Institutes* 1 (1937–38): 97ff.

29. Both F. Gilbert and Skinner stress the extent and importance of recognizing Machiavelli's continuity with the genre: "The Humanist Concept," pp. 451–52; *Foundations*, I:129. F. Gilbert's subsequent analysis of how Machiavelli's point of view "left its mark on the structure of *The prince*" ("The Humanist Concept," p. 477) established the now-standard reading of chapters 15–19 as refutative.

30. Neal Wood, "Machiavelli's Concept of *Virtù* Reconsidered," *Political Studies* 15 (1967): 159–72. I. Hannaford provides a critical rejoinder: "Machiavelli's Concept of *Virtù* in *The Prince* and *The Discourses* Reconsidered," *Political Studies* 20 (1972): 185–89.

31. Skinner, *Foundations*, I:122.

32. A. Gilbert, *Machiavelli's Prince*, p. 5.

33. Machiavelli quotes Tacitus (in chapter 13) and Livy (in chapter 26) without naming them, and, as Burd, Allan Gilbert, and others have documented, the work reflects the allusiveness characteristic of its educated author and his milieu. But, of course, other writers were allusive as well, and some *specula* were written without frequent citation of authorities. There are two key determinations guiding this analysis of Machiavelli's text. First, the use of another author's name usually is meaningful semiotically and rhetorically: the name operates as a sign of authorship that in turn constitutes at once a higher appeal to argumentative authority and a more limiting definition of the text's relationship to other texts and to the world. Second, the presence or absence of such signs can be determined to be significant only in respect to specific considerations of situation and strategy pertinent to that text. Rather than applying a universal linguistic rule, we need to determine in specific cases how the presence or absence of these signs functions, along with other textual dynamics, to create characteristic forms of consciousness. In this manner we can determine both patterns of usage, as with the genre, and moments of radical change, as with *The Prince*.

34. "Great parts of the *Discourses* are simply straight comments on succeeding chapters of Livy. In his other works he pursued traditional patterns still more slavishly" (F. Gilbert, *Machiavelli and Guicciardini*, p. 164).

35. I provide a third example, the English translation "with some marginal animadversions noting and taxing his errors" by Edward Dascres in 1640, in an earlier version of this essay, "Composing Modernity in Machiavelli's *Prince*," *Journal of the History of Ideas* 50 (1989): 3–29; reprinted in *Renaissance Essays II*, edited by William J. Connell, Library of the History of Ideas, X (Rochester, NY: University of Rochester Press, 1993).

36. Born, "Introduction," p. 29.

37. Ibid., p. 30.

38. Erasmus, *Education of a Christian Prince*, p. 200.

39. Augustini Niphi, *De regnandi peritia*, 1523.

40. A. Gilbert, *Machiavelli's Prince*, p. 23. The old debate about the two names for Machiavelli's work—*Il Principe* and *De principatibus*—covers the same ground Nifo is plowing. See, for examples, A. Gilbert, *Machiavelli's Prince*, pp. 8f., Burd, *Il Principe*, pp. 175–76.

41. F. Gilbert, "The Humanist Concept," pp. 457, 468.

42. Ibid., pp. 469 and 470.

43. F. Gilbert: "The dominating idea . . . is an appeal to recognize the crucial importance of force in politics" (*Machiavelli and Guicciardini*, p. 154). Skinner: Machiavelli denounces the other writers "for failing to emphasise the significance of sheer power in political life" (*Foundations*, I:129).

44. For one example of how "power" is a metaphysical term in modern politics: "The struggle for power is universal in time and space and is an undeniable fact of expe-

rience" (Hans Morgenthau, *Politics Among Nations,* 1st ed. [New York: Alfred A. Knopf, 1948], p. 17). For critique and discussion of the realists' contradictory stance of denigrating abstractions while relying on "power," see Joel H. Rosenthal, *Righteous Realists: Political Realism, Responsible Power, and American Culture in the Nuclear Age* (Baton Rouge: Louisiana State University Press, 1991), pp. 37ff. Rosenthal's nuanced discussion of the first generation of the realist school is an excellent study in realism as it was a substantive doctrine developed by sophisticated thinkers in a particular historical period. Their work obviously is richer than the outline of the realist style that I offer here, but nonetheless it also conforms to major characteristics of that style and reveals how realism need not be, but is disposed to be, congruent with authoritarian politics and an imperial state.

45. Friedrich Meinecke, *Machiavellianism: The Doctrine of Raison d'État and Its Place in Modern History,* translated by Douglas Scott (New Haven: Yale University Press, 1957). Note that Machiavelli is not describing the modern state; he is authoring a manner of speaking that became uniquely capable of fostering its development (or, more precisely, development of a particular conception of the state, and one that competes with other conceptions of it, for example, as a legal institution). See J. H. Hexter, "*Il principe* and *lo stato,*" especially pp. 126–30; also, Rabb, *The English Face of Machiavelli,* p. 256: "The evidence indicates that there was a consciousness of *statecraft* before there was a consciousness of the *state.*"

46. Perhaps this is the point to discuss the relationship between the doctrine of political realism and the persuasive repertoire of the realist style. Although there is a great deal of overlap, I have several, admittedly provisional, reasons for distinguishing them. Political realism refers to a specific set of propositions oriented much of the time toward foreign affairs. This doctrine generally includes assertions such as that human nature is self-interested and that anarchy prevails between nations, and usually it is applied to manifest and large-scale political problems. Although these assertions are easily composed within the realist style, it also can operate in respect to any subject, in any locale, and without attention to the substantive assertions about politics accumulated in international studies. Political realism also has acquired a particular intellectual history, especially as it has become articulated as the basis for the academic discipline of International Relations, and as realism has become the property of this discipline, it has acquired additional nuances and constraints. For the classic statement of the realist paradigm within the discipline, see Morgenthau, *Politics Among Nations.* He is credited as the founder of the discipline by Stanley Hoffmann, "An American Social Science: International Relations," *Daedalus* 106 (1977): 41–60, and acknowledged as the "unofficial dean of the realist school" by Rosenthal, *Righteous Realists,* p. 2. The changes across the book's several editions also are instructive of how the paradigm developed in response to intellectual and political challenges. More recently, John A. Vasquez has claimed that 90 percent of behavioral studies in international relations are based on realist assumptions; *The Power of Power Politics* (New Brunswick, NJ: Rutgers University Press, 1983), pp. 162–70. For review, criticism, and a bibliography of the disciplinary discourse of realism, see Francis A. Beer and Robert Hariman, eds., *Post-Realism: The Rhetorical Turn in International Relations* (East Lansing: Michigan State Univ. Press, forthcoming).

47. Quoted in Henry A. Kissinger, *A World Restored: Metternich, Castlereagh and the Problems of Peace, 1812–22* (Boston: Houghton Mifflin, 1957), p. 10.

207

48. Henry A. Kissinger, *For the Record* (Boston: Little, Brown, 1981), p. 161. See also his essay, "The White Revolutionary: Reflections on Bismarck," *Daedalus* 97 (1968): 888–924.

49. Kissinger, *For the Record*, p. 114. This statement is a good example of how the realist speaker often relies on truisms. Of course, diplomacy can't be learned from texts alone—what can be learned that way? He could just as well have noted that it requires the experience that comes with age. The truism is important not for what it says but for what it does: By opposing his practice to the reading of a text, Kissinger activates the realist's assumptions, attitudes, and preferred audience responses. For further analysis of Kissinger's use of realist tropes, see Robert Hariman, "Henry Kissinger: Realism's Rational Actor," in Beer and Hariman, eds., *Post-Realism.*

50. Richard M. Nixon, *Real Peace* (Boston: Little, Brown, 1984), p. 4. Consider this the sequel to Richard M. Nixon, *The Real War* (New York: Warner Books, 1980): For example, "American newsmen" presented Afghanistan as "a metaphor for all the dull and distant events that glazed the eyes of the American reader. But in real life Afghanistan is much more than that . . . Afghanistan has traditionally been one of the those points where the great thrusts of empire met" (p. 9). Nixon's vulgarity reveals how the realist style draws on other conventional oppositions in the general text of modernity, including not least of all the opposition between masculinity and femininity. Machiavelli did the same; see Hannah Fenichel Pitkin, *Fortune Is a Woman: Gender and Politics in the Thought of Niccolo Machiavelli* (Berkeley: University of California Press, 1984).

51. George Bush, remarks at the dedication ceremony of the social sciences complex at Princeton University, New Jersey, 10 May 1991 (*Weekly Compilation of Presidential Documents,* Monday, May 13, 1991, vol. 27, no. 19, pp. 589–92). Apparently we are to believe that the executive branch is innocent of paperwork. For the charge of usurpation, see Theodore Draper, "Presidential Wars," *New York Review of Books* 38 (26 September 1991): 64–74, and "The True History of the Gulf War," *New York Review of Books* 39 (30 January 1992): 38–45.

52. Of course, this continues the deconstructive movement of the text: a rhetoric of anti-rhetoric, it also sublimates social definition through the social process of attributing status. It is not enough to point this out, however, if one wants to understand the appeal of such discourse. Anders Stephanson provides an interesting preliminary discussion of the unresolved contradiction between George Kennan's appreciation of personal style in diplomacy and his belief in the reality of power. See his *Kennan and the Art of Foreign Policy* (Cambridge: Harvard University Press, 1989), pp. 195–203. Kennan couldn't recognize fully his stylistic capabilities because he lacked the means to describe them, and because his dominant style included the pretense that charm, ornament, grace, and other elements or standards of composition were unimportant for political action.

53. The key definition of prudence as the distinctive form of political intelligence is provided by Aristotle, *Nicomachean Ethics* 6.8–9 (1142b.20). For an earlier discussion of the "remarkable, but largely unremarked, affinity between *phronesis* and rhetoric," see Oscar L. Brownstein, "Aristotle and the Rhetorical Process," in *Rhetoric: A Tradition in Transition* edited by Walter Fisher, pp. 19–32 (East Lansing: Michigan State University Press, 1974). Lois S. Self argues that this connection supplies sufficient ethical grounding for rhetoric in "Rhetoric and *Phronesis*: The Aristotelian Ideal," *Philosophy and Rhetoric* 12 (1979): 130–45. For provocative discussions of the dialectic between more ethical and

208

more expedient conceptions of prudence, see Marcia L. Colish, "Cicero's *De Officiis* and Machiavelli's *Prince*," and particularly Garver, *Machiavelli and the History of Prudence.* Although following different methods, both Colish and Garver argue that Machiavelli avoids the reduction of prudence to cleverness. I respond to Colish in Hariman, "Composing Modernity," pp. 22–23. I discuss Garver's work, while providing another division between performative and calculative forms of prudence, in "Prudence/Performance," *Rhetoric Society Quarterly* 21 (1991): 26–35; an expanded version of this essay is forthcoming in John S. Nelson, ed., *Arguments Civic and Academic: Rhetorics of Professional Practices* (forthcoming). Morgenthau and other realists do use prudence as a titular term, but it quickly becomes a synonym for their ideas of calculative reasoning (or perhaps an escape hatch when those calculations fail).

54. Geerken, "Machiavelli Studies Since 1969," p. 361.

55. For the argument that Machiavelli is the founder of modern strategy and that he accomplished this through the *Prince* and the *Discourses* as much as in the *Art of War,* see Felix Gilbert, "Machiavelli: The Renaissance of the Art of War," in *Makers of Modern Strategy from Machiavelli to the Nuclear Age,* edited by Peter Paret (Princeton: Princeton University Press, 1986), pp. 11–31.

56. See also the discussion of Machiavelli's "economy of violence" by Sheldon S. Wolin, *Politics and Vision: Continuity and Innovation in Western Political Thought* (Boston: Little, Brown, 1960).

57. Neal Wood, "Machiavelli's Humanism of Action," in Parel, *The Political Calculus,* p. 41. Wood's most extended discussion of this idea occurs in his introduction to the revised edition of the Ellis Farneworth translation of Machiavelli's *The Art of War* (Indianapolis: Bobbs-Merrill, Library of Liberal Arts, 1965), especially section 5, "The Common Style of the Two Arts," pp. liii ff. The commentary on Machiavelli's use of *virtu* also offers a very useful discussion of strategic thinking. See, for example, Felix Gilbert, "On Machiavelli's Idea of *Virtu*," *Renaissance News* 4 (1951): 53–55, and discussion in volume 5: 21–23 and 70–71; Neal Wood, Machiavelli's Concept of *Virtù* Reconsidered," *Political Studies* 15 (1967): 159–72; Jerrold Seigel, "*Virtù* in and since the Renaissance," in *Dictionary of the History of Ideas* edited by Philip P. Wiener (New York: Scribner's, 1968), 4:476–86; Neal Wood, "Some Common Aspects of the Thought of Seneca and Machiavelli," *Renaissance Quarterly* 21 (1968): 11–23; John H. Geerken, "Homer's Image of the Hero in Machiavelli: A Comparison of *Areté* and *Virtù*," *Italian Quarterly* 14 (1970): 45–90; Russell Price, "*Virtu* in Machiavelli's *Il Principe* and *Discorsi*," *Political Science* 22 (1970): 43–49; I. Hannaford, "Machiavelli's Concept of Virtù in *The Prince* and *The Discourses* Reconsidered," *Political Studies* 20 (1972): 185–89; John Plamenatz, "In Search of Machiavellian *Virtù*," in Parel, *The Political Calculus,* pp. 157–78. Dietz discusses Machiavelli's strategic thinking in her essay, "Trapping the Prince," pp. 779–99. For discussion of the analogy between generalship and oratory in Renaissance humanism, see William Weithoff, "The Martial 'Virtue' of Rhetoric in Machiavelli's *Art of War*," *Quarterly Journal of Speech* 64 (1978): 304–12; and C. C. Bayley, *War and Society in Renaissance Florence: The De Militia of Leonardo Bruni* (Toronto: University of Toronto Press, 1961).

58. For a perhaps oversimplified attempt to discern a structure of political action within strategic thinking, see George Beam and Dick Simpson, *Political Action: The Key to Understanding Politics* (Athens, OH: Swallow Press, 1984). For a more sophisticated

approach, albeit one that relies on too limited a conception of rhetoric, see William Riker, *The Art of Political Manipulation* (New Haven: Yale University Press, 1986); Riker used the term "heresthetic" to define strategic thinking and argued (mistakenly, in my opinion) that it is more inclusive than rhetoric since the latter art concerns only words and not the structuring of situations.

59. For the argument that Machiavelli used portraits of political leaders as persuasive *exempla,* see Peter E. Bondanella, *Machiavelli and the Art of Renaissance History* (Detroit, MI: Wayne State University Press, 1973).

60. Skinner misses the point when reviewing Machiavelli's lack of concern about private immorality: "The classical idea of self-control is dismissed without a shrug" ("Introduction" to *The Prince,* p. xxii). Machiavelli's disregard of *cose vane* ("empty things," like sex or business) doesn't compromise his rigorous disciplining of the prince's persona, which is the mode of self-control appropriate to making decisions and influencing others in the competitive world of politics. This asceticism is genuine: pride in one's self-control is one characteristic of the realist style. Listen for the tone in these remarks by an Assistant Secretary for Far Eastern Affairs: "Precision, wisdom, realism: These require the utmost in cool and unemotional judgment and what I called earlier cool, deliberate analysis. Tough minds, analytical minds, are required . . . with steady nerves and unflinching will" (quoted in Philip Wander, "The Rhetoric of American Foreign Policy," *Quarterly Journal of Speech* 70 [1984]: 350). In bourgeois society, of course, private scruples are more important than they were for Machiavelli, and the realist ethos is likely to include more conventional restraints. I marvel at how Americans like G. Gordon Liddy and Oliver North can live so close to executive power and be so devoid of public morality, yet remain untainted by the ordinary corruptions that snare politicians such as the Kennedys, just to take a name out of the hat.

61. F. Gilbert, "The Humanist Concept," p. 470.

62. X (George F. Kennan), "The Sources of Soviet Conduct," *Foreign Affairs* 25 (1947): 566–82. The article was reprinted or excerpted extensively and provoked immediate and prolonged debate in both public and scholarly forums. There is more to be said about this essay, of course, as well as the "Long Telegram," both of which employ many other appeals as well, including Protestant providentialism (see the last paragraph of "Sources"), and which are laced with the bizarre political psychology of the time. For related discussion of Kennan's rhetoric, see Robert Ivie, "Realism Masking Fear: George F. Kennan's Political Rhetoric," in Beer and Hariman, eds., *Post-Realism.*

63. Kennan, "The Sources of Soviet Conduct," pp. 580, 573–76.

64. For review of discussion of the literary merits of Machiavelli's work, see Clark, "Machiavelli." My observation that many readers overlook Machiavelli's style does not refer to his treatment in Italy, of course, or especially to the work by Fredi Chiapelli and others, which involves careful examination of how Machiavelli's language is crafted and how his literary skill contributes to his political theory. This work has not been picked up by most readers of *The Prince,* however, and to a certain extent it remains inconclusive regarding political thought. See Chiapelli, "Machiavelli as Secretary," *Italian Quarterly* 14 (1970): 27–44, for an introduction to his project. Chiapelli has examined the full range of Machiavelli's work, including the documents he produced while working for the Florentine government, and he concludes that Machiavelli's artistic genius is evident from the begin-

210

ning of his career, that there is an essential unity of thought, personality, and expression in his work, and that "there is no essential distinction between the secretary and the writer" (p. 42). If only to make clear what I am not doing, let me identify two interlocking issues that a comprehensive study of the political significance of Machiavelli's prose style would have to consider (among others): first, how his word choices shape what he is saying about politics, and, second, how they influence use of his text as a model for acting politically. Both questions, but particularly the first, lead back to analysis of the Italian text and its relation to the conventional usage and artistic aspirations of his day. I have stepped over this task—I hope safely—to address the second question by identifying more general rhetorical forms and articulating the pattern of symbolic action I label a political style.

65. Witness the many remarks on the clarity and forcefulness of the text, remarks typically given as last word of a commentary: "It was there that Machiavelli first presented, with matchless clarity and force, his basic assumption that rulers must always be prepared to do evil if good will come of it" (Berlin, "Introduction" to *The Prince*, p. xxiv); "As long as this strain will remain in political thinking, so long will *The Prince* be found to have expressed in undying prose its intensity and its temper" (Lerner, "Introduction" to *The Prince and The Discourses*, p. xxxv).

66. There were several similar schemes: for example, the plain, middling, and grand (Cicero, *Orator* 69–112, especially 75–99) or the plain, elegant, forceful, and grand (Demetrius, *On Style* 36–304). I have adapted the classical scheme to account for one moment in the modern development of plain speech. Generally, I believe Cicero's scheme is weakest where it is most systematic—namely, when he aligns the three styles with the three functions of oratory—and that the modern valorization of plainness transforms every element in the classical theory: for example, instruction becomes explanation, naturalness becomes the representation of nature, and, in political discourse well after Machiavelli, the speaker's modesty becomes a democratic ethos. I trust that the basic distinctions (*mutatis mutandis*) and attention to such considerations as scope, function, speaker-subject-audience relations, effect, and the like can still prove useful. For a comprehensive account of the development of plain speech in the United States during the nineteenth century, see Kenneth Cmiel, *Democratic Eloquence: The Fight over Popular Speech in Nineteenth-Century America* (New York: William Morrow, 1990).

67. This translation is by George Bull, *The Prince* (London: Penguin, 1981). I have not used the Ricci translation here, as it uses a different syntax in the last sentence than the Italian text, probably to capture the subtle sense of amplification in the closing clause. In each case, I have chosen sound translations that have had wide circulation; I prefer the diction and cadence of the one, but use the other in this instance because its sentence construction is closer to the "original" and to many other translations at my point of critical interest.

68. Perhaps one qualification is needed here: The passage is not so much devoid of artistic ethos as characterized by purposively limited embellishment. The amplification provided by the first subordinate clause is focused on the restatement of the single term "all," the term "limb" is an explicit but very ordinary analogy, and although the last parallelism deftly weakens the logical entailments, it does so implicitly. The question then is, before whom is the author being so modest? It seems to me that the answer is, his

211

subject. Machiavelli still appeals to the skillful reader through his subtle artistry, but he also is crafting a more comprehensive trope that subordinates reader and writer to the material conditions to be described.

69. "Everyone knows that it is difficult to integrate chapter 26 with the rest of *The Prince;* at the very least there is an obvious shift in tone, and at most there could be real incoherence" (Garver, *Machiavelli and the History of Prudence,* p. 117).

70. Hans Blumenberg, *The Legitimacy of the Modern Age,* translated by Robert W. Wallace (Cambridge: MIT Press 1983), p. 14. I'm also attempting to correct an oversight by Blumenberg, who mentions Machiavelli only once, consistent with his view of the Renaissance as a brief and almost reactionary period of mystification. It does Blumenberg no harm to demonstrate how his theory can be extended and improved by incorporation of oblique cases.

71. Blumenberg's critique of the secularization thesis includes the following claims: it fails to meet basic standards of explanation, requires a muddled view of language, confuses or overlooks other forms of historical change, and counters one myth of modernity (the myth of an epoch created *ex nihilo*) only by smuggling in propositions that are inauthentic for "the understanding of reality that is itself characterized as 'worldly' " (*Legitimacy,* p. 5).

72. The attitude toward language initially guiding Blumenberg's theory is evident in his statement that "a metaphor is after all a rhetorical artifice, nothing serious and certainly nothing that can lead to any sort of knowledge" (p. 19). As William J. Bouwsma has remarked in a review of *Legitimacy:* "He is not only a philosopher but a philosopher of the Enlightenment, an element in his heritage that also limits his philosophical range" (*Journal of Modern History* 56 [1984]: 701). Like Ernst Cassirer before him, however, Blumenberg subsequently has modified his Kantianism to write a linguistic philosophy of originality and power. Compare the prior statement on metaphor with this formulation from his essay on rhetoric:

> The human relation to reality is indirect, circumstantial, delayed, selective, and above all 'metaphorical.' . . . Metaphor is not only a chapter in the discussion of rhetorical means, it is a distinctive element of rhetoric, in which rhetoric's function can be displayed and expressed in terms of its relation to anthropology. ("An Anthropological Approach," pp. 439–40)

See also Hans Blumenberg, *Work on Myth,* translated by Robert M. Wallace (Cambridge: MIT Press, 1985), and the review by William J. Bouwsma in *Journal of the History of Ideas* 48 (1987): 347–54. "A Bibliography of Blumenberg's Work and Responses to It" appears in *Annals of Scholarship* 5 (1987): 97–108. The same issue is devoted to a symposium on Blumenberg.

73. Two distinctions needed to be noted here to avoid likely misunderstandings of my point. First, there is a difference between the reoccupation model as it is presented in *Legitimacy* and as it is subsequently modified to incorporate Blumenberg's later engagement with language. As Blumenberg says of the concept of reoccupation, "I introduced and explained this concept in my *Legitimacy of the Modern Age* . . . but I did not yet see that it implies a rhetorical transaction" ("An Anthropological Approach," p. 451). As the subsequent modifications of the model still are underway, we should observe at this time only that the analysis of Machiavelli's composition of modern political discourse indicates that such modifications are necessary. Second, Blumenberg's assertion that the reoccupa-

212

tion is accomplished rhetorically does not yet commit him to the analysis of how discourses act by acting upon each other. His basic assertion is that since reoccupation occurs via transfers of meaning and power, its logical structure must be the structure of metaphor, that is, the structure presented in the term's etymology of "carrying over." My rhetorical analysis of *The Prince* suggests a further dynamic, however, which is that the relationship between modern ideas and modern patterns of composition is at least as determinative of both positive and negative articulations of modernity as is the relationship between the ideas of the modern epoch and the functional tendencies of the prior cultural system.

74. Bender and Wellbery provide an excellent synopsis of the pertinent changes in cultural practices; see the first chapter of their edited volume, *The Ends of Rhetoric,* pp. 3–39. The history of hermeneutics proper—itself an early-modern innovation—also follows the same course. Initially, "intention" referred to the implication of the genre or other basic designs of the text, and hermeneutical theory was explicitly modeled on rhetorical constructs (and so a continuation of classical textuality). After Friedrich D. E. Schleiermacher, intentionality is understood as self-assertion of the individual author's subjective life, and hermeneutics has achieved relative autonomy from the classical rhetorical tradition. For discussion and representative texts, see Kurt Mueller-Vollmer, *The Hermeneutics Reader* (New York: Continuum, 1985). As Bender and Wellbery summarize, "the insistence on the originating power of subjectivity is incompatible with rhetorical doctrine" (p. 19). Machiavelli's innovations in his account of political invention provide a prototype for this model of the relationship between language and the modern self.

75. David Quint, *Origin and Originality in Renaissance Literature: Versions of the Source* (New Haven: Yale University Press, 1983), p. 220. Quint also argues that "by obtaining a cultural autonomy from systems of authorized truth, literature gave up its right to be authoritative" (p. 219); once again, the self-assertion of the individual author coincides with the modern organization of social practices into separate, autonomous spheres of authority—for example, the realms of aesthetics, politics, ethics, and the natural sciences—and with that, the marginalizing of traditional sources of political wisdom. Such has been the legacy of Morgenthau's dictum that "the political realist maintains the autonomy of the political sphere, as the economist, the lawyer, the moralist maintain theirs" (*Politics Among Nations,* 2d ed. [New York: Alfred A. Knopf, 1954], p. 10).

76. There has been extensive discussion of this question in several periods and disciplines. For example, E. D. Hirsch, Jr., articulated a strong intentionalist position for literary studies in *Validity in Interpretation* (New Haven: Yale, 1967) that was the subject of considerable debate. Richard E. Palmer, *Hermeneutics: Interpretation Theory in Schleiermacher, Dilthey, Heidegger, and Gadamer* (Evanston: Northwestern University Press, 1969) observed that the American debate was a reprise of an earlier exchange between Hans Georg Gadamer and Emilio Betti. For a bibliography of the discussion in analytical philosophy, see Stephen Schiffer, *Remnants of Meaning* (Cambridge: MIT Press, 1987).

213

77. Kenneth Burke, *A Rhetoric of Motives* (Berkeley: University of California Press, 1969), p. 38.

78. See, for example, Michel Foucault, "What Is an Author?" in *The Foucault Reader,* edited by Paul Rabinow (New York: Pantheon, 1984), pp. 101–20; Michael Calvin McGee, "In Search of 'The People': A Rhetorical Alternative," *Quarterly Journal of Speech* 61 (1975): 235–49.

79. Geerken summarizes the debate regarding the relationship between *The Prince* and *The Discourses* ("Machiavelli Studies," pp. 357ff., 364ff.), as does F. Gilbert ("Machiavelli," pp. 19ff.—especially note 20), and Cochrane ("Machiavelli," pp. 132ff.). For the argument for their incompatibility, see Hans Baron, "Machiavelli: The Republican Citizen and the Author of The Prince," *English Historical Review* 76 (1961): 217–53. J. G. A. Pocock's *Machiavellian Moment* initiated and defined an extended debate regarding Machiavelli's influence on the development of Anglo-American civic republicanism. For a more accessible presentation of Machiavelli's republicanism, see Bruce James Smith, *Politics and Remembrance: Republican Themes in Machiavelli, Burke, and Tocqueville* (Princeton: Princeton University Press, 1985).

80. Geerken, "Machiavelli Studies," pp. 357ff.; Garver, *Machiavelli and the History of Prudence,* chapters 5 and 6; Berlin, "The Originality of Machiavelli," p. 181. Note Berlin's insight: "The vision—the dream—typical of many writers who see themselves as tough-minded realists—of the strong, united, effective, morally regenerated, splendid and victorious *patria,* whether it is saved by the *virtù* of one man or many—remains central and constant" (p. 181).

81. Pocock's emphasis on Machiavelli's significance within civic republicanism becomes questionable at the point where his analysis becomes sketchy—in the North American period. See the notes in chapter 4 on the republican style for the claim that Cicero also was a major and at times dominant influence on civic republican thought.

82. This insight comes from Struever, *Language of History,* p. 158.

83. See chapter 4 on the republican style's dependency on the practice of oratory and other verbal arts.

84. Here I am following Berlin, "The Originality of Machiavelli," pp. 197ff.

85. See Wolin's discussion of how "politics has become external to its participants," that is, not concerned with the improvement of interior life (*Politics and Vision,* pp. 236–37). No wonder realists are comfortable with the metaphor of containment. All values are contained within the state (while states face each other as extrinsic entities in a condition of anarchy), just as all value judgments are contained within the individual (while individuals face each other as emotivists in a condition of irrationality). From this perspective, it is sensible to see any threat as behavior to be contained rather than as the actions of someone with whom you might communicate.

86. Stephen Toulmin, *Cosmopolis: The Hidden Agenda of Modernity* (New York: Free Press, 1990), p. 209.

87. See, for example, James Boyd White, *When Words Lose Their Meaning: Constitutions and Reconstitutions of Language, Character, and Community* (Chicago: University of Chicago Press, 1984).

88. For contemporary affirmations of the ideal that "eloquence is one," see the essays on Renaissance rhetoric by Vickers and by Garin in Vickers, *Rhetoric Revalued.* The phrase comes from Cicero, *De oratore* 3.5.23: *"Una est enim . . . eloquentia, quascumque in oras disputationis regionesve delata est."*

Chapter Three: Kapuściński's Courtly Style

1. Georges Duby, *The Chivalrous Society,* translated by Cynthia Postan (Berkeley: University of California Press, 1977); Frank Whigham, *Ambition and Privilege: The Social Tropes of Elizabethan Courtesy Theory* (Berkeley: University of California Press, 1984);

Patricia Fumerton, *Cultural Aesthetics: Renaissance Literature and the Practice of Social Ornament* (Chicago: University of Chicago Press, 1991). Study of the English Renaissance has been influenced considerably by Stephen Greenblatt, *Renaissance Self-Fashioning: From More to Shakespeare* (Chicago: University of Chicago Press, 1980). Richard A. Lanham's earlier and equally impressive *Motives of Eloquence: Literary Rhetoric in the Renaissance* (New Haven: Yale University Press, 1976) follows similar interests to somewhat different conclusions, but often is overlooked. For historical studies inspired by an anthropological perspective, see Sean Wilentz, ed., *Rites of Power: Symbolism, Ritual, and Politics since the Middle Ages* (Philadelphia: University of Pennsylvania Press, 1985). The projects noted here have come the farthest in the direction of understanding the rhetorical and aesthetic dimensions of courtly politics. Although indicative of the methods and high standards of historical scholarship, they are not representative of the many historical studies of European monarchy that have paid little heed to its symbolic forms.

2. Norbert Elias, *The Court Society,* translated by Edmund Jephcott (New York: Pantheon, 1982).

3. Norbert Elias, *Power and Civility,* translated by Edmund Jephcott with notes and revisions by the author (New York: Pantheon, 1983); *The History of Manners,* translated by Edmund Jephcott (New York: Pantheon, 1978).

4. Clifford Geertz, *Negara: The Theatre State in Nineteenth-Century Bali* (Princeton: Princeton University Press, 1980); "Centers, Kings, and Charisma: Reflections on the Symbolics of Power," in Sean Wilentz, ed., *Rites of Power,* pp. 13–38. For other studies that emphasize ceremonial power in non-European court cultures, see David Cannadine and Simon Price, *Rituals of Royalty: Power and Ceremonial in Traditional Societies* (Cambridge: Cambridge University Press, 1987). The anthropological and historical perspectives have been melded, with excellent results, in Wilentz, ed., *Rites of Power.* See also Eric Hobsbawm and Terence Ranger, eds., *The Invention of Tradition* (Cambridge: Cambridge University Press, 1983). For study of a contemporary civic spectacle, see Ronald L. Grimes, *Symbol and Conquest: Public Ritual and Drama in Santa Fe, New Mexico* (Ithaca, NY: Cornell University Press, 1976).

5. Clifford Geertz, "Thick Description: Toward an Interpretive Theory of Culture," in *The Interpretation of Cultures* (New York: Basic Books, 1973).

6. The identification of a common style of courtliness is trickier than one might think: On the one hand, it is too easy to see variability among courts. Whereas realists claim that there is one reality, civic republicans see a common fate for all republics, and bureaucracies are supposed to be equally impersonal, courts are defined in part by the idiosyncrasies of the sovereign and often are claimed to embody the spirit of the age. I hope it is clear that I would question all of these attributions and that I think stylistic analysis should recognize the interaction between a general pattern of identification and the special characteristics of the particular case. On the other hand, when looking for similarities it is too easy to lose all sense of distinction between courtly ideals and other versions of the civilizing process with which they have been intertwined historically. Here Baldesar Castiglione's *The Book of the Courtier* (translated by George Bull [Harmondsworth: Penguin, 1976]) is exhibit A; Victoria Kahn has summarized the relationship within the Renaissance nicely: "I think it is fair to say that the rhetorical tradition of humanism continued alongside and entered into various relations with the interests of courtliness" (*Rhetoric, Prudence, and Skepticism in the Renaissance* [Ithaca: Cornell University Press,

1985], p. 188). C. Stephen Jaeger argues that court culture was an earlier development of classical humanism in *The Origins of Courtliness: Civilizing Trends and the Formation of Courtly Ideals, 939–1210* (Philadelphia: University of Pennsylvania Press, 1985). My interest is not in determining the precise proportions of influence within the historical process, but in setting out ideal types that can be used for the analysis of persuasive speech and conduct in our own period and perhaps others as well. For additional discussion of ideal type analysis, see chapter 6.

7. Ethiopia's position as the interface of two geopolitical orders is featured in its mythology, which includes the stories that its monarchy is the issue of the Queen of Sheba and King Solomon, that it is the repository of the original Ark of the Covenant, and others like these. This definition has been reinforced by its distinctive Jewish and Christian communities, its intermediate position in both colonialism and the cold war, and its experience of both "international" relief campaigns and African tribal separatism. While its status in the West fluctuates, it remains (for the West) a fundamentally ambiguous construct, always an intermediate or mixed state capable of moving toward one side or the other but incapable of full identification with either. See, for example, Haile Selassie I, *'My Life and Ethiopia's Progress,' 1892–1937: The Autobiography of Emperor Haile Sellassie I,* translated by Edward Ullendorff (Oxford: Oxford University Press, 1976); Harold G. Marcus, *Haile Sellassie I: The Formative Years, 1892–1936* (Berkeley: University of California Press, 1987); Bahru Zewde, *A History of Modern Ethiopia, 1855–1974* (London: James Curry, 1991); Mulatu Wubneh and Yohannis Abate, *Ethiopia: Transition and Development in the Horn of Africa* (Boulder, CO: Westview Press, 1988); John H. Spencer, *Ethiopia at Bay: A Personal Account of the Haile Sellassie Years* (Algonac, MI: Reference Publications, 1984); Patrick Gilkes, *The Dying Lion: Feudalism and Modernization in Ethiopia* (New York: St. Martin's Press, 1975); Donald N. Levine, *Wax and Gold: Tradition and Innovation in Ethiopian Culture* (Chicago: University of Chicago Press, 1965).

8. Ryszard Kapuściński, *The Emperor: Downfall of an Autocrat,* translated by William R. Brand and Katarzyna Mroczkowska-Brand (New York: Harcourt Brace Jovanovich, 1983), p. 5. Subsequent citations are found in the text as parenthetical page references. For discussion by an expert in Ethiopian studies of typical responses to the book, see Harold G. Marcus, "Prejudice and Ignorance in Reviewing Books about Africa: The Strange Case of Ryszard Kapuściński's *The Emperor* (1983)," *History in Africa* 17 (1990): 373–78. I should caution against reading Kapuściński's account too literally, for area scholars can identify errors of fact and other implausibilities, and some would dispute the assessment of the Selassie government encouraged by the book. I am indebted to Professor Marcus for consultation on this point; see his review article for elaboration of expert concerns. To the extent that the discussion involves Ethiopia directly, I would note that Kapuściński's account does address an acknowledged gap in the understanding of the emperor's "charisma" and that important principles of the account are supported by or consistent with other sources, as when John Spencer observes Selassie's "addiction to pomp and protocol" (*Ethiopia at Bay,* p. 134). From my perspective, the questions of local veracity are to be taken seriously in their place, but only there. Important works in the literature of political studies have involved similar "distortions" of the particular case: *The History of the Peloponnesian War* includes speeches fabricated by the author to represent debates he did not witness, *The Prince* includes idealized portraiture of actual

216

rulers known or only known of by the author, and *The Trial* and *The Castle* rely on obvious exaggeration of the author's experience as a bureaucrat. One might say that in each of these works the literary license has been used to "perfect" the symbolic forms that are of the greater interest politically in order to represent them more clearly.

9. Kenneth Burke, *A Rhetoric of Motives* (Berkeley: University of California Press, 1969), p. 226.

10. Some will insist at this point that every regime of any sort ultimately is based on coercion. Let me suggest several counterpoints: First, much of the time the coercive possibility doesn't matter, or doesn't matter any more than any other "ultimate" motivation, because more apparent and proximate elements are determinative. Second, as even Machiavelli recognized, successful rule depends on legitimation of authority through the use of political symbols, not to mention actual provision of governmental services. So it is that raw coercion produces not only obedience but also resistance and revolution, and some of the time regimes persist long after their ability to coerce has passed. Third, the reduction to coercion provides a weak account of the persistence of ideals of political order and sacrifice in their name. Finally, for elite participants, social status usually is far more commanding than force.

11. I am scanting this familiar feature of courtly life as it has been documented thoroughly in historical, sociological, and anthropological studies, and I couldn't improve on Frank Whigham's analysis of its major tropes; see *Ambition and Privilege,* chapter 3.

12. Burke, *A Rhetoric of Motives,* p. 232. Of course, "Mystery" read less appreciatively is "mystification," which can be read more or less ideologically. Nonetheless, Burke deserves great credit for emphasizing how hierarchy is one of the basic patterns of human motivation that can never be entirely suppressed.

13. More precisely, Burke is after "the purely dialectical motives (ultimate verbal motives) behind the rhetorical convertibility between terms for social hierarchy and terms for theologic hierarchy" (*A Rhetoric of Motives,* p. 232).

14. Burke, *A Rhetoric of Motives,* pp. 301–13.

15. Elias, *The Court Society,* p. 104.

16. Ernst H. Kantorowicz, *The King's Two Bodies: A Study in Mediaeval Political Theology* (Princeton: Princeton University Press, 1957), p. 7. Note the use of male pronouns to refer to a female monarch; as with Lulu, the natural body at court is a tissue of signifiers.

17. Lynn Hunt, *Politics, Culture, and Class in the French Revolution* (Berkeley: University of California Press, 1984), p. 55.

18. Michel Foucault, *Power/Knowledge: Selected Interviews and Other Writings, 1972–1977,* translated by Colin Gordon et al. (New York: Pantheon Books, 1980), p. 55.

19. You can see one of His Majesty's fifty-two pillows in any picture of him sitting. My favorite is the frontispiece picture for Selassie's autobiography (*'My Life and Ethiopia's Progress'*), in which he is posed with his feet on the pillow and a little dog (Lulu?) sitting erect between his legs.

20. Michel Foucault, *Discipline and Punish,* translated by Alan Sheridan (New York: Pantheon, 1977).

21. For example, see Wilentz, ed., *Rites of Power.*

22. For an informative study of courtly spectacles, see Roy Strong, *Art and Power:*

217

Renaissance Festivals, 1450–1650 (Berkeley: University of California Press, 1984). "Under the impact of renaissance humanism the art of festival was harnessed to the emergent modern state as an instrument of rule" (p. 19).

23. This observation about the intersection of aesthetic tendencies should not obscure the differences between them. Perhaps there is an affinity, however, between the courtly style and a liberal visual aesthetic that depicts social problems by featuring common people in individual portraiture.

24. See the discussion of this "universal rule which seems to apply more than any other in all human actions or words," in Castiglione, *The Book of the Courtier,* p. 67 and preceding pages.

25. Elias, *The Court Society,* p. 87.

26. Mary Douglas, *Natural Symbols* (New York: Vintage, 1973), p. 99.

27. Ambiguity is not limited to courtly politics, of course. Murray Edelman identifies how the ambiguity characteristic of much political discourse allows both individual advantage and collective flexibility: see *Constructing the Political Spectacle* (Chicago: University of Chicago Press, 1988). See also William E. Connolly, *Politics and Ambiguity* (Madison: University of Wisconsin Press, 1987). The emperor's ambiguity is distinguished by its identification with speech while being placed within a particular hierarchy of modes of communication.

28. For a related example of courtly control of speech, see Michael V. Fox, "Ancient Egyptian Rhetoric," *Rhetorica* 1 (1983): 9–22. "The first canon of Egyptian rhetoric is *silence*" (p. 12). Full understanding of the role of silence at court would require identifying other forms of silence as well. See, for example, Robert L. Scott, "Rhetoric and Silence," *Western Journal of Speech Communication* 36 (1972): 146–58, and "Dialectical Tensions of Speaking and Silence," *Quarterly Journal of Speech* 79 (1993): 1–18; Barry Brummett, "Towards a Theory of Silence as a Political Strategy," *Quarterly Journal of Speech* 66 (1980): 289–303.

29. Elias, *The Court Society,* pp. 86–87.

30. Barbara Tuchman, *The March of Folly* (New York: Alfred A. Knopf, 1984), p. 8.

31. P'u Yi, *From Emperor to Citizen: The Autobiography of Aisin-Gioro P'u Yi,* translated by W. J. F. Jenner (Oxford: Oxford University Press, 1987), p. 41. Like *The Emperor,* this text reports personal experience of the court yet is written from another, reformed vantage—in this case, the perspective provided by P'u Yi's political re-education and state involvement in the writing and publication of the book.

32. Thomas Carlyle, *The French Revolution: A History,* 2 vols. (New York: Harper & Brothers, 1870), I:6.

33. Carlyle, *The French Revolution,* I: 27, 28, 2, 10ff.

34. Ibid., II:303–5. This passage also reveals one of the affinities between the courtly and realist styles—as each subordinates speech to compose power, authority, or legitimacy—while still illustrating marked differences between them.

35. Sei Shōnagon, *The Pillow Book of Sei Shōnagon,* translated and edited by Ivan Morris (New York: Columbia University Press, 1991). The original text was circulated circa 996 and completed subsequently. The many, many examples include: on rank and splendor, 34–35, 56, 109–10, 132–34, 146–47, 155, 181, 192–93, 228–29, 232; on decorum, 47–48, 71–72; on laughter, 24, 28, 48, 101, 104, 109, 113, 162, 251. Shōna-

gon's observations perfectly confirm Burke's discussion of the cult of laughter (*Rhetoric of Motives,* pp. 226–27).

36. Nakanoin Masatada, *The Confessions of Lady Nijō,* translated by Karen Brazell (Garden City, NY: Doubleday/Anchor, 1973). The original text dates from 1307. Tears are an oft-used device: for example, pp. 5, 9–11, 28, 35, 44, 48, 66, 253.

37. Whigham, *Ambition and Privilege,* pp. 38–39.

38. Ibid., p. 39. Although Whigham's statement pertains to a court obsessed with sheer performance, I believe it applies, *mutatis mutandis,* to any courtly culture and ultimately to all institutional life.

39. Frank Lentricchia, *Criticism and Social Change* (Chicago: University of Chicago Press, 1983), pp. 106–7.

40. S. R. F. Price provides succinct summary of the difference between the conventional (realist, rationalist) analysis of power, which defines power as the possession of individuals who efficiently employ force or control an administrative apparatus, and the contrasting (dramatistic, constructivist) perspective, which defines power as the property of a structure of relations constituted by symbolic acts. See his *Rituals and Power: The Roman Imperial Cult in Asia Minor* (Cambridge: Cambridge University Press), pp. 9–11 and 240ff.

41. Lanham, *Motives of Eloquence,* pp. 155, 156.

42. The literature on modern subjectivity is enormous, of course. Representative criticisms include Christopher Lasch, *The Culture of Narcissism* (New York: Basic Books, 1978), and Richard Sennett, *The Fall of Public Man* (New York: Random House/Vintage, 1978). For a careful defense, see Charles Taylor, *Sources of the Self: The Making of Modern Identity* (Cambridge: Harvard University Press, 1989) and *The Ethics of Authenticity* (Cambridge: Harvard University Press, 1992).

43. Lanham, *Motives of Eloquence,* pp. 147–48, 152, 155.

44. Whigham, *Ambition and Privilege.*

45. Elias, *The Court Society,* pp. 104–16.

46. Geertz, in Wilentz, *Rites of Power,* p. 33.

47. As Thomas Rosteck and Michael Leff summarize Kenneth Burke's understanding of this point, "The systematic rejection of one perspective does not yield an absence, but generates adherence to a new and equally systematic principle of order" ("Piety, Propriety, and Perspective; An Interpretation and Application of Key Terms in Kenneth Burke's *Permanence and Change,*" *Western Journal of Speech Communication* 53 [1989]: 328).

48. Burke, *A Rhetoric of Motives,* pp. 221, 232.

49. Lewis H. Lapham, *The Wish for Kings: Democracy at Bay* (New York: Grove Press, 1993); "Adieu, Big Bird: On the Terminal Irrelevance of Public Television," *Harper's* (December 1993): 35–43. In part, the difference between Lapham's account and my own is the difference between public commentary and academic writing—a comparison much to his advantage, I realize. Let's also grant that his primary interest is in challenging the powers that be, while mine is in identifying political artistry that can be used for good or ill. It is one thing to call a foundation executive a prince and another to discern that she does indeed craft speech and conduct according to conventions of high decorousness, status hierarchy, fixation on the body of the sovereign, and the like. The two approaches

219

are thoroughly complementary, however, particularly when the different writers share civic republican sentiments.

50. Eric Konigsberg, "No Hassle," *The New Republic* (1 March 1993): 22.

51. Ibid.

52. Ibid.

53. For additional discussion of Madonna, see Cathy Schwichtenberg, ed., *The Madonna Connection: Representational Politics, Subcultural Identities, and Cultural Theory* (Boulder, CO: Westview Press, 1993). This collection is a good example of the tendency in cultural studies to use poststructuralist vocabularies while still pursuing the modernist problematic regarding the reality behind the performance, the authenticity of the performer, and the politics of artistic representation. My interest is more modest and my assumptions quite different: I am considering only how Madonna's performances articulate a particular political style, and I believe that questions of ontological status, authenticity, and representation can be impediments to understanding persuasive texts. There is no doubt that popular culture is overdetermined and multiply coded, however, and I have bracketed ideological criticism in part because it is done well by others. Like cultural studies generally, *The Madonna Connection* raises the stakes and provides both method and insight for the analysis of popular culture.

54. This suggestion could be easily overstated. To take it a step further, however, perhaps the modern instantiation of this style gives us the double irony of courtliness without a court and a queen's body for the king. Oprah and Madonna are the highest paid women entertainers in the world, and the style seems to be present but less active with male entertainers. Although Ed McMahon began every Johnny Carson show with a stock gesture of obedience toward his sovereign (palms together and pointed out from the chest while the head is bowed) and Carson himself ended every monologue with his characteristic gesture of a golf swing (once a sign of aristocracy), the show was relatively disembodied. By contrast, Joan Rivers used her body as a persistent subject of humor and register of her reactions while trying to create the ambiance of a salon. Certainly there is a difference in the coverage of Prince Charles and Lady Di: Both are locked into a rhetoric of clothing and revealing the body, but her body receives far greater coverage and is more readily a subject for scandal. In addition, all of these cases suggest that whatever the degree to which the style operates, it allows the actor to develop a reputation for liberal expression while reaffirming the status quo.

55. There is little doubt regarding two basic differences in advertisers' portrayals of men and women: Advertising consistently portrays men and women according to the conventional ideals of masculinity and femininity, and it features images of women far more than men. Recent discussions of these most pervasive designs include Diane L. Barthel, *Putting on Appearances: Gender and Advertising* (Philadelphia: Temple University Press, 1988) and Alice E. Courtney and Thomas W. Whipple, *Sex Stereotyping in Advertising* (Lexington, MA: Lexington Books, 1983). For additional examples and commentary, see Erving Goffman, *Gender Advertisements* (Cambridge: Harvard University Press, 1979); Trevor Millum, *Images of Woman: Advertising in Women's Magazines* (Totowa, NJ: Rowman and Littlefield, 1975); Joseph E. Dispenta, *Advertising the American Woman* (Dayton, OH: Pflaum Publishing, 1975). It is difficult to underestimate the manner and extent to which advertising constructs gender within a patriarchal frame. If I slight this concern, it is only to focus specifically on how a political style can be inscribed in the text along with

the ideological code, and also because more comprehensive analyses of gender coding already are available. For a superb elaboration of Walter Benjamin's perspective on the relationships between modern representational media, culture, and ideology, see John Berger, *Ways of Seeing* (New York: Viking Press, 1973). The claim that women's bodies are more frequently partitioned is demonstrated more by showing than by telling, for example, in Goffman. It is discussed as a more general feature of sexist representation by Susan R. Bordo, "The Body and the Reproduction of Femininity: A Feminist Appropriation of Foucault," in *Gender/Body/Knowledge: Feminist Reconstructions of Being and Knowing*, edited by Alison M. Jaggar and Susan R. Bordo, pp. 13–33 (New Brunswick, NJ: Rutgers University Press, 1989).

56. Analysis of the rhetorical effects of images of bodies and body parts need not commit one irrevocably to either side of the debates regarding the priority of the uninscribed body in the process of inscription, or the critique of the structuralist distinction between nature and order, etc. Judith Butler's *Gender Trouble: Feminism and the Subversion of Identity* (New York: Routledge, 1990) provides a cogent discussion of some of these issues (pp. 128ff.) and argues on behalf of a conception of gender "as *a corporeal style*, an 'act,' as it were, which is both intentional and performative, where *'performative'* suggests a dramatic and contingent construction of meaning" (p. 139). Butler's argument also is representative of many recent studies of the inscription of social meaning and ideological design onto bodies, as she draws on the continental problematics of structuralism/poststructuralism and psychoanalysis/feminism as well as on the work in Anglo-American cultural anthropology, featured by Mary Douglas and Victor Turner, to develop a perspective on the role of ritual social dramas, now defined as "*stylized repetition of acts*" (p. 140). She does this in order to overturn essentialist conceptions of subjectivity and advance Foucault's materialist conception of discursive practices. For another brief review, see Bordo, "The Body and the Reproduction of Femininity." For earlier work, see, for example, Beverley Brown and Parveen Adams, "The Feminine Body and Feminist Politics," *M/F* 3 (1979): 35–50. See also the essays in Susan Rubin Suleiman, ed., *The Female Body in Western Culture: Contemporary Perspectives* (Cambridge: Harvard University Press, 1986). See also the bibliography in Catherine Burroughs and Jeffrey Ehrenreich, eds., *The Body as Social Text* (Iowa City: University of Iowa Press, 1993).

57. Richard Harvey Brown, *Society as a Text: Essays on Rhetoric, Reason, and Reality* (Chicago: University of Chicago Press, 1987), pp. 57–58.

58. Suleiman, *The Female Body*, p. 1.

59. Fragmentation is highlighted in important critiques of the cultural construction of gender through the discourses of medicine and of law: In *The Woman in the Body: A Cultural Analysis of Reproduction* (Boston: Beacon Press, 1987), Emily Martin examines the discourse of medicine. In particular, Martin draws on the work of Paul Schlider, *The Image and Appearance of the Human Body* (London: Kegan Paul, Trench, and Trubner, 1935), to emphasize the association of bodily fragmentation with neurosis and of bodily integrity with mental health. For profound analysis of the relationship between the body and symbolic and social order, see Elaine Scarry, *The Body in Pain: The Making and Unmaking of the World* (New York: Oxford University Press, 1985), particularly the discussion of torture. For discussion of fragmentation through the discourse of law, see Zillah R. Eisenstein, *The Female Body and the Law* (Berkeley: University of California Press, 1981). Ellyn Kaschak discusses fragmentation as an effect characteristic of the construction of

221

women in *Engendered Lives: A New Psychology of Women's Experience* (New York: Basic Books, 1992), pp. 111–13, 203–4.

60. For critique of the role of the dialectic of fragmentation and integrity in the construction of gender and of sex roles, see Monique Wittig, "One Is Not Born a Woman," pp. 9–20 in *The Straight Mind and Other Essays* (Boston: Beacon Press, 1992), and *The Lesbian Body*, translated by Peter Owen (New York: Avon, 1976). Where men are typically portrayed whole, and women largely in bodily fragments, the two images operate as complementary tropes. The major trope of female fragmentation becomes defined by the minor trope of male bodily integrity (and, of course, the further alignment of the male with the realm of the not pictured because not bodied).

61. Since both the fetishist and the courtier are drawn to metonymy, the trope provides them with a common ground, whether for eroticizing courtly politics or dominating erotic discourse. The fetish operates through the double substitution of the metonym: substituting part for part while substituting focalized attention on an object for abstract conception. As the breast, and then the bra, becomes the object of desire, so does the definition of desire work by displacement and by incarnating all of erotic awareness and mystery in the substituted part and its characteristic ornament. I should add that my interpretation is completely independent of any psychoanalytical account of the origin of the fetish, which I view as one version of "the pun whereby the logically prior can be expressed in terms of the temporally prior, and *v.v.*" (Kenneth Burke, *A Grammar of Motives* [Berkeley: University of California Press, 1969], p. 430). In addition, I am attempting to steer clear of debates about both the Freudian and Lacanian systems. Two comments in that regard: First, I am considering the fetish as it is a generalized phenomenon—not a specific "perversion" of "deviant" individuals, but part of all the gender representations and sexual relations in our society. For a similar perspective, see Katie Berkeley, "The Fetish in *Sex, Lies & Videotape*: Whither the Phallus," in Arthur and Marilouise Kroker, eds., *The Hysterical Male: New Feminist Theory* (New York: St. Martin's Press, 1991): "In the 'society of the spectacle,' however, fetishistic transactions may be characteristic of signification in the scopic economies, rendering somewhat 'normal' the 'perversions' that preoccupied Freud (although he also noted that a 'disposition to perversions is an original disposition of the human sexual instinct')" (p. 174). Second, if, as is posited within the Lacanian system, fragmentation is the child's experience of the body prior to transformation from the Real into symbolic organization, then fragmentation of the image of the adult body would be a transformation back out of order into primal (natural, organic) meaninglessness and, therefore, a powerful means for both the representation of political disorder (as during the decline or usurpation of a court) and for the subordination of women. For Jacques Lacan's account of the infant's bodily experience, see *Écrits: A Selection*, translated by Alan Sheridan (New York: W. W. Norton, 1977), pp. 4–5. For discussions of body signification through the recent feminist engagement with psychoanalysis, see, for example, Elizabeth Grosz, *Jacques Lacan: A Feminist Introduction* (New York: Routledge, 1990); Teresa Brennan, ed., *Between Feminism and Psychoanalysis* (London: Routledge, 1989); Jane Gallop, *The Daughter's Seduction: Feminism and Psychoanalysis* (Ithaca, NY: Cornell University Press, 1982); Elizabeth Gross, "The Body of Signification," in *Abjection, Melancholia, and Love: The Work of Julia Kristeva*, edited by John Fletcher and Andrew Benjamin (London: Routledge, 1990).

62. Michael Novak, *Choosing Our King* (New York: Macmillan 1974), p. 19.

63. For a related argument from a very different perspective, see Jürgen Haber-mas's account of "refeudalization" of the public sphere in *The Structural Transformation of the Public Sphere,* translated by Thomas Burger and Frederick Lawrence (Cambridge: MIT Press, 1989). For Habermas, whose social theory is oblivious to the aesthetic dimen-sion of practical communication, refeudalization is a long and gradual process determined by institutional changes; I am suggesting it (or something like it) can occur rapidly via stylistic changes.

64. For example, Diane Rubenstein argues that "the pathological policies of Iran Contra are discursively framed by Reagan's hospital stays and surgical interventions" ("Open Letters/Covert Operations: Rhetorical Readings of Iran Contra," in *Rhetorics of International Relations: Analyzing the Arguments, Myths, and Symbols of Foreign Affairs,* edited by John S. Nelson, [forthcoming]). For a wide-ranging account of the internalization of the trope of the king's two bodies by American presidents, see also chapter 3, "The King's Two Bodies: Lincoln, Wilson, Nixon, and Presidential Self-Sacrifice," in Michael Paul Rogin, *Ronald Reagan, The Movie, and Other Episodes in Political Demonology* (Berkeley: University of California Press, 1987).

65. Peggy Noonan, *What I Saw at the Revolution: A Political Life in the Reagan Era* (New York: Random House, 1990), p. 48. These aristocratic moments recall earlier debates about the style fitting to the presidency: See John C. Miller, *The Federalist Era* (New York: Harper and Row, 1960), pp. 6–12; Henry Ford James, *Washington and His Colleagues* (New Haven: Yale University Press, 1921), pp. 1–25. Elias argues in *The History of Manners* that conceptions of decorum were one site for the class conflict between the expanding middle class and ruling aristocracies in the eighteenth and nineteenth cen-turies. The tension between aristocratic and democratic aesthetic norms continues to shape social practices and cultural critique: see Debora Silverman, *Selling Culture: Bloomingdale's, Diana Vreeland, and the New American Aristocracy of Taste in Reagan's America* (New York: Pantheon, 1986).

66. Larry Speakes with Robert Pack, *Speaking Out: The Reagan Presidency from Inside the White House* (New York: Charles Scribner's Sons, 1988), p. 202.

Chapter Four: Cicero's Republican Style

1. Robert A. Ferguson, *Law and Letters in American Culture* (Cambridge: Harvard University Press, 1984), pp. 74n. 58, 76. Stephen Botein reminds us that Cicero was not only an influence, but an appropriation; "Cicero as Role Model," *Classical Journal* 73 (1978): 313–21. The role of antiquity, and of Cicero in particular, is chronicled vividly in the scholarly literature on civic republicanism in the Constitutional period: for example, "They found their ideal selves, and to some extent their voices, in Brutus, in Cassius, and in Cicero, whose Catilinarian orations the enraptured John Adams, age 23, declaimed aloud, alone at night in his room" (Bernard Bailyn, *The Ideological Origins of the Ameri-can Revolution* [Cambridge: Harvard University Press, 1967], p. 26). See also Gordon S. Wood, *The Creation of the American Republic, 1776–1787* (Chapel Hill: University of North Carolina Press, 1969) and *The Radicalism of the American Revolution* (New York: Alfred A. Knopf, 1992). See also Garry Wills, *Cincinnatus: George Washington and the Enlightenment* (Garden City, NY: Doubleday, 1984).

2. The letters recently have received superb presentation by D. R. Shackleton Bai-ley: *Cicero's Letters to Atticus* (Cambridge: Cambridge University Press, 1965–70);

223

Cicero: Epistulae ad Familiares (1977); *Cicero: Epistulae ad Quintum Fratrem et M. Brutum* (1980). The first work includes Latin text, English translation, and commentary; the translation also is available in paperback: D. R. Shackleton Bailey, *Cicero's Letters to Atticus* (New York: Penguin, 1978). The others provide Latin text with commentary. The Loeb Library collection remains available as well. Typically the letters have been used for linguistic analyses, or as marginalia when explicating other, more public Ciceronian texts, or as the inspiration and material for more general histories of their author and his world. Works based on the letters include Gaston Boissier, *Ciceron et ses Amis* (Paris, 1897), available in English translation by Adnah David Jones, *Cicero and His Friends* (New York: Cooper Square Publishers, 1970); Warren Stone Gordin, *The Estimates of Moral Values Expressed in Cicero's Letters: A Study of the Motives Professed or Approved* (Chicago: University of Chicago Press, 1905); Anna Bertha Miller, *Roman Etiquette of the Late Republic as Revealed by the Correspondence of Cicero* (Lancaster, PA: Press of the New Era, 1914); E. B. Sihler, *Cicero of Arpinum,* 2d corrected ed., (New York: G. E. Stechert, 1933); J. P. V. D. Balsdon, "Cicero the Man," in *Cicero,* edited by T. A. Dorey, pp. 171–214 (New York: Basic Books, 1965); D. R. Shackleton Bailey, *Cicero* (London: Duckworth, 1971); Magnus Wistrand, *Cicero Imperator: Studies in Cicero's Correspondence, 51–47* B.C. (Gothenburg, Sweden: Acta Universitatis Gothoburgensis, 1979). In addition, there are a number of biographies of Cicero, most following the same chronological pattern and themes. Besides those already mentioned, I would single out, for various reasons: H. J. Haskell, *This Was Cicero: Modern Politics in a Roman Toga* (New York: Alfred A. Knopf, 1942), which includes an annotated bibliography of prior biographies (pp. 368–76); R. E. Smith, *Cicero the Statesman* (Cambridge: Cambridge University Press, 1966); D. Stockton, *Cicero: A Political Biography* (Oxford: Oxford University Press, 1971); W. K. Lacey, *Cicero and the End of the Roman Republic* (New York: Harper and Row, 1978); Elizabeth Rawson, *Cicero: A Portrait,* rev. ed. (Ithaca, NY: Cornell University Press, 1983); Christian Habicht, *Cicero the Politician* (Baltimore: Johns Hopkins University Press, 1990); Thomas N. Mitchell, *Cicero: The Ascending Years* (New Haven: Yale University Press, 1979) and *Cicero: The Senior Statesman* (New Haven: Yale University Press, 1991). For general background, see Claude Nicolet, *The World of the Citizen in Republican Rome,* translated by P. S. Falla (Berkeley: University of California Press, 1980).

3. Neal Wood provides a succinct account of the historical fluctuations in Cicero's status as a political philosopher: *Cicero's Social and Political Thought* (Berkeley: University of California Press, 1988), pp. 1–13. The most virulent attack in modern scholarship was by the German classicist Theodor Mommsen: for example, Cicero "was a statesman without insight, idea, or purpose, . . . and was never more than a shortsighted egotist" who must "revolt every reader of feeling and judgment"; in his literary work, he was "a dabbler, . . . a journalist in the worst sense of that term"; as a man, he was the epitome of "thinly varnished superficiality and heartlessness" (*Mommsen's History of Rome,* translated by William P. Dickson [New York: Scribner's, 1899], vol. 4, pp. 724–25). The bases for Mommsen's judgment are revealed in part, first, by a related comment on Cicero— "his importance rests on his mastery of style, and it is only as a stylist that he shows confidence in himself" (p. 724)—and his corresponding judgment of Caesar's character—"thoroughly a realist and a man of sense; and whatever he undertook and achieved was pervaded and guided by the cool sobriety which constitutes the most marked peculiarity of his genius" (p. 540). The accuracy of Mommsen's judgment is indicated by his

assessment of Cicero's oratorical skill: "Cicero had no conviction and no passion; he was nothing but an advocate, and not a good one" (p. 726). Even more balanced assessments of the time emphasize that Cicero "was formed of pliable stuff, . . . always under the sway of the moment and therefore little qualified to be a statesman. . . . Hence the attempts he made to play a part in politics served only to lay bare his utter weakness" (*Teuffell's History of Roman Literature,* revised and enlarged by Ludwig Schwabe, translated by George C. W. Warr [London: George Bell, 1891], vol. 1, p. 276). Wood concludes that "the Cicero who has endured throughout the ages is the supreme political moralist, not the masterful politician" (p. 204). Wood's discussion parallels my own, as he contests the modern dismissal of Cicero by looking to "some of the Roman's lesser-known writings" for "perceptive thoughts on the nature of political activity" that can be understood as an "art of politics" (p. 176).

4. The most recent exposition of the civic republican perspective is also its best: Wood, *The Radicalism of the American Revolution.* The revival of scholarly interest began with Wood's earlier work, *The Creation of the American Republic,* along with Bailyn's *The Ideological Origins of the American Revolution.* Major impetus came from J. G. A. Pocock, "Virtue and Commerce in the Eighteenth Century," *Journal of Interdisciplinary History* 3 (1972): 119–34, and *The Machiavellian Moment: Florentine Political Thought and the Atlantic Republican Tradition* (Princeton: Princeton University Press, 1975). For sympathetic presentation of the republican ideal, see Ferguson, *Law and Letters.* Several of Garry Wills's books have helped cut the trail as well, despite some differences in theme and nomenclature: *Inventing America: Jefferson's Declaration of Independence* (Garden City, NY: Doubleday, 1978), *Explaining America: The Federalist* (Garden City, NY: Doubleday, 1981), and *Cincinnatus.* Daniel T. Rodgers provides an excellent review of the scholarly literature in "Republicanism: The Career of a Concept," *Journal of American History* 79 (1992): 11–38. Liberal objections to the revisionary project are exemplified by John Patrick Diggins, *The Lost Soul of American Politics: Virtue, Self-Interest, and the Foundations of Liberalism* (New York: Basic Books, 1984); Thomas L. Pangle, *The Spirit of Modern Republicanism: The Moral Vision of the American Founders and the Philosophy of Locke* (Chicago: University of Chicago Press, 1988); and Joyce Appleby, *Capitalism and a New Social Order: The Republican Vision of the 1790s* (New York: New York University Press, 1984). Appleby attempts to articulate an intermediate position in her most recent work, *Liberalism and Republicanism in the Historical Imagination* (Cambridge: Harvard University Press, 1992). For a more detailed record of the debate, see Rodgers, "Republicanism," p. 23, especially note 26.

5. Rodgers observes that "the concept of republicanism was one of the success stories of the 1980s," and he documents how it was used in colonial history, labor history, Southern history, and the like ("Republicanism: The Career of a Concept," p. 11). Ferguson describes the predominance of the Ciceronian model in federalist and Jeffersonian America (*Law and Letters,* pp. 20n. 22 and 74ff.). See also Kenneth Cmiel's rich synopsis of the period's culture of eloquence in *Democratic Eloquence: The Fight over Popular Speech in Nineteenth-Century America* (New York: William Morrow, 1990), chapter 1. Ferguson provides an apt example of how Cicero, and the *Letters to Atticus,* have been featured even in caricatures of the republican model: "'The South was an aggregate of farms and plantations, presided over by our composite agrarian hero, Cicero Cincinnatus. . . . the old gentleman in Kentucky who sat every afternoon in his front yard under an

225

old sugar tree, reading Cicero's Letters to Atticus' " (*Law and Letters,* pp. 295–96; quotation from Allen Tate, "A Southern Mode of the Imagination," *Collected Essays* [Denver, CO: Alan Swallow, 1959], pp. 563–64).

6. The major challenge to liberal individualism in contemporary political theory has been the communitarian revival, which in turn draws on a civic republican model. This debate is reviewed by Michael J. Sandel, ed., *Liberalism and Its Critics* (New York: New York University Press, 1984), and Shlomo Avineri and Avner de-Shalit, eds., *Communitarianism and Individualism* (Oxford: Oxford University Press, 1992). See, in particular, Sandel's influential essay, "The Procedural Republic and the Unencumbered Self," *Political Theory* 12 (1984): 81–96, reprinted in Avineri and de-Shalit, *Communitarianism and Individualism,* pp. 12–28. The discussion of civic republicanism in legal scholarship offers specific examples of how it is used to counter both conservative authority and liberal hegemony. Frank Michelman's "Law's Republic" was written in part to attack neoconservative judicial "authoritarianism" (*Yale Law Journal* 97 (1988): 1493–1513); see also "The Supreme Court: 1985 Term—Foreward: Traces of Self-Government," *Harvard Law Review* 100 (1986): 4–77. See also the additional essays in that issue, as well as in *William and Mary Law Review* 29 (1987), and *Florida Law Review* 41 (1989). Stanley Ingber turns to the literature on republicanism to equip himself for a communitarian interpretation of the first amendment in "Rediscovering the Communal Worth of Individual Rights: The First Amendment in Institutional Contexts," *Texas Law Review* 69 (1990): 1–108. As another mark of their republican sensibility, both Michelman and Ingber exemplify a somewhat more principled and literary sense of the law than the dominant orientation toward technical reasoning within bureaucratic structures; on this basic (and in part aesthetic) difference in legal thought, see Ferguson, *Law and Letters,* chapter 3 and ff., and pp. 281–90. I would also include the work in women's history as an example of recuperating republicanism as a means for countering authoritarianism, in this case, the rule of patriarchy; see Rodgers, "Republicanism," n. 43. This strategy is complicated by the historical association of republicanism with unduly limiting definitions of citizenship, and particularly by the masculinist tenor of the republican literature, which regularly associated masculinity, martial virtues, eloquence, and the preservation of the republic; see, for example, Wood, *Creation,* pp. 52–53. For a general sense of the masculinist definition of oratory, see Kathleen Hall Jamieson, *Eloquence in an Electronic Age: The Transformation of Political Speechmaking* (New York: Oxford University Press, 1988), chapter 4. For discussion of the affinities between feminism and republicanism, see Suzanne Sherry, "Civic Virtue and the Feminine Voice," *Virginia Law Review* 72 (1986): 543–616. For discussion of how gendered language could function in a more complicated manner in republican discourse, see James Jasinski, "The Feminization of Liberty, Domesticated Virtue, and the Reconstitution of Power and Authority in Early American Political Discourse," *Quarterly Journal of Speech* 79 (1993): 146–64. For criticism of the reactionary tone of some republican scholars, see Isaac Kramnick, *Republicanism and Bourgeois Radicalism: Political Ideology in Late Eighteenth-Century England and America* (Ithaca, NY: Cornell University Press, 1990), chapter 1. This attention to the political and ideological designs in the scholarly literature on civic republicanism does not contradict Rodgers' argument that the literature flourished because it solved interpretive crises in a number of subdisciplines. As for Cicero, there is no question that he was an elitist and that he did not avoid the practices of slavery, patriarchy, class domination, and imperialism that were part of

—
226

the fabric of Roman life. But these ideological discourses play little part in his artistry and receive no promotion by his example, and he was no Pompey or Caesar either. As for the republican style, it can carry political attitudes ranging from the reactionary to the progressive and serve as a code for both elitist presumptions and communitarian ideals. Rather than assume that any of these positions are likely outcomes, I consider them issues negotiated within its practice.

7. See, for example, William M. Sullivan, *Reconstructing Public Philosophy* (Berkeley: University of California Press, 1986), especially chapter 5, "A Renewal of Civic Philosophy." My criticism is not intended to denigrate such work, only to identify a crucial limitation. Mark V. Tushnet describes civic republican arguments in legal scholarship as one version of an antiformalism that he believes is merely utopian ("Anti-Formalism in Recent Constitutional History," *Michigan Law Review* 83 [1985]: 1544). His argument turns in part on the assessment that due to changes in the social formation "it is unclear that the republican tradition is readily available to us" (p. 1540). Although the point is a good one, it also is the case that generally recuperation appears to be a problem for those who assume that (1) discursive changes always are epiphenomenal, never determinative, (2) the tradition has to be recovered whole, and (3) it has to be recovered as a coherent set of ideas. I hope it is obvious that I am working from contrary assumptions.

8. Rodgers, "Republicanism," p. 37.

9. Ibid., pp. 35–38. The term "cult of eloquence" comes from Ferguson, *Law and Letters*, pp. 72–78, who stresses the republicans' mastery of diverse genres of expression. See also Isaac Kramnick, "The 'Great National Discussion': The Discourse of Politics in 1787," *William and Mary Quarterly* 45 (1988): 3–32. Kramnick observes a "profusion and confusion of political tongues" (p. 4), which he identifies as the four idioms of civic republicanism, Lockean liberalism, work-ethic Protestantism, and state-centered theories of power and sovereignty.

10. Rodgers concludes that consolidating the republican paradigm shift "required a more strategic sense of language than the ideational and linguistic structures for which republicanism's inventors and borrowers often yearned" ("Republicanism," p. 38).

11. Christopher Lasch dismissed the revisionary project for this reason: "A republican synthesis was no better than a liberal synthesis when such terms expanded to cover every political persuasion" (*The True and Only Heaven: Progress and Its Critics* [New York: W. W. Norton, 1991], p. 176).

12. Here I would apply the common sense of practical criticism: One can reasonably conclude that a particular political style is the means for the composition of political experience to the extent that all of its conventions are present and arrayed coherently, applied to the topics and tasks at hand comprehensively (broadly and deeply), controlling other appeals both through placement and characteristic interactions (as some appeals overrule or neutralize others), and connected to decision and action. It might be available in fragments, or prevail only by providing a basis for compromise, or be inconsistent with specific statements of intention, yet still be determinative. If it is present only in parts and incoherently, or occasionally and incidentally, etc., it probably should be considered inconsequential. (Even so, the criteria can shift a bit for particular styles; see the related discussion in chapter 3.) This book focuses primarily on identifying important elements of specific styles and their characteristic forms of coherence. I also suggest occasionally how they might work in respect to particular tasks, interact with other styles, and result in

227

particular outcomes, although much, much more could be said about these additional concerns.

13. Hans-Georg Gadamer, *Truth and Method*, 2d, rev. ed., translated by Joel Weinsheimer and Donald G. Marshall (New York: Continuum, 1993), pp. 384ff. I recognize that Gadamer has disavowed any intention of offering a model of interpretive technique. I am among those admirers who believe he has bent over too far backwards on this question of the relation between philosophical and technical hermeneutics, however. *Truth and Method* contains profound insights regarding how to begin an interpretation, which I have tried to put to good use here.

14. Gadamer, *Truth and Method*, 2d, rev. ed., pp. 386–88; see also p. 306.

15. Ibid., pp. 373ff.

16. Ibid., p. 387.

17. Ibid., p. 386.

18. Translations are by Shackleton Bailey, *Cicero's Letters to Atticus*. Parenthetical notes provide first the numbers used for his edition and then the traditional book and letter numbers of the Latin texts. I do not cite similar instances of an example, although typically they are available—for example, for another testimonial to Atticus, see 17/1.17. I hope I have solved the problem of providing enough examples to interest readers in classical studies while avoiding those that would be obscure for readers less familiar with the period. In any case, my primary purpose is to use the letters as a pretext for identifying the republican style. I like to think that this interpretation could be extended further into the classical language and literature by those with the expertise I lack and that other readers might turn to Cicero's letters and speeches to experience firsthand his genius.

19. This emotionally driven sense of action is consistent with Cicero's rhetorical theory, which distinguished between three basic functions of the persuasive act: one could persuade by teaching, pleasing, or moving the audience. Although he stressed that the complete oration should fulfill all three of these offices, the most important task was to set the emotional charge that would impel the audience to act on the orator's plea. "To prove is a necessity, to please a delight, to move brings victory" (my translation of *Orator* 69).

20. The passage translates four Greek rhetorical terms: περίοδοι, καμπαί, ἐνθυμήματα, κατασκευαί.

21. Jay Fliegelman's analysis of the rhetorical norms of the founders of the American republic is an intriguing approach to the problem of getting inside this culture of oratorical performance. Unfortunately, I discovered *Declaring Independence: Jefferson, Natural Language, and the Culture of Performance* (Stanford: Stanford University Press, 1993) only late in the revision of my manuscript. The affinities between Fliegelman's study and my own include our appreciation of the rhetorical tradition and our general interest in the relationship between "the dynamics of persuasion" and "the dynamics of political authority," as well as specific correspondences between his observations on the founders' culture and mine on the republican style. These common elements include (in my terms) the primacy of oratory, the sense of artistic (and acoustic) performance, the ideal of consensus, the composition and display of character, the importance of imitation, the role of emotion, the anxieties and paradoxes of practice, and the norm of civility, among others. There are differences as well: most importantly, Fliegelman emphasizes how more mod-

228

ern conceptions of self-expression, affective identity, and natural language were emerging and altering eighteenth-century political culture. In sum, Fliegelman illuminates some of the elements of the republican style as they were generally disseminated at the time but presents them as elements of a different whole—a transitional repertoire of classical republican and modern liberal appeals. By contrast, my analysis is not limited to one period and focuses on the elements cohering in an explicitly republican ideal type.

22. Cicero, *Orator* 71, translated by H. M. Hubbell, Loeb Library (Cambridge: Harvard University Press, 1962). Note that this extension still maintains oratory as the master art. For additional discussion of the importance of decorum within Cicero's conception of rhetoric, see A. E. Douglas, "A Ciceronian Contribution to Rhetorical Theory," *Eranos* 55 (1971): 18–26; Elaine Fantham, "Orator 69–74," *Central States Speech Journal* 35 (1984): 123–25; Michael Leff, "Decorum and Rhetorical Interpretation: The Latin Humanistic Tradition and Contemporary Critical Theory," *Vichiana* 3a series, 1 (1990): 107–26.

23. Cicero, *Orator* 74.

24. Cicero, *De officiis,* translated by Harry G. Edinger, Library of Liberal Arts (Indianapolis: Bobbs-Merrill, 1974), 1.111.

25. Francesco Petrarca, *Letters on Familiar Matters:* Rerum familiarium libri *XVII–XXIV,* translated by Aldo S. Bernardo (Baltimore: Johns Hopkins University Press, 1985), 24.4. Note how Petrarch recuperates Cicero by celebrating him first as a philosopher (rather than a politician), and then (24.5) as a literary stylist.

26. Note how Cicero also is activating for the moment the master trope of the realist style: He makes Cato appear unrealistic by marking him as discursive, under the sway of Plato's dialogue; the full implication is that Cato's alternative policy could only work in the idealistic, fictional world outlined in *The Republic.* The republican speaker can play the realist adroitly, but not without risk of being cut by the same sword. (The realist style and its effect on republicanism is discussed in chapter 2.) Realism is not necessary when defending Cicero's expediency, however. For example, see his zestful caricature of Cato's Stoicism in *Pro Murena* 61–66.

27. For an excellent essay on behalf of Cicero's perspective, see Paul F. Izzo, "Cicero and Political Expediency," *Classical World* 42.11 (7 March 1949): 168–72.

28. "It was Cicero's presentation of the orator that was particularly attractive to Renaissance humanists" (Victoria Kahn, *Rhetoric, Prudence, and Skepticism in the Renaissance* [Ithaca, NY: Cornell University Press, 1985], p. 36). Kahn's summary of the quattrocento humanists' attitudes toward rhetoric aptly captures Cicero's fusion of appropriate speech and effective political action: "practical certainty is in turn seen to be manifest in the *consensus omnium* of linguistic usage, rhetorical convention, and social custom. Philology and rhetoric (as the theory and practice of linguistic consensus) and politics (as the theory and practice of social consensus) are then judged to be analogous and inseparable" (p. 27). See also Nancy S. Struever, *The Language of History in the Renaissance: Rhetoric and Historical Consciousness in Florentine Humanism* (Princeton: Princeton University Press, 1970).

29. The American appropriation of civic humanism and veneration of Cicero is documented ably by Ferguson, *Law and Letters,* pp. 74–84, Cmiel's *Democratic Eloquence,* and others noted above. One text bears special mention: Caleb Bingham's widely

read *Columbian Orator* (1797) exemplifies the equation of eloquence and republican polity, as well as their mutual dependence on a pedagogy of imitation. One wonders if it shouldn't be reprinted today and perhaps updated as well.

30. Cmiel, *Democratic Eloquence,* p. 39.

31. Ferguson, *Law and Letters,* p. 78.

32. Perhaps the ephemeral nature of public address also had allegorical significance for civic republicans, obsessed as they were with the republic's stability while equating eloquence with liberty; or perhaps a political culture grounded in public address is more likely than others to have a strong sense of the transitory. The ephemeral nature of public address also poses special problems for both artistic appreciation and composition; how can one admire what is vanishing, and why emulate what will be forgotten? The republican cult of eloquence, and especially its reliance on imitation of classical texts, can be understood as one response to such problems. For discussion of these problems in the scholarly study of public address; see Herbert A. Wichelns, "The Literary Criticism of Oratory," in *Studies in Rhetoric and Public Speaking in Honor of James Albert Winans* edited by A. M. Drummond, pp. 181–216 (New York: Russell & Russell, 1925).

33. The imagined injunction is even sharper in the Latin—"dic, M. Tulli"—and the contrast heightened by the cadence and tone of the following line: "Quid dicam? 'Exspecta, amabo te, dum Atticum conveniam'?" See also 126/7.3, 130/7.7, and 171/9.5. Given his status as ex-consul, Cicero would have been the first or one of the first called on to speak.

34. See Bailyn, *Ideological Origins.*

35. This constitutive function goes all the way down: Cicero's rhetorical theory begins with the assertion that speech has been the primary agency of the civilizing process: *De inventione,* 1.2. The source for this assertion is Isocrates, *Antidosis* 253–54.

36. Ferguson observes how Rufus Choate "once spoke with such vehemence that he feared internal injury, and he was always sick and exhausted after a speech" (*Law and Letters,* p. 83); Cmiel quotes a reaction to Webster: " 'Three or four times I thought my temples would burst with the gush of blood' " (*Democratic Eloquence,* p. 23). The task of producing a community through discourse requires unusual emotional energy in the speaker and powerful emotional responses from the audience. Cicero's story of Galba offers a model of how the orator should exhaust himself while inflaming his audience: The moral of the story is that

> of the two chief qualities which the orator must possess, accurate argument looking to proof and impressive appeal to the emotions of the listener, the orator who inflames the court accomplishes far more than the one who merely instructs it; that in short Laelius possessed precision, Galba power. (*Brutus,* translated by G. L. Hendrickson, Loeb Classical Library [Cambridge: Harvard University Press, 1971], 85–89)

37. Ferguson, *Law and Letters,* pp. 80–84.

38. Cicero's *De oratore* provides extensive discussion of his conception and ranking of the various arts. Oratory is the supreme form of human artistry and the essential constituent of political practice. It is indispensable because of the inherent limitations of human nature, and its operation cannot be reduced to a knowledge of technique. Eloquence requires mastery of all human faculties, draws on and ranges across all other arts of civilization, and is realized through mastery of style. Consequently, the best preparation

230

for the art of oratory involves instruction in a wide range of disciplines. See, for example, *De oratore* 1.16–19, 30–34, 3.74–76, 122–24. Cicero is reproducing many of Isocrates' arguments regarding the nature and status of rhetoric; see, for example, *Against the Sophists* 12 and *Antidosis* 253–54, 271.

39. The republican appeal to consensus is a complicated idea that will have to include specific cultural presumptions and political practices. This richness can be developed by analysis of those concepts that accompany it. In antiquity, the idea resonated with *friendship,* which included but went well beyond the modern sense of affectionate or companionable relationships and provided the model for civic life. To press the point, let me suggest that Aristotle's analysis of friendship in the *Nicomachean Ethics* is crucial to his understanding of politics and that Cicero's dialogue *De amicitia* is another statement of his political ideals, a poetic complement to *De officiis.* The idea of *balance* (aesthetic and political; gestural and communal) also figured in Cicero's understanding of consensus, and apparently was important in the North American constitutional period as well; see Fliegelman, *Declaring Independence,* pp. 100–107, and 189–90. (Fliegelman is especially good at showing how the classical idea underwent modern redefinition.) According to Peter B. Knupfer, the idea of *compromise* also undergirded constitutional debates and became the dominant appeal for consensus during the conflict over slavery in the next century; see his *The Union As It Is: Constitutional Unionism and Sectional Compromise, 1787–1861* (Chapel Hill: University of North Carolina Press, 1991). Consider how each stage included the ideas of its predecessor, although each idea waned over time. Today the classical ideal of friendship is all but extinct (evident only in such phrases as "he's a good friend of the union"), balance is primarily a matter of diet and physical fitness, and compromise seems to be losing its energy amidst urban identity politics and suburban enclaves. In addition, to the extent that each of these ideas are versions of republican practice, they draw on a relatively optimistic view of human nature: one that doesn't deny our vices but holds out the likelihood that we can act in accord with "the better angels of our nature." Alburt Furtwangler illustrates how this ideal informs the style of the *Federalist* papers in *The Authority of Publius: A Reading of the Federalist Papers* (Ithaca, NY: Cornell University Press, 1984), pp. 78–79.

40. Habicht, *Cicero the Politician,* p. 99. This self-promotion has had other effects, of course, such as making Cicero a favorite whipping boy for more authoritarian intellectuals such as Mommsen.

41. On the persistence and literary character of Cicero's depiction of his relationship to the republic, see John Glucker, "As has been rightly said . . . by me," *Liverpool Classical Monthly* 13 (1988): 6–9. Cicero's later alignment of himself with the republic is most evident in the Second Philippic, which begins: "Members of the Senate: to what fatality of mine should I ascribe the fact that in these twenty years there was never an enemy of the Commonwealth who did not at the same time declare war on me?" Cicero, *Philippics,* edited and translated by D. R. Shackleton Bailey (Chapel Hill: University of North Carolina Press, 1986), 2.1.

42. James M. May provides a succinct discussion of Cicero's use of this figure, particularly in the speeches following his return from exile; see chapter 4 of *Trials of Character: The Eloquence of Ciceronian Ethos* (Chapel Hill, NC: University of North Carolina Press, 1988).

43. *De officiis* 1.117. I have substituted "person" for "man" in the translation.

231

44. *De officiis* 1.124.

45. Cicero, *De oratore,* translated by E. W. Sutton and H. Rackham, Loeb Classical Library (Cambridge: Harvard University Press, 1976), 2.310. Cf. May, *Trials of Character,* p. 167.

46. May, *Trials of Character,* pp. 11–12, 166. As May charts Cicero's career, the orator beings with the ethos of the *novus homo,* then assumes the Consular authority, recovers himself *post reditum* by identifying himself more explicitly with the idea of the Republic, and completes his career through intensified use of this figure in the *Philippics.*

47. Shackleton Bailey, *Cicero,* p. 114. Forrest McDonald, *Ordo Seclorum: The Intellectual Origins of the Constitution* (Lawrence: University of Kansas Press, 1985) provides an instructive discussion of how the founders of the American republic saw the love of fame as the most noble passion and a pillar of republican government (pp. 189–90). Earlier, Douglass Adair had argued that the republican love of fame transmuted crass self-interest into good government; see "Fame and the Founding Fathers," in *Fame and the Founding Fathers: Essays by Douglass Adair,* edited by Trevor Colbourn, pp. 3–26 (New York: W. W. Norton, 1974). See also, James M. Farrell, "John Adam's *Autobiography:* The Ciceronian Paradigm and the Quest for Fame," *New England Quarterly* 62 (1989): 505–28.

48. Leo Braudy, *The Frenzy of Renown: Fame and Its History* (New York: Oxford University Press, 1986), pp. 77–78.

49. Hannah Arendt, *The Human Condition* (Chicago: University of Chicago Press, 1958), p. 21.

50. Wills, *Cincinnatus,* says the same of the American constitutional period: "Fame was thus a social glue, a structural element, for the republic in its early days" (p. 129). Certainly modern thought has drifted far from Alexander Hamilton's charge that Aaron Burr threatened liberty because he lacked a love of glory; see Gerald Stourzh, *Alexander Hamilton and the Idea of Republican Government* (Stanford: Stanford University Press, 1970), pp. 98–102. See also David F. Epstein, *The Political Theory of the Federalist* (Chicago: University of Chicago Press, 1984), pp. 179–85. Pocock provides a succinct discussion of the role of *onore* in the republican tradition in *The Machiavellian Moment,* pp. 248–53.

51. Braudy, *The Frenzy of Renown,* p. 75.

52. Balsdon, "Cicero the Man," p. 194.

53. This is why it has been important to restore some balance to the historical record: The argument begins by noting that it is unfair to compare Cicero's record of his inner life with his competitors' public pronouncements; he is penalized because his letters survived and theirs did not. At perhaps its farthest reach, it reconsiders what constitutes success and failure, for example, noting that Caesar was assassinated first and that some elements of Cicero's republic were preserved against considerable odds. The major essays on Cicero each address these questions one way or another. Habicht's *Cicero the Politician* and Woods's *Cicero's Social and Political Thought* are recent statements in his defense.

54. John Milton, from the *Second Defense,* as rendered by Antonia Fraser, *Cromwell: The Lord Protector* (New York: Dell, 1975), p. 113.

55. Furtwangler advances similar claims about the American constitutional debates. In particular, the *Federalist* was crafted to "develop a national spirit of good will"

232

that had to go "beyond the winning of a few grudged ballots or narrow majorities" if the new government was to prevail (*Authority*, p. 69), and the authors did this through a carefully developed ethos that featured "a tone—and an authority—of high, privileged civility in debate" (pp. 94 and ff.).

56. The usage is legion, but for one example of how the style structures analysis, see George F. Will, *Statecraft as Soulcraft: What Government Does* (New York: Touch-stone/Simon and Schuster, 1983). Will invokes Cicero as the guiding spirit of the volume, focuses on government's inevitable influence and dependence on character, defines virtue as self-control for public ends, and concludes, in part, with this injunction: "to revitalize politics and strengthen government, we need to talk about talk. We need a new, respect-ful rhetoric—respectful, that is, of the better angels of mankind's nature. It must be more Ciceronian, more Lincolnesque" (p. 159). This last melding of polity, public talk, and decorousness reproduces a republican sensibility, albeit one that is both aesthetically restrained and ideologically oriented as well. I can agree with Will's call for improved public discourse as long as the ideological code also at work in the passage is kept sealed—that is, as along as the sentiment is not applied to censor categorically some forms of liberal and radical speech, as Will certainly would see fit to do. Also note that there are considerable differences between traditional republicanism and conservatism. Although both believe that virtues are the key to polity and that cultural institutions are the means for inculcating virtue, the virtues have changed radically (for example, from courage to piety) and, not surprisingly, the idea that commerce is the chief threat to civic virtue has disappeared entirely. Nonetheless, progressives probably will be quick to dismiss any af-firmation of the republican style as a conservative rhetoric. This would be a mistake simi-lar to their abandonment of the Bible to fundamentalist interpretation and nativist politics.

57. Walter Lippmann illustrates how one can join republican appeals with a con-servative vision to dupe a liberal audience. In his *Essays in the Public Philosophy* (Boston: Little, Brown, 1955), Lippmann draws heavily on the commonplaces of conservative rheto-ric—the decline of the West, due in part to its abandonment of natural law, etc.—and concludes by calling for a "Defense of Civility" that melds liberal public-spiritedness with a reactionary politics.

58. For example, Michael Walzer, "Civility and Civic Virtue in Contemporary America," *Social Research* 41 (1975): 593–611. Walzer's essay distinguishes between civic republican and more recent liberal versions of civility, in favor of the latter, while holding out for a more "socialist and democratic" version of civic virtue. These twists and turns suggest that "civility" and "civic virtue" are concepts being activated to manage rather serious, and at times unnamed, difficulties within liberalism. In fact, it has be-come a familiar appeal, particularly in peroration, by liberal apologists and administra-tors. It also is used across an ideological spectrum of theorists, although usually reflecting a bias toward the right. Alasdair MacIntyre provides the most notorious claim in *After Virtue: A Study in Moral Theory*, 2d ed. (Notre Dame, IN: University of Notre Dame Press, 1984): "What matters at this stage is the construction of local forms of community within which civility and the intellectual and moral life can be sustained through the new dark ages which are already upon us" (p. 245). For sharp criticism of this sentiment, but guarded use of its vocabulary, see Benjamin Barber, *The Conquest of Politics: Liberal Philosophy in Democratic Times* (Princeton: Princeton University Press, 1988), pp. 190ff. The most systematic case for civility comes from Michael Oakeshott, "The Voice of Poetry

233

in the Conversation of Mankind," in *Rationalism in Politics and Other Essays* (New York: Basic Books, 1962), and *On Human Conduct* (Oxford: Clarendon Press, 1975). The easy substitution of one of Oakeshott's terms, "conversation," for another, "civility," has been the key for translating his argument into the liberal idiom by theorists such as Richard Rorty and Richard Bernstein. See also the discussion by Fred R. Dallmyer, *Polis and Praxis: Exercises in Contemporary Political Theory* (Cambridge: MIT Press, 1984), pp. 190ff. These varied responses cohere if considered as a response to the legitimation crisis of late modern liberalism, and one that is coincident with the shift from positivist to linguistic conceptions of rationality. Influential discussion of this latter shift includes Richard J. Bernstein, *Beyond Objectivism and Relativism: Science, Hermeneutics, and Praxis* (Philadelphia: University of Pennsylvania Press, 1985), and Richard Rorty, *Contingency, Irony, and Solidarity* (Cambridge: Cambridge University Press, 1989). For discussion of this shift in respect to university politics, see Robert Hariman, "The Liberal Matrix: Pluralism and Professionalism in the American University," *Journal of Higher Education* 62 (1991): 451–66, especially 459ff. The influence of Robert N. Bellah et al., *Habits of the Heart: Individualism and Commitment in American Life* (Berkeley: University of California Press, 1985), is indicative of the wide appeal of republican themes once they are translated into the vernacular of modernist social theory (no mean feat). The more modest success of the sequel, *The Good Society* (New York: Alfred A. Knopf, 1991), is indicative of the difficulty of the basic problem the work tackles, which is extending those themes within institutional politics. There are other difficulties as well, many related to the authors' insufficient attention to such considerations as the importance of persuasion and the role of imitation. Finally, Richard Sennett, *The Fall of Public Man: On the Social Psychology of Capitalism* (New York: Random House/Vintage, 1978), provides an insightful defense of civility, including the observation that its demise "makes of the individual *an actor deprived of an art*" (p. 264).

59. For an example of how norms of civility can inform anarchist oratory, see Thomas Rosteck and Michael Leff, "Piety, Propriety, and Perspective: An Interpretation and Application of Key Terms in Kenneth Burke's *Permanence and Change*," *Western Journal of Speech Communication* 53 (1989): 327–41.

60. Vaclav Havel, "Paradise Lost," translated by Paul Wilson, *New York Review of Books* 39 (9 April 1992): 6–8; "Politics, Morality, and Civility," in *Summer Meditations*, translated by Paul Wilson (New York: Alfred A. Knopf, 1992); *Time*, 3 August 1992, pp. 46–48. Havel sounds additional themes of civic republican thought as well: He defines the transformation of the state as a "crisis of civility" and a struggle between vices and virtues, he defines the ideal politician as someone who has the "decorum and good taste" to work midway between deceit and principle, and he emphasizes that democratic government requires comprehensive cultural revival:

234

> Culture in the widest possible sense of the word, including everything from what might be called the culture of everyday life—or 'civility'—to what we know as high culture, including the arts and sciences. . . . I am convinced that we will never build a democratic state based on rule of law if we do not at the same time build a state that is—regardless of how unscientific this may sound to the ears of a political scientist—humane, moral, intellectual and spiritual, and cultural. (*Summer Meditations*, pp. 12, 18)

The civic republican tenor of these ideas can be highlighted by noting the strong similarity with the philosophy of Leonardo Bruni. As summarized by Pocock, Bruni's "idealization of Florentine civility" defined the citizen as one "who can develop as many forms of human excellence as possible and develop them all in the service of the city, . . . The case for the open society, as Bruni saw it, was that the excellence of one could only flourish when developed in collaboration with the diverse excellences of others" (*Machiavellian Moment,* p. 88). See also chapter 5, "Imitation, Rhetoric, and Quattrocento Thought in Bruni's *Laudatio,*" in Hans Baron, *From Petrarch to Leonardo Bruni: Studies in Humanistic and Political Literature* (Chicago: University of Chicago Press, 1968), and in the same volume the text of the *Laudatio Florentinae Urbis,* pp. 232–63. The concept of civility shapes Havel's promotion as well (or, is promoted further through portraits of Havel): Theodore Draper's account of a meeting with Adamec, when "both sides behaved with the utmost civility," is at once so solemn and mundane that it becomes silly ("A New History of the Velvet Revolution," *New York Review of Books* 40 [14 January 1992]: 17).

61. Havel, "Paradise Lost," pp. 7–8.

62. Havel's thoroughgoing European modernism is evident in, for example, "A Dream for Czechoslovakia," translated by Paul Wilson, *New York Review of Books* 39 (25 June 1992). For provocative discussion of the relationship between modernity and manners in the European context, see John Murray Cuddihy, *The Ordeal of Civility: Freud, Marx, Lévi-Strauss, and the Jewish Struggle with Modernity* (New York: Basic Books, 1974).

63. MacIntyre, *After Virtue,* p. 220. MacIntyre has given his argument extensive additional development, for example, in *Whose Justice? Which Rationality* (Notre Dame: University of Notre Dame Press, 1988). I am among those who believe that *After Virtue* remains the more challenging work, despite its flaws, and that the promise of MacIntyre's project is more likely to be realized through engagement with his most provocative statement than by following the road he has taken since, which leads back into some of the professional attitudes and assumptions that he had rightly criticized before.

64. Cicero, *Post reditum in Senatu,* translated by D. R. Shackleton Bailey, *Back From Exile: Six Speeches upon His Return* (Atlanta, GA: Scholars' Press, 1991), p. 1.

65. This ethical stance also accounts for his error in judgment when he ordered the execution of the conspirators without trial. If the survival of the republic had depended on such quick, decisive action, the violation of custom and law would have been excused; as it did not, it seemed only hurried and became a violation of the countervailing norm of civility. The judgments involved were not so much a matter of setting aside or holding to the legal code, but more a matter of ethical consideration, and both his rationalization and others' unease were justifiable in terms of republican precepts.

66. As Jean-Claude Schmitt summarizes, Cicero stands at the beginning of a tradition of reflection upon gesture that was thoroughly ethical in its orientation ("The Ethics of Gesture," in *Fragments for a History of the Human Body,* edited by Michel Feher, pp. 128–47 [New York: Zone, 1989]). Michel Foucault's work is instructive here as well, as when he claims, while quoting Aristotle's *Rhetoric,* that classical sexual morality came not from derivation of a systematic code of rules, but rather from "prudence, reflection, and calculation in the way one distributed and controlled his acts," that is, a strategic process of "variable adjustment" accomplished through one's performance according to

235

considerations of need, timeliness, and status. As prudence signified the transformation of raw desire into acceptable gesture, it served as a program both for disciplining the body for the composition of meaning and for the production of the system of knowledge and authority regulating the social body. See Michel Foucault, *The Use of Pleasure,* translated by Robert Hurley (New York: Vintage, 1990), p. 54.

67. Cicero, *Orator* 74. For similar statement and development, see also *De officiis* 1.126–41.

68. Obviously, the list of examples here could be endless. For an interesting case study, see Lawrence W. Rosenfield, "Central Park and the Celebration of Civic Virtue," in *American Rhetoric: Context and Criticism,* edited by Thomas W. Benson, pp. 221–66 (Carbondale: University of Southern Illinois Press, 1989). I also find Henry Fairlie's promotion of republican sensibilities to be noteworthy: for example, "The Politician's Art," *Harper's* (December 1977): 33–46, 123–24, and "The Decline of Oratory," *The New Republic* (28 May 1984): 15–19. The best example of a contemporary text that could serve as a primer in the republican style is *Congressional Anecdotes* by Paul F. Boller, Jr. (New York: Oxford University Press, 1991). Each of the elements I have identified (and additional nuances) are displayed repeatedly, and some of them function as well to establish its superiority over bureaucratic or courtly alternatives. One should consider how civics curricula today would be improved if this collection, as well as the *Columbian Orator* and other such collections of public discourse (which now would include, say, the Port Huron statement and the Redstocking Manifesto, among others) were added to the reading of the Constitution, itself increasingly a text used in public discourse without any sense of intertextuality.

69. The best instruction for a contemporary reader in the use of classical models probably is Garry Wills's superb study, *Lincoln at Gettysburg: The Words that Remade America* (New York: Simon and Schuster, 1992).

70. Marshall S. Shapo, letter to the editors, *The New Republic* (29 November 1993): 7.

71. This is the sense of literary or lexical style embedded within republican composition. American republican diction initially was created out of a tension between admiration of Cicero's amplified style and identification with a plain speech providing symbolic contrast with the language of monarchy. Thus, republican literary composition would have to be some kind of intermediate rhetoric. The artistic potential of a language of elevated simplicity was revealed in the Gettysburg Address; Wills, in *Lincoln at Gettysburg,* discusses Lincoln's stylistic achievement and influence. Cmiel, in *Democratic Eloquence,* provides extended discussion of the many factors contributing to the development of a middling style that has prevailed in the twentieth century.

72. Cicero, *In Catilinam,* translated by C. MacDonald, Loeb Classical Library (Cambridge: Harvard University Press, 1977), 3.26.

73. Cicero, *Pro Murena,* translated by C. MacDonald, Loeb Classical Library (Cambridge: Harvard University Press, 1977), 52. Unfortunately, this translation dulls the effect of *illa lata insignique lorica.*

74. Those familiar with the secondary literature on civic republicanism will recognize that this concluding argument parallels the foundational debate in that literature regarding the influence historically of Lockean and civic republican doctrines. Rodgers, "Republicanism," pp. 12ff., reviews these debates.

75. This position has been developed most successfully by John Rawls, *A Theory of Justice* (Cambridge: Belknap/Harvard University Press, 1971). Rawls's position is widely understood as the major statement of the dominant frame of reference in Anglo-American political culture. Other defenses of modern subjectivity include Jürgen Habermas's *The Philosophical Discourse of Modernity: Twelve Lectures,* translated by Frederick Lawrence (Cambridge: MIT Press, 1987), and Charles Taylor's *Sources of the Self: The Making of Modern Identity* (Cambridge: Harvard, 1989) and *The Ethics of Authenticity* (Cambridge: Harvard University Press, 1992). Each of these works illustrates how far modernity has gone beyond the classical literature and republican sensibilities and also how the philosophical construction of modern identity occurs without consideration of social and political practices that have been both pervasive and important, particularly in North America. For critique of Rawls, see Michael J. Sandel, *Liberalism and the Limits of Justice* (Cambridge: Cambridge University Press, 1982). For an important break with the liberal emphasis upon rights, see Mary Ann Glendon, *Rights Talk: The Impoverishment of Political Discourse* (New York: Free Press, 1991).

76. See MacIntyre's statement of this argument in *After Virtue.*

77. Sandel, *Liberalism and Its Critics,* pp. 5–6.

78. Studies of Cicero's prose style naturally are focused on his orations and other public works, while studies of the letters subordinate style to other concerns, and generally classical studies are focused on use of the classical language and literary practices of the time. See A. D. Leeman, *Orationis Ratio: The Stylistic Theories and Practice of the Roman Orators, Historians, and Philosophers,* 2 vols. (Amsterdam: Adolf J. Hakkert, 1963); Harold Gotoff, *Cicero's Elegant Style* (Urbana: University of Illinois Press, 1979); Walter Ralph Johnson, *Luxuriance and Economy: Cicero and the Alien Style* (Berkeley: University of California Press, 1971). The first observation on Cicero's letters from this perspective would be that they are distinguished from his other works by being written in the plain style (one of the *tria genera dicendi*): "It is everyday language without vulgarity, the conversational language of the upper-class. We find it in Terence's comedies, in the *sermones* of Horace, and in Cicero's letters" (Leeman, *Orationis ratio,* I:31). There is more to be said, of course, and the letters pose an interesting problem for Cicero's rhetorical theory are well: if they are examples of the plain style, they confound his alignment of the three styles with the three functions of persuasion (plain/teaching, middle/pleasing, and grand/moving); if they are read as compendia of the several styles, then they demonstrate a facility for changing one's voice frequently and fluidly that is not adequately accounted for in his theory, despite the argument that the orator should be capable of using all three modes. In each case, Cicero's practice is the better guide than his theory.

79. Gadamer, *Truth and Method,* 2d, rev. ed., pp. 383–88.

80. Arendt, *The Human Condition.* See also, Sennett, *Fall of Public Man.*

81. This "*locus of the irreparable*" is the rhetorical figure sustaining the sense of temporality that Pocock has identified as a crucial characteristic of modern republicanism. His argument is developed across the length of *The Machiavellian Moment;* the figure is discussed in Chaim Perelman and L. Olbrechts-Tyteca, *The New Rhetoric: A Treatise on Argumentation,* translated by John Wilkinson and Purcell Weaver (Notre Dame: University of Notre Dame Press, 1969), pp. 91–93.

82. McDonald, *Ordo Seclorum,* illustrates how "to understand Washington and to understand the species of republican virtue provided for a few by the theory of the

passions, one must begin with the recognition that Washington was ever concerned, almost obsessively, with creating and then living up to what he called his 'character'—what in the twentieth century would be called his reputation or public image" (p. 193). For a similar account, see Wills, *Cincinnatus,* especially chapter 8, "Fame," and chapter 9, "Role." See also Fliegelman, *Declaring Independence,* pp. 180ff. Both Wills and McDonald argue that Washington composed himself by drawing heavily on Joseph Addison's widely influential play, *Cato.* Whatever the particular hero chosen for emulation, the republican rhetor chooses in order to repeat the hero's persuasive victory of becoming perceived to be the embodiment of the republic. By comparing these republican icons with other leading Romans, we see how embodiment includes but exceeds an ethos of civic virtues.

83. Observe his disgust over how he had been stripped of his dignity on the one hand by Pompey's vacillation and on the other by Caesar's aggressiveness:

> Only one thing remains to fill up the cup of our friend's dishonour—not to go to Domitus' help. "But nobody doubts that he will go." *I* don't think so. . . . Well, I know whom to flee but I don't know whom to follow. You praise that "memorable" saying of mine, that I prefer defeat with Pompey to victory with those others. Why, so I do, but with Pompey as he then was or as I thought him to be. But *this* Pompey, who takes to his heels before he knows where he is running or whom he is running from, who has surrendered all that is ours, has abandoned Rome, is abandoning Italy—well, if I preferred defeat with him I have my wish, defeated I am. For the rest, I can't bear the sight of things I never feared to see, nor, I will add, of the man who has robbed me not only of what I had but of what I was. (155/8.7)

Whereas too often today reputation is understood as external to the individual—as a commodity that can be manipulated—for Cicero, reputation is the substance of one's relationships with others, something that is at once objective and keenly felt, a form of conscience and a political resource held in common with both friends and adversaries.

84. It seems there is a growing support in historical scholarship for this idea of composite rhetorics. Michael Lienesch provides a thoughtful discussion of how the transition from classical republicanism to modern liberalism was "inconclusive, neither clear nor complete, and the result was a hybrid mixture that combined republican and liberal themes in a creative but uneasy collaboration" (*New Order of the Ages: Time, the Constitution, and the Making of Modern American Political Thought* [Princeton: Princeton University Press, 1988], p. 7). For arguments that the traditions are convergent or symbiotic, see, for example, Jeffrey C. Isaac, "Republicanism vs. Liberalism? A Reconsideration," *History of Political Thought* 9 (1988): 349–77, and Dorothy Ross, *The Origins of American Social Science* (Cambridge: Cambridge University Press, 1991), chapter 2. The possibilities for convergence and combination of liberal and civic republican precepts are more easily comprehended once they are understood as stylistic choices. This does not eliminate conflict between them, particularly when the liberal doctrine is articulated in a legalist style, as now is often the case, but it does help in identifying how they function together persuasively despite philosophical contradictions. See also Thomas Gustafson, *Representative Words: Politics, Literature, and the American Language, 1776–1865* (Cam-

238

bridge: Cambridge University Press, 1992), which I regret I discovered too late to incorporate into this essay.

Chapter Five: Kafka's Bureaucratic Style

1. Walter Benjamin, "Franz Kafka: On the Tenth Anniversary of His Death," in *Illuminations,* edited by Hannah Arendt (New York: Schocken, 1969), p. 122.

2. Max Weber, *The Protestant Ethic and the Spirit of Capitalism,* translated by Talcott Parsons (New York: Scribner, 1958), p. 181; Jürgen Habermas, *The Theory of Communicative Action,* vol. 2, *Lifeworld and System: A Critique of Functionalist Reason,* translated by Thomas McCarthy (Boston: Beacon, 1987), and *The Philosophical Discourse of Modernity: Twelve Lectures,* translated by Frederick Lawrence (Cambridge: MIT Press, 1987).

3. Awareness of the moral ambivalence of bureaucracy has been available since Weber and was articulated during an important time in the formation of American social theory by Alvin W. Goulder, "Metaphysical Pathos and the Theory of Bureaucracy," *American Political Science Review* 49 (1955): 496–507. It should be emphasized, moreover, that this ambivalence is not based on the claim that bureaucracy is morally neutral. There is a difference between seeing something as neither good nor evil, and seeing it as both good and evil. I don't deny that bureaucracies are means for controlling workers and populations, or that given uncontested installation in a society, as in the former Soviet bloc, they have made communal life unrelentingly dreary, or that they can be forms of violence that disrupt local community and rationalize the destruction of human beings. The ambivalence comes from admitting that they also are enormously productive means for achieving the good life. Consider bureaucracy as another of modernity's gambles, similar to betting on technological development that could liberate us from scarcity, if the resource consumption sustaining that development in the meantime doesn't result in suicide. The focus of my analysis is not on the summary judgment, but on identifying choices in everyday communicative practice that determine this form of life. For an analysis that is compatible with my perspective, see Peter Miller, "Accounting and Objectivity: The Invention of Calculating Selves and Calculable Spaces," *Annals of Scholarship* 9 (1992): 61–86, reprinted in Allan Megill, ed., *Rethinking Objectivity* (Durham, NC: Duke University Press, 1994), pp. 239–64.

4. Benjamin remarked that theological interpretation of *The Castle* has "become the common property of Kafka criticism" (*Illuminations,* p. 127). For excellent discussion of the theological significance of *The Castle,* as well as succinct review of other critical approaches to the text, see Hans Küng and Walter Jens, *Literature and Religion,* translated by Peter Heinegg (New York: Paragon House, 1991), pp. 261–96. For representative examples of the critical literature, see Peter F. Neumeyer, ed., *Twentieth Century Interpretations of* The Castle (Englewood Cliffs, NJ: Prentice-Hall, 1969); Kenneth Hughes, ed. and trans., *Franz Kafka: An Anthology of Marxist Criticism* (Hanover: University Press of New England, 1981); Alan Udoff, ed., *Kafka and the Contemporary Critical Performance* (Bloomington: Indiana University Press, 1987); Mark Anderson, ed., *Reading Kafka: Prague, Politics, and the Fin de Siècle* (New York: Schocken, 1989); Ritchie Robertson, *Kafka: Judaism, Politics, and Literature* (Oxford: Clarendon, 1985); Stanley Corngold, *Franz Kafka: The Necessity of Form* (Ithaca, NY: Cornell University Press, 1988); Clayton

239

Koelb, *Kafka's Rhetoric: The Passion of Reading* (Ithaca, NY: Cornell University Press, 1989). For a bibliography, see Flores Angel, *A Kafka Bibliography: 1908–1976* (New York: Gordian Press, 1976).

5. Harold Garfinkel, *Studies in Ethnomethodology* (Oxford: Polity Press, 1967), p. 45.

6. Ibid.

7. Ibid. See also Harold Garfinkel, ed., *Ethnomethodological Studies of Work* (New York: Routledge, 1987). Basic discussions of ethnomethodology include John Heritage, *Garfinkel and Ethnomethodology* (Cambridge: Polity Press, 1984); Kenneth Leiter, *A Primer on Ethnomethodology* (New York: Oxford University Press, 1980); Wes Sharrock and Bob Anderson, *The Ethnomethodologists* (New York: Tavistock, 1986); Roy Turner, ed., *Ethnomethodology* (Harmondsworth: Penguin, 1974). For ethnomethodological analysis of bureaucratic work, see, for example, Donald Zimmerman, "Record Keeping and the Intake Process in a Public Welfare Agency," in *On Record: Files and Dossiers in American Life*, edited by Stanton Wheeler, pp. 319–54 (New York: Sage, 1969), and the essays by Aaron Cicourel, Garfinkel, David Sudnow, and D. L. Wieder in Turner, ed., *Ethnomethodology*.

8. Garfinkel, *Studies in Ethnomethodology*, p. 11.

9. Ibid., p. 45.

10. Franz Kafka, *The Castle*, translated by Willa and Edwin Muir (New York: Schocken Books, 1982), pp. 47–48. Subsequent page citations are given in the text.

11. Earlier critics have noted this peculiar characteristic of Kafka's literary style: for example, "He sees everything solidly and ambiguously at the same time; and the more visually exact he succeeds in making things, the more questionable they become" (Edwin Muir, "Introductory Note," *America*, translated by Edwin and Willa Muir [London, 1938], p. vii).

12. For biographies of Kafka, see, for example, Frederick Robert Karl, *Franz Kafka, Representative Man* (New York: Ticknor and Fields, 1991); Ernst Pawel, *The Nightmare of Reason: A Life of Franz Kafka* (New York: Farrar, Straus, Giroux, 1984); Ronald Hayman, *Kafka: A Biography* (New York: Oxford University Press, 1992).

13. Garfinkel, *Studies in Ethnomethodology*, p. 46.

14. Benjamin, *Illuminations*, p. 129. See also Karl J. Kuepper, "Gesture and Posture as Elemental Symbolism in Kafka's *The Trial*," *Mosaic* 3 (1970): 143–52, reprinted in James Rolleston, ed., *Twentieth Century Interpretations of* The Trial (Englewood Cliffs, NJ: Prentice-Hall, 1976). For an example of how Kafka used his sense of gesture to regulate himself and particularly his writing, see "Resolutions," in *The Penal Colony: Stories and Short Pieces*, translated by Willa and Edwin Muir (New York: Schocken Books, 1948), pp. 28–9: " . . . A characteristic movement in such a condition is to run your little finger along your eyebrows."

15. Benjamin, *Illuminations*, p. 127.

16. Ibid., p. 121.

17. Ibid., p. 124.

18. Ibid., p. 120.

19. Franz Kafka, *The Trial*, translated by Willa and Edwin Muir, revised by E. M. Butler (New York: Schocken Books, 1984), p. 2. Subsequent page citations are given in the text.

20. Benjamin, *Illuminations*, p. 122. My comparison with ethnomethodology need

not deny that Kafka also uses other, and perhaps more literary, means for inducing alien-ation. I feature only those that are pertinent to the political style that is the object of my investigation, however. See Richard Sheppard, *On Kafka's Castle: A Study* (New York: Barnes and Noble, 1973), for analysis of eight other alienation techniques: "parallelisms, discrepancies, leitmotivs, changes of register, reflection, indirect narrational comment, direct comment on K. by others, and breaks in narrative perspective" (p. 35).

21. I don't wish to become entangled at this point in an argument about generic classifications. *The Trial* usually has been read in either of two ways: as either a criticism of a sociopolitical system or an account of an existential condition. For representative examples of each approach, see Hannah Arendt, "Franz Kafka," in Hughes, ed. and trans., *Franz Kafka: An Anthology of Marxist Criticism,* and Ingeborg Henel, "The Legend of the Doorkeeper and Its Significance for Kafka's Trial," translated by James Rolleston, in Rol-leston, ed., *Twentieth Century Interpretations of* The Trial. Either way, many readers con-clude that the story is "a modern tragedy." It is a tragedy because it features a protago-nist who fails in his struggle with fate, perhaps because of a flaw of character, and it is modern because of its low mimetic characterization and its focus on self-consciousness. My terminology comes from Northrup Frye, *Anatomy of Criticism: Four Essays* (Princeton: Princeton University Press, 1957). Ultimately, this focus on self-consciousness makes tragedy an epistemological drama—a struggle for knowledge and, particularly, knowledge of one's self; this perspective is evident in the influential text by Cleanth Brooks and Robert B. Heilman, *Understanding Drama* (New York: Holt, Rinehart and Winston, 1966), and developed in Henel's finely argued criticism. For the suggestion that the tragic form arises with the ascendancy of a *"forensic"* mentality, see Kenneth Burke, *Attitudes To-ward History,* rev. 2d ed., (Boston: Beacon Press, 1961), p. 38.

22. For documentation of K.'s lack of credibility, see Erwin R. Steinberg, "K. of The Castle: Ostensible Land-Surveyor," *College English* 32 (1965): 1985–89, reprinted in Neumeyer, ed., *Twentieth Century Interpretations of* The Castle; Walter Sokel, *Franz Kafka* (New York: Columbia University Press, 1966), pp. 39–44, reprinted as "K. as Impos-tor: His Quest for Meaning" in Neumeyer, ed., *Twentieth Century Interpretations of* The Castle.

23. The point is unchanged if one accepts the alternative ending where K. dies a natural death but receives partial acceptance into the village.

24. See, for example, the Mayor's hilarious account of the Castle's obviously hap-hazard and error-ridden infallibility (pp. 82–97).

25. Max Weber, *Economy and Society: An Outline of Interpretive Sociology,* 3 vols., edited by Guenther Roth and Claus Wittich (New York: Bedminster Press, 1968), vol. 1, p. 223.

26. Some readers in organizational studies will object at this point, arguing that Weber and Kafka were worlds apart since Weber celebrated the rationality and efficiency of bureaucracies while Kafka portrayed their irrationality and inefficiency. Others might take a similar path by claiming that Kafka was satirizing a relatively premodern bureau-cracy and that, although his critique might apply to the West as a *reducto ad absurdum,* it can't be taken as a documentary account. I could quibble, for example, by noting where Weber was somewhat ambivalent, recalling Kafka's conscientious work as a modern bu-reaucrat, emphasizing how Western readers consistently see his work as the premier cri-tique in modern literature of bureaucratic order, and questioning any critic's inclination

241

to let the modern world off the hook. But there is more to it. Ultimately, it doesn't matter whether you see bureaucracies as highly efficient machines (which they often are) or as absurd exercises in deferral and rationalization (which they can be at any time), because they work much the same in any case. Whether for good or ill, the bureaucratic mentality draws on the same set of rhetorical practices, and enters into specific paradoxes, and receives equally unexamined veneration, whatever it is doing.

27. The scheme of system and lifeworld is most obvious in the relationships between the Castle and the village. Kafka's comic effects frequently stem from the incongruity between officials' behavior and bureaucratic norms: for example, the norms of "precision, speed, unambiguity, knowledge of the files, continuity, discretion, unity, strict subordination, reduction of friction and of material and personal costs—these are raised to the optimum point in the strictly bureaucratic administration, especially in its monocratic form" (Weber, *Economy and Society,* vol. 3, p. 973). For a correspondence of decor or agency, compare Weber's observation that bureaucracy depends on modern communication technologies (*Economy and Society,* vol. 1, p. 224; vol. 3, p. 973), with K.'s first communication with the Castle, which occurs over a telephone (p. 5). K. considers the phone a surprising development for the village, though one he also expected—because, we can assume, of the proximity of the Castle.

28. The first principle of bureaucratic organization is "the principle of official *jurisdictional areas,* which are generally ordered by rules, that is, by laws or administrative regulations" (Weber, *Economy and Society,* vol. 3, p. 956).

29. This has been the typical liberal humanist reading since the 1950s; for example, Hannah Arendt, "Franz Kafka: A Revaluation," *Partisan Review* 11 (1944): "Since his demands are nothing more than the inalienable rights of man, . . ." (p. 415). From Weber's perspective, K.'s insistence on his individuality would appear more as insistence on a more primitive social order: one structured by status rather than by offices. So it is that K. can see himself insisting on his rights as a person, while the others see him as someone asking for a privileged (and unwarranted) relationship with the organization.

30. Garfinkel and others have demonstrated the point that deviation from rational procedures can be essential for rational action. See, for example, chapter 6, "'Good' Organizational Reasons for 'Bad' Clinic Records," in Garfinkel, *Studies in Ethnomethodology.*

31. "The principles of *office hierarchy* and of channels of appeal (*Instanzenzug*) stipulate a clearly established system of super- and sub-ordination in which there is a supervision of the lower offices by the higher ones. Such a system offers the governed the possibility of appealing, in a precisely regulated manner, the decision of a lower office to the corresponding superior authority" (Weber, *Economy and Society,* vol. 3, p. 957).

32. I hope it is apparent that there are significant differences between the appeals to hierarchy in the bureaucratic and courtly styles, although the obvious similarities provide a strong basis for coordination between them. Even without regard to substantive variation—namely, who or what is actually referred to—all hierarchies are not alike, although each resonates with all others.

33. Kenneth Burke, *A Rhetoric of Motives* (Berkeley: University of California Press, 1969), p. 141.

34. Ibid., p. 237.

35. This passage offers another angle on bureaucratic deferral when read as a strange loop: "The 'Strange Loop' phenomenon occurs whenever, by moving upwards (or

downwards) through the levels of some hierarchical system, we unexpectedly find ourselves right back where we started" (Douglas R. Hofstadter, *Godel, Escher, Bach: An
Eternal Golden Braid* [New York: Basic Books, 1979], p. 10).

36. Here I have condensed Weber's fourth, fifth, and sixth criteria into a single
category. As Weber observed, "Office management, at least all specialized office management—and such management is distinctly modern—usually presupposes thorough
training in a field of specialization." In addition, "official activity demands the *full working
capacity* of the official." Finally, as "the management of the office follows *general rules,*"
"knowledge of these rules represents a special technical expertise which the officials
possess" (Weber, *Economy and Society,* vol. 3, p. 958). My emphasis comes from shifting
from a sociological to a rhetorical perspective: Whereas Weber was identifying elements
of bureaucratic operation in organizational settings, I am identifying elements of bureaucratic discourse dominant in those settings (that is, reciprocally constitutive of those practices) but not limited to those settings.

37. The irony here is priceless, but also unstable: at first, it seems that he
wouldn't rise because the organization actually is the opposite of what it claims to be;
as we learn more of his zeal for procedure, however, one also has to consider that he
couldn't rise because the organization could never function if its managers were so totally
dedicated to correct detail. As ethnomethodologists have suggested, the effectiveness of
the system requires some inefficiency by the individual manager.

38. Weber, *Economy and Society,* vol. 1, p. 225.

39. Ibid., vol. 1, p. 219; vol. 3, p. 957. Weber's claim has since been developed
extensively by scholars in anthropology, classical studies, communication studies, and
other disciplines who have investigated the relationships between orality, literacy, and
polity. As Jack Goody has concluded, "writing is critical in the development of bureaucratic states" (*The Logic of Writing and the Organization of Society* [Cambridge: Cambridge University Press, 1986], p. 91, see also pp. 89–92, 124–25). Influential work on
orality and literacy includes Erik A. Havelock, *The Literate Revolution in Greece and Its
Cultural Consequences* (Princeton: Princeton University Press, 1982) and *The Muse Learns
to Write: Reflections on Orality and Literacy from Antiquity to the Present* (New Haven:
Yale University Press, 1986), and Walter J. Ong, *The Presence of the Word: Some Prole-
gomena for Cultural and Religious History* (New Haven: Yale University Press, 1967) and
Orality and Literacy: The Technologizing of the Word (New York: Methuen, 1982). See
also Richard Leo Enos, ed., *Oral and Written Communication: Historical Approaches* (London: Sage, 1990).

40. This scene also neatly captures the interpenetration of the two orders of
Castle and village—the sense in which everyone occupies an intermediate position in a
hierarchy potentially extending infinitely above, into the system, and below, into the lifeworld. Momus is given beer, and then ink, marking his rise from ordinary person to official; the person is defined by the necessities of organic life and the simple pleasures of
ordinary sociality, and the official is defined by the requirements of organizational life and
the not-so-simple pleasures of institutional authority. At the end of the scene, the document has been put down while he picks up this food and drink; the change from ink to
beer is a declension, a shift away from the Castle back into village life.

41. As Jack Goody states: "By creating a text 'out there,' . . . the written word
can become the subject of a new kind of critical attention. That is not only because it is

243

'out there,' but because we cannot, as Plato observed, pose questions which the text itself can answer back, unlike the human beings to whom we talk. Moreover the text is often more difficult to understand since it lacks the context of speech, may well be abbreviated, cryptic and generalized, and may not relate primarily to the present at all, . . . In all these ways the text requires interpretation, explanation, even translation. Moreover the creation of the legal text involves a formalization (e.g., a numbering of the laws), a universalization (e.g., an extension of their range by the elimination of particularities) and an ongoing rationalization. This latter must be understood not in the sense of a process opposed to the modes of thought of oral communities, but one that reorders and reclassifies, sometimes in ways that do not necessarily clarify, the words, phrases, sentences, items with which the text is dealing, as well as leading to further commentaries, either written in the first instance or summarizing the oral elaborations of scholars upon the original work" (*The Logic of Writing,* p. 129).

42. Weber, *Economy and Society,* vol. 3, p. 1111.

43. This standoff is exemplified by Robertson, *Kafka* vs. Koelb, *Kafka's Rhetoric.* Although Koelb's analysis of Kafka's "rhetoricity" corresponds at some points to my sense of how *The Castle* mirrors another discourse, generally I believe his inquiry is, like other late modern critical projects, subject to Robertson's criticism of those who contend that Kafka's works "have nothing substantive to say, however indirectly, about the world, but are designed to frustrate the reader's desire for meaning and force him to reflect on the unreliability of his own mental operations"—Robertson concludes that this view is not "compatible with admiration of Kafka as a great writer" (p. ix). Similarly, although Kafka's profound engagement with the act of interpretation is well known, critics have scanted its importance in organizational life. For another, very difficult, account of Kafka's writing that I think has some affinities with my argument, see Gilles Deleuze and Felix Guattari, *Kafka: Toward a Minor Literature,* translated by Dana Polan (Minneapolis: University of Minnesota Press, 1986).

44. I am indebted to Robertson's discussion of the importance for Kafka of the problematic of Jewish assimilation. Like many of the Jewish intelligentsia of the early twentieth century, Kafka faced a choice between incompatible worlds. On the one hand, he lived in a Christianized and self-consciously modern, liberal, European culture. This choice offered much: protection by the state from persecution and entry into middle-class authority. Kafka's cousin, Bruno Alexander Kafka, exemplified how far one could go. He became a Professor of Law and Rector of the German University at Prague, editor of Czechoslovakia's oldest German-language newspaper, a founder of the German Democratic Liberal Party, and member of the Czech parliament—and a convert to Catholicism (q.v., *Encyclopedia Judaica*). Yet, by this time it already was becoming apparent that loyalty to liberalism was "a lost cause" (Robertson, *Kafka,* p. 4) and, in any case, assimilation ultimately demanded full price for only a portion of the goods. On the other hand, the discovery of the many organic, Orthodox Jewish communities of Eastern Europe confronted modernized Jews with the extent of their deprivation. For the first time, the choice of a Jewish identity seemed preferable: It promised acceptance, sustenance, historical continuity, polity. But it also was far to the east, came with all the constraints of premodern village culture, and lay open to periodic persecution. For someone like Kafka, the clear determination of one's identity appeared to be a choice between two forms of shame. The result was something else: a sense that one was a boarder in one's own home.

244

45. This interpenetration of the two orders is evident from the beginning: K. enters the village to obtain access to the Castle; he soon becomes fixated on meeting Klamm, the chief official for the village; to do so, he courts Klamm's mistress, Frieda, which results in K. and Frieda making love for three hours on the beer-splattered floor of the barroom outside of Klamm's door. As he is about to surrender completely to an experience of blissful intimacy, they are interrupted. "From Klamm's room a deep, authoritative, impersonal voice called for Frieda. 'Frieda,' whispered K. in Frieda's ear, passing on the summons. With a mechanical instinct of obedience Frieda made as if to spring to her feet" (p. 54). This scene captures perfectly the manner in which modern organization is suffused with a drama of power. An unseen, impersonal authority issues a command, an invisible but powerful system interrupts the lifeworld, and suddenly we must choose between two orders of being. Moreover, the responses to that choice reveal that the system already has been at work within. Frieda's incipient gesture shows that she is disposed to react mechanically, though still capable of acting contrary to the command. K.'s reactions have the same elements of a capacity for choice and a disposition to obey, but weighted in the other direction. He is not so much shocked as comforted by the voice, and scrambles to refasten her "disordered" blouse and send her to her master. His reactions mark his ambition to become completely identified with the bureaucratic order, just as they prefigure his abandonment of Frieda and the lifeworld she represents.

46. Chaim Perelman and L. Olbrechts-Tyteca, *The New Rhetoric: A Treatise on Argumentation,* translated by John Wilkinson and Purcell Weaver (Notre Dame: University of Notre Dame Press, 1969), pp. 411–59.

47. Jacques Derrida, *Of Grammatology,* translated by Gayatri Chakravorty Spivak (Baltimore: Johns Hopkins University Press, 1976), p. 157.

48. It also suggests that even Frieda's love for K. is because of his supplemental relationship to the possibility of another world outside of the closed system of the Castle. Note her yearning for escape to France for a life of love without deference to a higher authority (pp. 180 and 328), as well as the German connotations of *der Schloss.* K., of course, will have none of it.

49. Other readings are not exempt from the temptation to erase the chain, however: ethnomethodology also leads to the same end, implying that we can indeed describe the actual moment of social consciousness, the unmediated presence of the social structure. This approach is corrected by Benjamin's realization that Kafka's gestures lead only to endless interpretation. The correction also could lead to announcement of a hermeneutical essence, but Benjamin wisely does not do so.

50. Derrida, *Grammatology,* pp. 144–45.

51. Consider how comprehensively academic practices are composed according to the conventions of the bureaucratic style: Academic work is conducted within a politics of certification and documentation governed by the jurisdictional autonomy of the disciplines and the organizational hierarchy of the particular institution. The professoriate is legitimated and regulated by their professional ethos, while academic politics often turns on skillful use of the tropes of textual interpretation. Scholarly inquiry itself is subject to the continual reifying of its rules, investigative protocols, and specialized languages, which become discourses for the perpetual deferral of their objects of inquiry. Thorstein Veblen's contempt for this transformation of intellectual culture has long been replaced by a natural attitude that overlooks whatever costs have accompanied the enormous increases in

productivity and institutional authority. See Thorstein Veblen, *The Higher Learning in America: A Memorandum on the Conduct of Universities by Business Men* (New York: Hill and Wang, 1967).

52. Nor do I wish to imply that there is no middle ground between systems management and more reflective or critical commentary. See, for example, Donald A. Schon, *The Reflective Practitioner: How Professionals Think in Action* (New York: Basic Books, 1983). For an intellectual history of management theory, see Stephen P. Waring, *Taylorism Transformed: Scientific Management Theory since 1945* (Chapel Hill: University of North Carolina Press, 1991).

53. Other theorists have recognized this elision of public meaning within bureaucratic order. Hannah Arendt characterized bureaucracy as the epitome of the "social" mentality that opposed her (classical, somewhat republican) model of authentic political organization (see *The Human Condition* [Chicago: University of Chicago Press, 1958]). Although taking pains to register his ambivalence regarding the role of instrumentalism in modern identity, Charles Taylor also recognizes that bureaucratic order and its critics—whether rationalist (specifically, Habermas, "partly inspired by Weber") or romantic—together have displaced "an 'objective' order in the classical sense of a publicly assessable reality" (Charles Taylor, *Sources of the Self: The Making of Modern Identity* [Cambridge: Harvard University Press, 1989], p. 510).

54. Weber, *Economy and Society,* vol. 3, pp. 1404–5.

55. Obviously, this portrait mirrors my account of the republican style. Rather than consider the correspondences or reactions between the bureaucratic and republican styles, perhaps we should emphasize that each can provide a corrective for the other. If so, often the best results will come from those capable of alternating between or blending together elements of the two styles to complete the task at hand.

56. Kafka, *The Trial,* pp. 213ff. The episode also is published separately as the parable "Before the Law."

57. Benjamin, "Some Reflections on Kafka," in *Illuminations,* p. 144.

Chapter Six: Conclusion

1. Kenneth Burke, *Attitudes Toward History,* rev. 2d ed. (Boston: Beacon, 1959), p. 107.

2. Ibid., pp. 39–44, 166–75.

3. Burke's major works are *A Grammar of Motives* (Berkeley: University of California Press, 1969); *A Rhetoric of Motives* (Berkeley: University of California Press, 1969); *Language as Symbolic Action: Essays On Life, Literature, and Method* (Berkeley: University of California Press, 1966); *The Rhetoric of Religion: Studies in Logology* (Berkeley: University of California Press, 1970). For an excellent collection of early responses to his work, see William H. Reuckert, ed., *Critical Responses to Kenneth Burke* (Minneapolis: University of Minnesota Press, 1969). The most extensive application of Burke's work to social theory was provided by Hugh Dalziel Duncan, *Communication and Social Order* (New York: Bedminster Press, 1962), *Symbols in Society* (New York: Oxford University Press, 1968), *Symbols and Social Theory* (New York: Oxford University Press, 1969). See also James E. Combs and Michael W. Mansfield, *Drama in Life: The Uses of Communication in Society* (New York: Hastings House, 1976); Dennis Brissett and Charles Edgley, eds., *Life as Theater: A Dramaturgical Sourcebook,* 2d ed. (New York: Aldine

de Gruyter, 1990). Clifford Geertz both criticizes and promotes the perspective in "Blurred Genres: The Refiguration of Social Thought," *American Scholar* 49 (1980): 165–79.

4. Burke, *A Rhetoric of Motives,* p. 26.

5. For discussion of the relationship between textual fragments and ideological structures, see Michael Calvin McGee, "Text, Context, and the Fragmentation of Contemporary Culture," *Western Journal of Speech Communication* 54 (1990): 274–89; Raymie E. McKerrow, "Critical Rhetoric: Theory and Praxis," *Communication Monographs* 56 (1989): 91–111. Even in conventional stylistics, "knowledge of style is usually 'tacit': it is a matter of habits properly acquired (internalized) and appropriately brought into play. . . . It is the goal of music theorists and style analysts to explain what the composer, performer, and listener know in this tacit way" (Leonard B. Meyer, "Toward a Theory of Style," in *The Concept of Style,* revised and expanded edition, edited by Berel Lang (Ithaca, NY: Cornell University Press, 1987), p. 31.

6. Kenneth Burke, "Literature as Equipment for Living," in *The Philosophy of Literary Form: Studies in Symbolic Action,* 3rd ed. (Berkeley: University of California Press, 1973), pp. 293–304.

7. Burke, *Attitudes Toward History,* p. 107.

8. Burke's ideas on the relationship between symbolic structure and perception are summarized in his essay on "terministic screens," in *Language as Symbolic Action,* pp. 44–62.

9. Anthony Giddens, *The Constitution of Society: Outline of a Theory of Structuration* (Berkeley: University of California Press, 1984).

10. Allan Megill, "What Does the Term 'Postmodern' Mean?" *Annals of Scholarship* 6 (1989): 142ff.

11. For discussion of the classical concept, see Michael Leff, "Decorum and Rhetorical Interpretation: The Latin Humanistic Tradition and Contemporary Critical Theory," *Vichiana* 3a series, 1 (1990): 107–26; Robert Kaster, "Decorum," Paper presented at the annual meeting of the American Philological Association, Philadelphia, 29 December 1982. For discussion of its reappropriation in the Renaissance, see Nancy Struever, *The Language of History in the Renaissance: Rhetoric and Historical Consciousness in Florentine Humanism* (Princeton: Princeton University Press, 1970): "Of all the rhetorical canons, the principle of decorum is probably the most crucial, since it predicates the synthesis of the other criteria of expression. . . . Since the Humanists' critical apparatus was rhetorical analysis, the concept of decorum became the framework of their attempts to establish internal coherence in their texts" (pp. 67–68). See also Victoria Kahn, *Rhetoric, Prudence, and Skepticism in the Renaissance* (Ithaca, NY: Cornell University Press, 1985); Daniel Javitch, *Poetry and Courtliness in Renaissance England* (Princeton: Princeton University Press, 1978). See also Eric C. White, *Kaironomia: On the Will to Invent,* (Ithaca, NY: Cornell University Press, 1987); James Kinneavy, "Kairos: A Neglected Concept in Classical Rhetoric," in *Rhetoric and Praxis,* edited by J. Dietz Moss (Washington, DC: Catholic University Press, 1986).

12. Cicero, *Orator* 70, translated by G. L. Hendrickson and H. M. Hubbell, Loeb Classical Library (Cambridge: Harvard University Press, 1971).

13. Kaster, "Decorum," p. 5.

14. Cicero, *De oratore* 3.215.

15. Aristotle, *Rhetoric* 3.18.7.

247

16. Quintilian, *Institutio oratoria* 11.1.9.

17. Hans-Georg Gadamer provides the most thoroughgoing discussion of classical rhetoric as a hermeneutical enterprise in *Truth and Method*, 2d, revised edition, translated by Joel Weinsheimer and Donald G. Marshall (New York: Continuum, 1993). Paul Ricoeur provides careful discussion of the methodological issues shaping a modern interpretive science in "The Model of the Text: Meaningful Action Considered as a Text," *Social Research* 38 (1971): 529–62.

18. For other discussions of the affinities between rhetoric and social theory, see David Zarefsky, "How Rhetoric and Sociology Rediscovered Each Other," in *The Rhetoric of Social Research: Understood and Believed,* edited by Albert Hunter, pp. 158–70 (New Brunswick, NJ: Rutgers University Press, 1990); Richard Harvey Brown, "Rhetoric, Textuality, and the Postmodern Turn in Sociology," *Sociological Theory* 8 (1990): 189–97.

19. Protagoras, Fr. B 1, Hermann Diels and Walther Kranz, *Die Fragmente Der Vorsokratiker,* 10th ed., 3 vols. (Berlin: Weidmann, 1960); Rosamond Kent Sprague, ed., *The Older Sophists: A Complete Translation by Several Hands of the Fragments in* Die Fragmente Der Vorsokratiker *Edited by Diels-Kranz with a New Edition of Antiphon and of Euthydemus* (Columbia: University of South Carolina Press, 1972). See discussions of this passage in W. K. C. Guthrie, *The Sophists* (Cambridge: Cambridge University Press, 1971), pp. 188–92; G. B. Kerferd, *The Sophistic Movement* (Cambridge: Cambridge University Press, 1981), pp. 85ff.; Edward Schiappi, *Protagoras and Logos: A Study in Greek Philosophy and Rhetoric* (Columbia: University of South Carolina Press, 1991), pp. 117–33. See also A. Thomas Cole, "The Relativism of Protagoras," in Allan Parry, ed., *Yale Classical Studies,* vol. 22 (Cambridge: Cambridge University Press, 1972), pp. 19–45.

20. This chapter's discussion draws on Max Weber, *Economy and Society: An Outline of Interpretive Sociology,* edited by Guenther Roth and Claus Wittich, 3 vols. (New York: Bedminster Press, 1968); Georg Simmel, *The Sociology of Georg Simmel,* translated and edited by Kurt Wolf (Glencoe, IL: The Free Press, 1957); Alfred Schutz, *The Phenomenology of the Social World,* translated by George Walsh and Frederick Lehnert (Evanston: Northwestern University Press, 1967); Alfred Schutz and Thomas Luckmann, *The Structures of the Lifeworld,* translated by Richard M. Zaner and H. Tristram Engelhardt, Jr., 2 vols. (Evanston: Northwestern University Press, 1973–89); Peter L. Berger and Thomas Luckmann, *The Social Construction of Reality: A Treatise in the Sociology of Knowledge* (New York: Doubleday, 1966). I am particularly indebted to the succinct discussion of Schutz's contribution to interpretive social theory provided by John Heritage, *Garfinkel and Ethnomethodology* (Cambridge: Polity Press, 1984). For a more extensive discussion of the phenomenological project, see Herbert Spiegelberg, *The Phenomenological Movement: A Historical Introduction,* 2d ed., 2 vols. (The Hague: Martinus Nijhoff, 1976).

21. Burke, *Grammar,* pp. 281ff., provides one definition of pragmatism as the philosophical articulation of a sense of agency.

22. I am not presuming to contribute in this discussion to the complex discussion of the ideal type as a hermeneutical construct. See, for example, Schutz, *Phenomenology,* pp. 176–201. For succinct statement of the relationship between type and individual consciousness, see Karl Mannheim, *Ideology and Utopia: An Introduction to the Sociology of Knowledge,* translated by Louis Wirth and Edward Shils (New York: Harcourt, Brace & World, 1936), p. 210. It is important to emphasize that interpretive social theory begins

at the same point as Protagoras's art of rhetoric: subjective consciousness is "essentially inaccessible" (Schutz, *Phenomenology*, p. 99).

23. Schutz, *Phenomenology*, p. 194.

24. Ibid.

25. Mannheim, *Ideology and Utopia*, pp. 307–8. This distinction obviously is similar to Ferdinand Saussere's division between synchronic and diachronic explanation in his *Course in General Linguistics*, translated by Wade Baskin (New York: McGraw-Hill, 1966).

26. Isocrates, *Against the Sophists*, in *Isocrates II*, translated by George Norlin, Loeb Library (Cambridge: Harvard University Press, 1932), 12.

27. Quoted in Heritage, *Garfinkel and Ethnomethodology*, p. 73. Note also Heritage's comment that Schutz's characters act like the players in "Grandma's footsteps," who move as long as your back is turned, then freeze. Perhaps recent attempts at theorizing performance and at performing research also can be understood as attempts to solve this problem.

28. Aristotle, *Nicomachean Ethics* 1094b.20–5, 1098a.30, 1104a.1–10.

29. Isocrates, *Antidosis* 271, in *Isocrates II*.

30. Hans Blumenberg, "An Anthropological Approach to the Contemporary Significance of Rhetoric," in *After Philosophy: End or Transformation*, edited by Kenneth Baynes, James Bohman, and Thomas McCarthy (Cambridge: MIT Press, 1987), p. 439.

31. For example, see Weber, *Economy and Society*, pp. 1104ff. For extensive argument on this point, see Duncan, *Symbols and Social Theory*. Duncan also illustrates how resistance to inquiry into socio-aesthetic phenomena has been a persistent feature of American sociology. For an attempt to place the contemporary concept of a lifestyle within classical social theory, see Bryan S. Turner, *Status* (Minneapolis: University of Minnesota Press, 1988). For discussion of the operation of status appeals in discourse theory, see Robert Hariman, "Status, Marginality, and Rhetorical Theory," *Quarterly Journal of Speech* 72 (1986): 38–54.

32. Simmel, *Sociology of Georg Simmel*, pp. 42–43. Simmel also emphasized the autonomy of art (and other highly developed cultural forms) from all other practices, and this modernist emphasis obviously works against my interest in the aesthetic dimension of practical activities. For perceptive commentary in this direction, see his note on "adornment" (pp. 338–44), which considers how aesthetic objects synthesize social forces.

33. John Dewey, *Democracy and Education: An Introduction to the Philosophy of Education* (New York: Macmillan, 1961), p. 6.

34. George Herbert Mead, "The Nature of Aesthetic Experience," in *Selected Writings*, edited by Andrew J. Reck (Chicago: University of Chicago Press), pp. 297–98. This aesthetic attitude is at once end and means, as it "accompanies, inspires, and dedicates common action" (p. 298).

35. Harold Garfinkel, *Studies in Ethnomethodology* (Oxford: Polity Press, 1967), pp. 35ff.; Heritage, *Garfinkel and Ethnomethodology;* Kenneth Leiter, *A Primer on Ethnomethodology* (New York: Oxford University Press, 1980); Wes Sharrock and Bob Anderson, *The Ethnomethodologists* (New York: Tavistock, 1986); Roy Turner, ed., *Ethnomethodology* (Harmondsworth: Penguin, 1974).

36. Erving Goffman, *Presentation of Self in Everyday Life* (New York: Anchor

249

Books, 1959), *Interaction Ritual* (New York: Pantheon, 1967), *Strategic Interaction* (Philadelphia: University of Pennsylvania Press, 1969), *Relations in Public* (New York: Harper and Row, 1971), *Frame Analysis* (New York: Harper and Row, 1974), *Forms of Talk* (Philadelphia: University of Pennsylvania Press, 1981).

37. Pierre Bourdieu, *Outline of a Theory of Practice* (Cambridge: Cambridge University Press, 1977); Michel de Certeau, *The Practice of Everyday Life* (Berkeley: University of California Press, 1984); "Everyday Life," special issue of *Yale French Studies* 73 (New Haven: Yale University Press, 1987), which continues the work of Henri Lefebvre, for example, *Everyday Life in the Modern World,* translated by Sacha Rabinovitch (New York: Harper and Row, 1971). For related work in American sociology, see Dorothy Smith, *The Everyday World as Problematic: A Feminist Sociology* (Boston: Northeastern University Press, 1987), *The Conceptual Practices of Power: A Feminist Sociology of Knowledge* (Boston: Northeastern University Press, 1990), and *Texts, Facts, and Femininity: Exploring the Relations of Ruling* (New York: Routledge, 1990). For discussion of Smith's work, see *Sociological Theory* 10, no. 1 (1992); for discussion in light of the themes raised earlier in this essay, see the essay in that issue by Charles Lemert, "Subjectivity's Limit: The Unsolved Riddle of the Standpoint," pp. 63–72. For other feminist discussion of the problems of interpreting everyday life, see Nancy Fraser, *Unruly Practices: Power, Discourse, and Gender in Contemporary Social Theory* (Minneapolis: University of Minnesota Press, 1989).

38. Michel de Certeau, *The Practice of Everyday Life,* pp. 30, 47, also 24. Note also the parallels with Kenneth Burke, as when de Certeau claims that language functions to provide tools for living and even uses the proverb as his representative case (pp. 18–24; cf. Kenneth Burke, "Literature as Equipment for Living." Readers of Burke are accustomed to seeing his insights replicated in contemporary social theories of practice, micropolitics, cultural semiotics, and the like. For one discussion of this relationship, see Frank Lentricchia, *Criticism and Social Change* (Chicago: University of Chicago Press, 1983).

39. Victor Turner has been a major influence: *The Forest of Symbols: Aspects of Ndembu Ritual* (Ithaca, NY: Cornell University Press, 1967), *Dramas, Fields, and Metaphors: Symbolic Action in Human Society* (Ithaca, NY: Cornell University Press, 1974).

40. Clifford Geertz, *Negara: The Theatre State in Nineteenth-Century Bali* (Princeton: Princeton University Press, 1980); see also *The Interpretation of Cultures* (New York: Basic Books, 1973), *Local Knowledge: Further Essays in Interpretive Anthropology* (New York: Basic Books, 1983). Geertz has been strongly criticized on grounds of both accuracy and intrusiveness. See, for example, Vincent Crapanzano, "Hermes' Dilemma: The Masking of Subversion in Ethnographic Description," in James Clifford and George E. Marcus, *Writing Culture: The Poetics and Politics of Ethnography* (Berkeley: University of California Press, 1986), pp. 51–76. For Geertz's somewhat dismissive response, see *Works and Lives: The Anthropologist as Author* (Stanford: Stanford University Press, 1988), particularly the last chapter, "Being Here." Fortunately, these disputes need not constrain many appropriations of anthropological insights, particularly by those of us who are not conducting ethnography. See also David Cannadine and Simon Price, *Rituals of Royalty: Power and Ceremonial in Traditional Societies* (Cambridge: Cambridge University Press, 1987); Sean Wilentz, ed., *Rites of Power: Symbolism, Ritual, and Politics since the Middle Ages* (Philadelphia: University of Pennsylvania Press, 1985); Eric Hobsbawm and

250

Terence Ranger, eds., *The Invention of Tradition* (Cambridge: Cambridge University Press, 1983).

41. Richard Harvey Brown, *A Poetic for Sociology: Toward a Logic of Discovery for the Human Sciences* (New York: Cambridge University Press, 1977), *Society as a Text: Essays on Rhetoric, Reason, and Reality* (Chicago: University of Chicago Press, 1987), *Social Science as Civic Discourse: On the Invention, Legitimation, and Uses of Social Theory* (Chicago: University of Chicago Press, 1989). For an important earlier statement on this perspective, see Paul Ricouer, "The Model of the Text."

42. Brown, *Society as a Text,* pp. 57–58.

43. S. R. F. Price, *Rituals and Power: The Roman Imperial Cult in Asia Minor* (Cambridge: Cambridge University Press, 1987), pp. 240–41.

44. Hannah Arendt, *The Human Condition* (Chicago: University of Chicago Press, 1958). See also her concept of "doing beauty," in "Thinking and Moral Considerations: A Lecture," *Social Research* 38 (1971): 437. For sympathetic discussion of this idea, see J. Glen Grey, "The Winds of Thought," *Social Research* 44 (1977): 53ff.

45. Michael Oakeshott, *Rationalism in Politics* (New York: Basic Books, 1962); Bernard Crick, *In Defense of Politics,* 2d ed. (London: Pelican, 1982); Henry Fairlie, "The Politician's Art," *Harper's* (December 1977): 33–46, 123–24 and "The Decline of Oratory," *The New Republic* (28 May 1984): 15–19.

46. Ronald Beiner, *Political Judgment* (Chicago: University of Chicago Press, 1983).

47. J. Peter Euben, *The Tragedy of Political Theory: The Road Not Taken* (Princeton: Princeton University Press, 1990).

48. Terry Eagleton, *Ideology of the Aesthetic* (Cambridge: Basil Blackwell, 1990).

49. For succinct statement of the position, see Herbert Marcuse, *The Aesthetic Dimension: Toward a Critique of Marxist Aesthetics* (Boston: Beacon, 1978). The basic elements of the critique of popular culture (in advanced capitalism) were articulated by Max Horkheimer and Theodore W. Adorno, *Dialectic of Enlightenment,* translated by John Cumming (New York: Continuum, 1972) during their residency in America. In any case, critical theory seems committed to analyses of the economic determination and political function of the arts, on the one hand, and of popular culture, on the other, but unaware of or uninterested in inquiry about the aesthetic dimension of ordinary political practices. As for Eagleton, his criticism of "the later Frankfurt School, before Habermas assumed its mantle" (p. 407), should not be overestimated. His own social criticism relies heavily on an ideal of aesthetic autonomy and a corresponding attitude of seriousness; see especially chapter 14, "From the *Polis* to Postmodernism."

50. Dick Hebdige, *Subculture: The Meaning of Style* (New York: Methuen, 1979). A citation count of *Subculture* would index much of the large amount of relevant work in cultural studies. The conjunction of aesthetics and politics in postmodern culture is featured in Hebdige's *Hiding in the Light* (New York: Routledge, 1988).

51. The number of texts here is increasing rapidly. For representative works see, for example, Dan Nimmo and Keith R. Sanders, *Handbook of Political Communication* (Beverly Hills: Sage, 1981); Dan Nimmo and James E. Combs, *Mediated Political Realities,* 2d ed. (New York: Longman, 1990); Robert E. Denton, Jr., and Gary C. Woodward, *Political Communication in America* (New York: Praeger, 1985), and many of the titles in

251

the Praeger Series in Political Communication edited by Denton. Much of the work on political symbolism has been inspired by Murray Edelman, *The Symbolic Uses of Politics* (Urbana: University of Illinois Press, 1964), *Politics as Symbolic Action: Mass Arousal and Quiescence* (New York: Academic Press, 1971), *Constructing the Political Spectacle* (Chicago: University of Chicago Press, 1988).

52. Again, a burgeoning literature. See, for example, Robert E. Denton, Jr., and Dan F. Hahn, *Presidential Communication: Description and Analysis* (New York: Praeger, 1986); Roderick P. Hart, *The Sound of Leadership: Presidential Communication in the Modern Age* (Chicago: University of Chicago Press, 1987); Jeffrey Tulis, *The Rhetorical Presidency* (Princeton: Princeton University Press, 1987); Mary E. Stuckey, *The President as Interpreter-in-Chief* (Chatham, NJ: Chatham House, 1991). For an unusual analysis closer to my approach, see Barry Brummett, "Gastronomic Reference, Synecdoche, and Political Images," *Quarterly Journal of Speech* 67 (1981): 138–45.

53. Richard F. Fenno, Jr., *Home Style: House Members in Their Districts* (Boston: Little, Brown, 1978); Morris P. Fiorina and David W. Rohde, eds., *Home Style and Washington Work: Studies in Congressional Politics* (Ann Arbor: University of Michigan Press, 1989); G. Robert Boynton, "When Senators and Publics Meet at the Environmental Protection Subcommittee," *Discourse and Society* 2 (1991): 131–56, "The Expertise of the Senate Foreign Relations Committee," in *Artificial Intelligence and International Relations* edited by Valerie Hudson (Boulder, CO: Westview, 1991); with C. L. Kim, "Political Representation as Information Processing and Problem Solving," *Journal of Theoretical Politics* 3 (1991): 437–61.

54. Arthur B. Sanders, *Making Sense of Politics* (Ames: Iowa State University Press, 1990). These results have finally emerged despite academic survey research being controlled rigidly by highly modernist (rationalist and institutionalist) assumptions about the nature of politics and citizenship. For both the standard model and signs of change, see Richard R. Lau and David O. Sears, eds., *Political Cognition* (Hillsdale, NJ: Lawrence Erlbaum, 1986).

index

256

Machiavelli: and civic humanism, 202n.11; and civic republicanism, 45–47; influence, 13

Machiavelli, works by:

— *The Discourses on Livy,* 45–46, 200n.1, 206nn.33, 34, 214nn.79, 80, 81

— *The Prince,* 13–49; and genre, 15–16, 17, 24, 25, 202n.10; history of interpretation, 13, 14, 15–16, 28, 200n.2; literary style, 37–40; relation to *The Discourses on Livy,* 45–46, 206n.34; structure, 37–40

MacIntyre, Alasdair, 126, 199n.11, 233n.58, 235n.63

McKerrow, Raymie E., 247n.5

Madonna, 83–85, 220nn.53, 54

Mannheim, Kurt, 248n.22, 249n.25

Mansfield, Michael W., 246n.3

Marcus, George E., 250n.40

Marcuse, Herbert, 251n.49

Martin, Emily, 221n.59

Masatada, Nakanoin, 219n.36

mass media, 52–53, 78, 79–81, 86–90, 92, 112, 122, 133, 138–39, 193

May, James M., 117, 231n.42, 232n.46

Mead, George Herbert, 181, 187–88, 249n.34

Megill, Allan, 179–80, 199nn.8, 9, 247n.10

Meinecke, Friedrich, 207n.45

Meyer, Leonard B., 247n.5

Michelman, Frank, 226n.6

Miller, Anna Bertha, 224n.2

Miller, John C., 223n.65

Miller, Peter, 239n.3

Millum, Trevor, 220n.55

Mitchell, Thomas N., 224n.2

modernity, 6–7, 10, 12, 40–43, 51, 71, 78, 141, 167, 168, 170, 171, 193, 198nn.3, 5, 208n.50, 219n.42, 235n.62, 237n.75, 239n.3

Mommsen, Theodor, 224n.3

Morgenthau, Hans, 206n.44, 207n.46, 209n.53, 213n.75

Moss, Roger, 201n.6

Moulakas, Athanasios, 200n.2

Mueller-Vollner, Kurt, 213n.74

Muir, Edwin, 240n.11

Murphy, James J., 197n.1, 201n.7

N

Nelson, John S., 199n.8

Nicolet, Claude, 224n.2

Nifo, Augustino, 26–28, 206nn.39, 40

Nimmo, Dan, 251n.51

Nixon, Richard M., 29, 208n.50

Noonan, Peggy, 92–93, 223n.65

Novak, Michael, 99, 222n.62

Novick, Peter, 200n.13

O

Oakeshott, Michael, 189, 233n.58, 251n.45

Olbrechts-Tyteca, L., 204n.24, 237n.81, 245n.46

Ong, Walter J., 243n.39

P

Palmer, Richard E., 213n.76

Pangle, Thomas L., 225n.4

Parel, Anthony, 201n.5

Pawel, Ernst, 240n.12

Perelman, Chaim, 171, 204n.24, 237n.81, 245n.46

Peters, John Durham, 200n.12

Petrarch, Francesco, 107, 229n.25

Pirkin, Hannah Feniche, 208n.50

Plamenatz, John, 209n.57

Plato, 229n.26

Pocock, J. G. A., 201n.7, 214nn.79, 81, 225n.4, 232n.50, 235n.60

political communication, study of, 190

political realism: definition of, 14; relationship with realist style, 207n.46

political style: analysis, levels of, 168; as analytical construct, 3–4; defined, 4, 187; identification of, in mirror texts, 4–5, 6–7, 177; as political theory, 4, 71, 96, 207n.46; research agenda, 191–92; as drama of social order, 64, 119, 168–71

politics, multiple discourses of, 12

postmodernity, 6–7, 9, 53, 86, 168, 198nn.3, 4, 251n.50

Poulakos, John, 197n.1

presidential studies, 191

Price, S. R. F., 189, 215n.4, 219n.40, 250n.4, 251n.43

Protagoras, 182

prudence, 10, 30, 39, 48, 112, 124, 198n.8, 208n.53, 235n.66

public opinion research, 191

Purcell, Edward A., 200n.13

P'u Yi, Aisin-Gioro, 68, 218n.31

Q

Quint, David, 43, 204n.23, 213n.75

Quintilian, 248n.16

R

Raab, Felix, 13, 207n.45

Ranger, Terence, 215n.4